# THE FLASH

## MERCURY FALLING

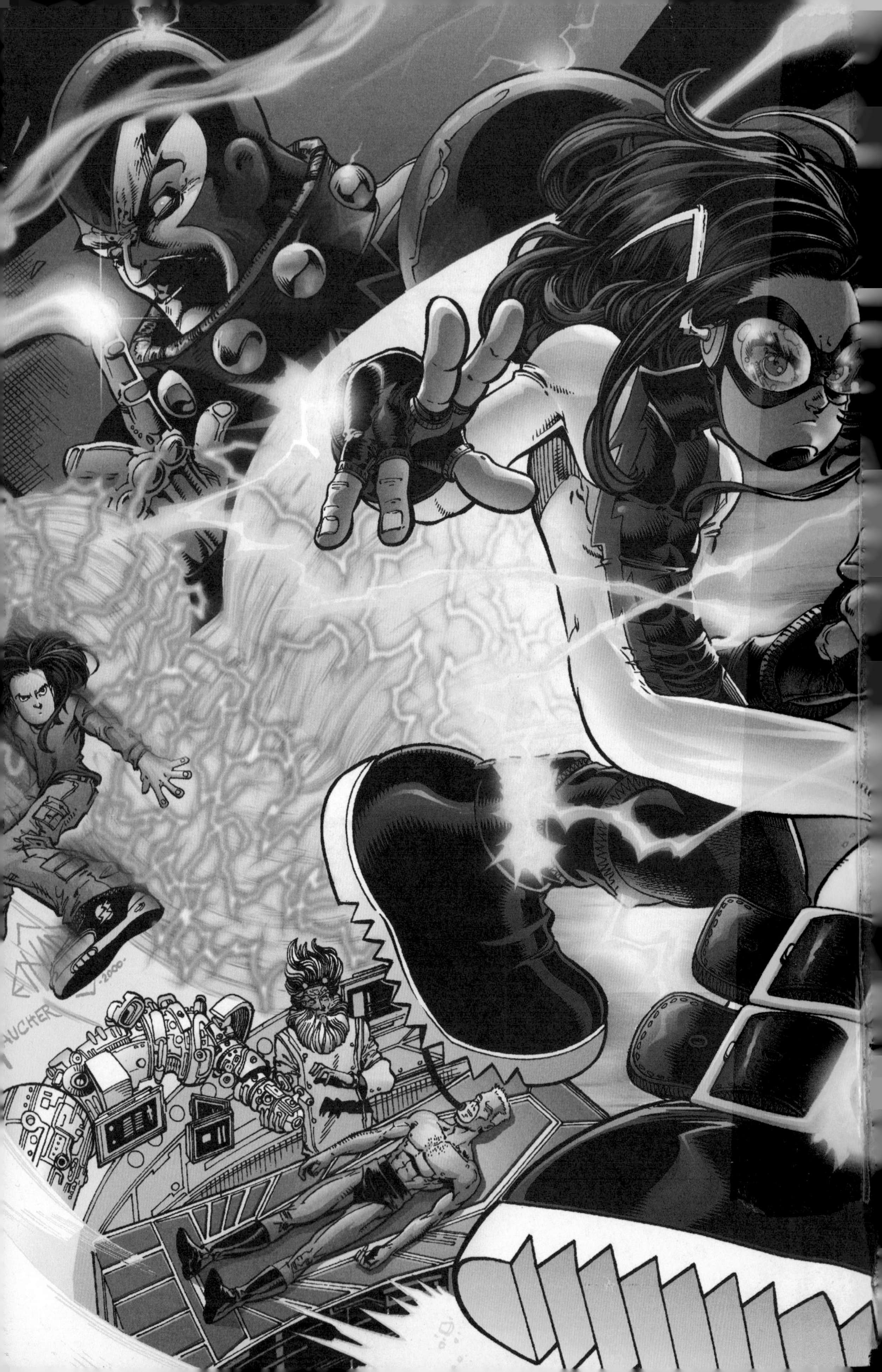

-2000-

# THE FLASH

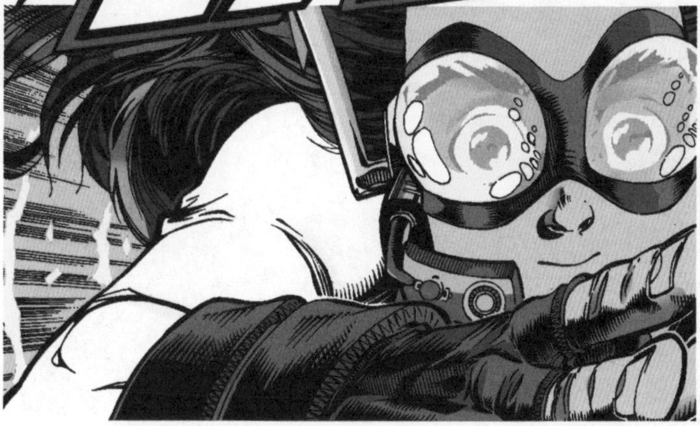

# MERCURY FALLING

**Todd Dezago**
Writer

**Ethan Van Sciver**
**Eric Battle**
Pencillers

**Barbara Kaalberg**
**John Stokes**
**Prentis Rollins**
**Andrew Hennessy**
Inkers

**Rick Taylor**
**Jason Scott Jones**
**Tom J. McCraw**
Colorists

**Jamison**
Separations

**Janice Chiang**
Letterer

**Ethan Van Sciver & Wayne Faucher**
Original series covers

IMPULSE created by Mark Waid & Mike Wieringo



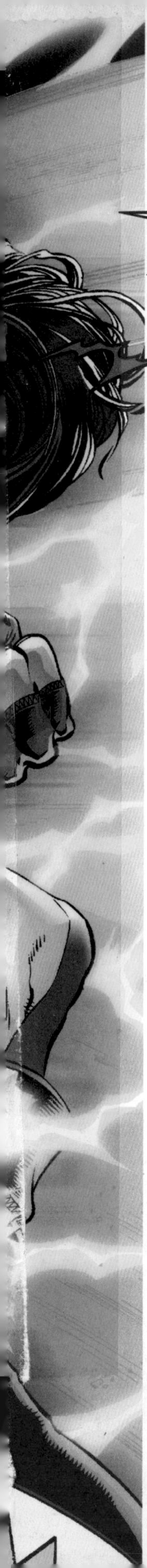

**Dan DiDio** Senior VP-Executive Editor

**L.A. Williams** Editor-original series

**Sean Mackiewicz** Editor-collected edition

**Robbin Brosterman** Senior Art Director

**Paul Levitz** President & Publisher

**Georg Brewer** VP-Design & DC Direct Creative

**Richard Bruning** Senior VP-Creative Director

**Patrick Caldon** Executive VP-Finance & Operations

**Chris Caramalis** VP-Finance

**John Cunningham** VP-Marketing

**Terri Cunningham** VP-Managing Editor

**Amy Genkins** Senior VP-Business & Legal Affairs

**Alison Gill** VP-Manufacturing

**David Hyde** VP-Publicity

**Hank Kanalz** VP-General Manager, WildStorm

**Jim Lee** Editorial Director-WildStorm

**Gregory Noveck** Senior VP-Creative Affairs

**Sue Pohja** VP-Book Trade Sales

**Steve Rotterdam** Senior VP-Sales & Marketing

**Cheryl Rubin** Senior VP-Brand Management

**Alysse Soll** VP-Advertising & Custom Publishing

**Jeff Trojan** VP-Business Development, DC Direct

**Bob Wayne** VP-Sales

Cover by Ethan Van Sciver & Wayne Faucher

**THE FLASH: MERCURY FALLING**

DC Comics, 1700 Broadway, New York, NY 10019
A Warner Bros. Entertainment Company
Printed in Canada. First Printing.

ISBN: 978-1-4012-2260-4

SUSTAINABLE FORESTRY INITIATIVE | Certified Fiber Sourcing
www.sfiprogram.org

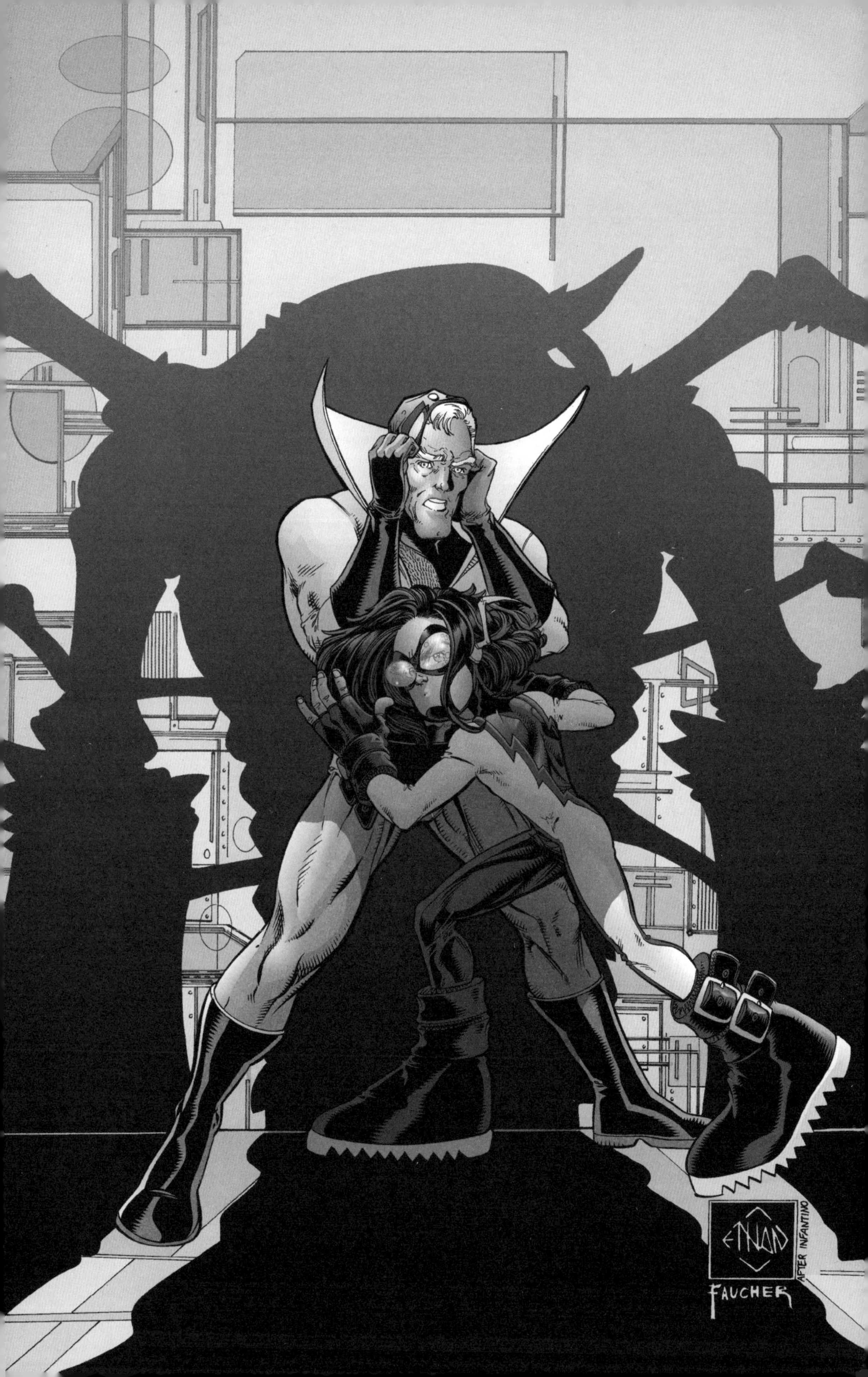
AFTER INFANTINO
FAUCHER

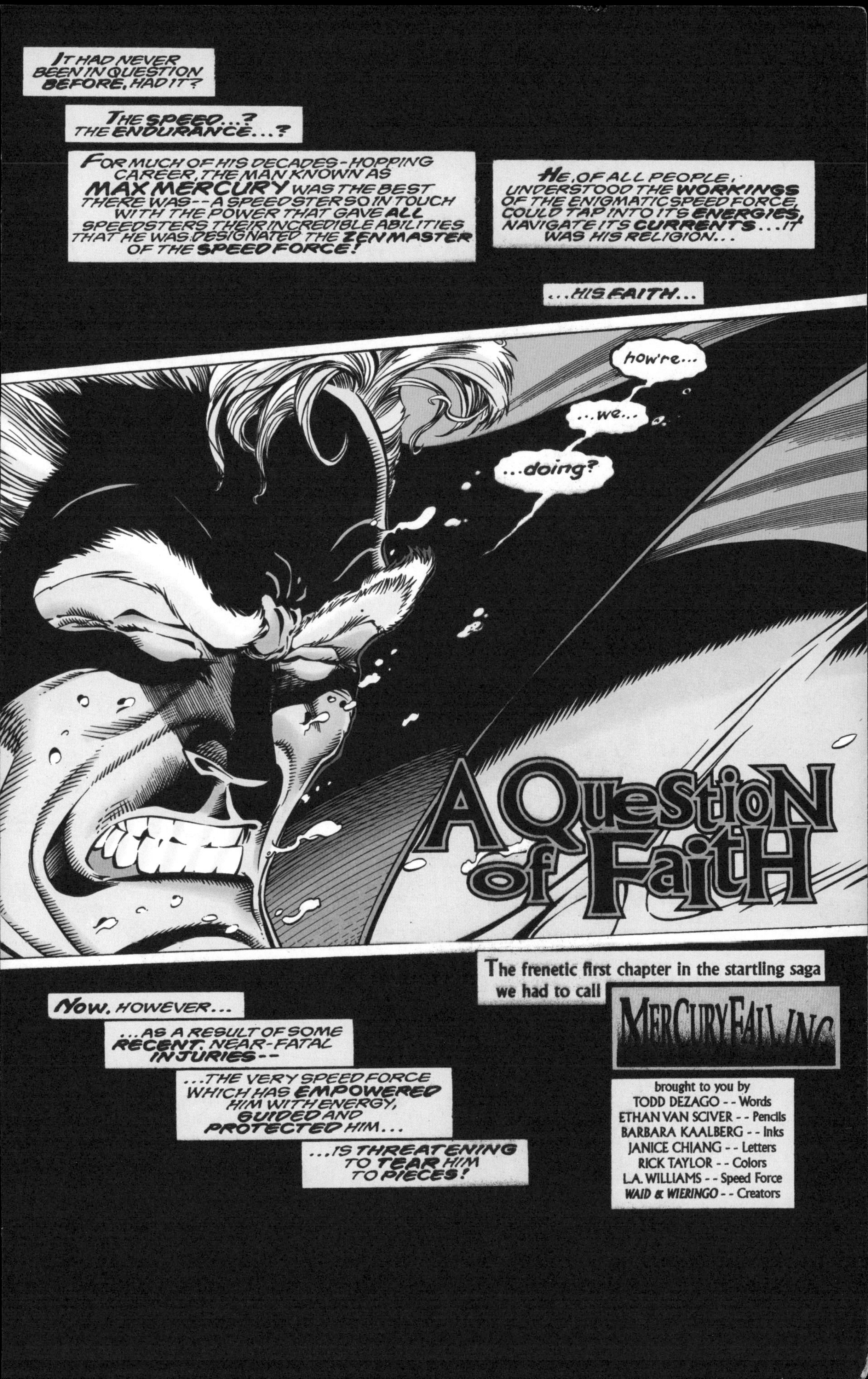

IT HAD NEVER BEEN IN QUESTION BEFORE, HAD IT?
THE SPEED...? THE ENDURANCE...?
FOR MUCH OF HIS DECADES-HOPPING CAREER, THE MAN KNOWN AS MAX MERCURY WAS THE BEST THERE WAS--A SPEEDSTER SO IN TOUCH WITH THE POWER THAT GAVE ALL SPEEDSTERS THEIR INCREDIBLE ABILITIES THAT HE WAS DESIGNATED THE ZEN MASTER OF THE SPEED FORCE!
HE, OF ALL PEOPLE, UNDERSTOOD THE WORKINGS OF THE ENIGMATIC SPEED FORCE, COULD TAP INTO ITS ENERGIES, NAVIGATE ITS CURRENTS...IT WAS HIS RELIGION...
...HIS FAITH...
how're...
...we...
...doing?
A QUESTION OF FAITH
The frenetic first chapter in the startling saga we had to call
MERCURY FALLING
NOW, HOWEVER...
...AS A RESULT OF SOME RECENT, NEAR-FATAL INJURIES--
...THE VERY SPEED FORCE WHICH HAS EMPOWERED HIM WITH ENERGY, GUIDED AND PROTECTED HIM...
...IS THREATENING TO TEAR HIM TO PIECES!
brought to you by
TODD DEZAGO - - Words
ETHAN VAN SCIVER - - Pencils
BARBARA KAALBERG - - Inks
JANICE CHIANG - - Letters
RICK TAYLOR - - Colors
L.A. WILLIAMS - - Speed Force
WAID & WIERINGO - - Creators

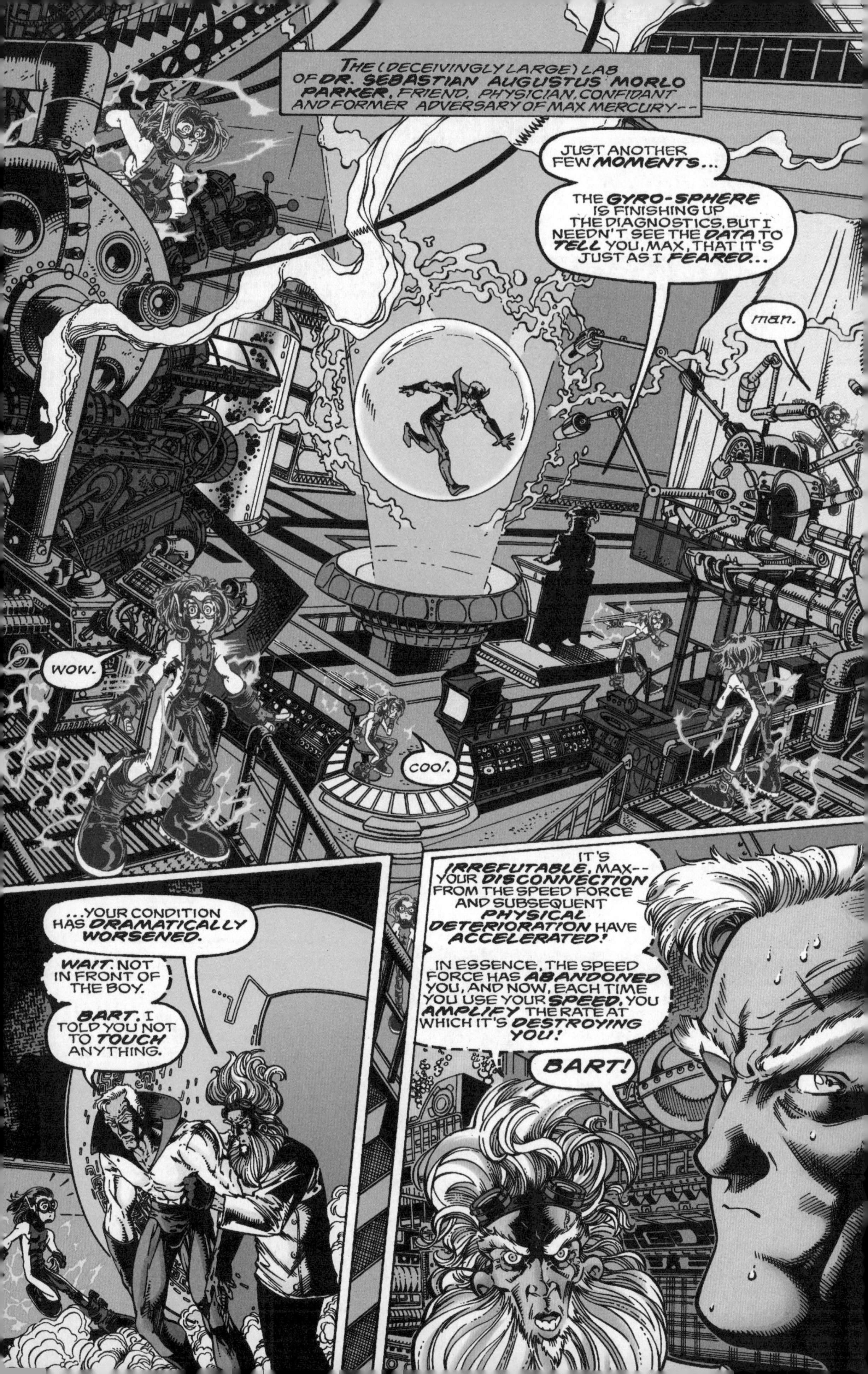
THE (DECEIVINGLY LARGE) LAB OF DR. SEBASTIAN AUGUSTUS MORLO PARKER, FRIEND, PHYSICIAN, CONFIDANT AND FORMER ADVERSARY OF MAX MERCURY--
JUST ANOTHER FEW MOMENTS...
THE GYRO-SPHERE IS FINISHING UP THE DIAGNOSTICS, BUT I NEEDN'T SEE THE DATA TO TELL YOU, MAX, THAT IT'S JUST AS I FEARED...
man.
WOW.
cool.
...YOUR CONDITION HAS DRAMATICALLY WORSENED.
WAIT. NOT IN FRONT OF THE BOY.
BART. I TOLD YOU NOT TO TOUCH ANYTHING.
IT'S IRREFUTABLE, MAX-- YOUR DISCONNECTION FROM THE SPEED FORCE AND SUBSEQUENT PHYSICAL DETERIORATION HAVE ACCELERATED!
IN ESSENCE, THE SPEED FORCE HAS ABANDONED YOU, AND NOW, EACH TIME YOU USE YOUR SPEED, YOU AMPLIFY THE RATE AT WHICH IT'S DESTROYING YOU!
BART!

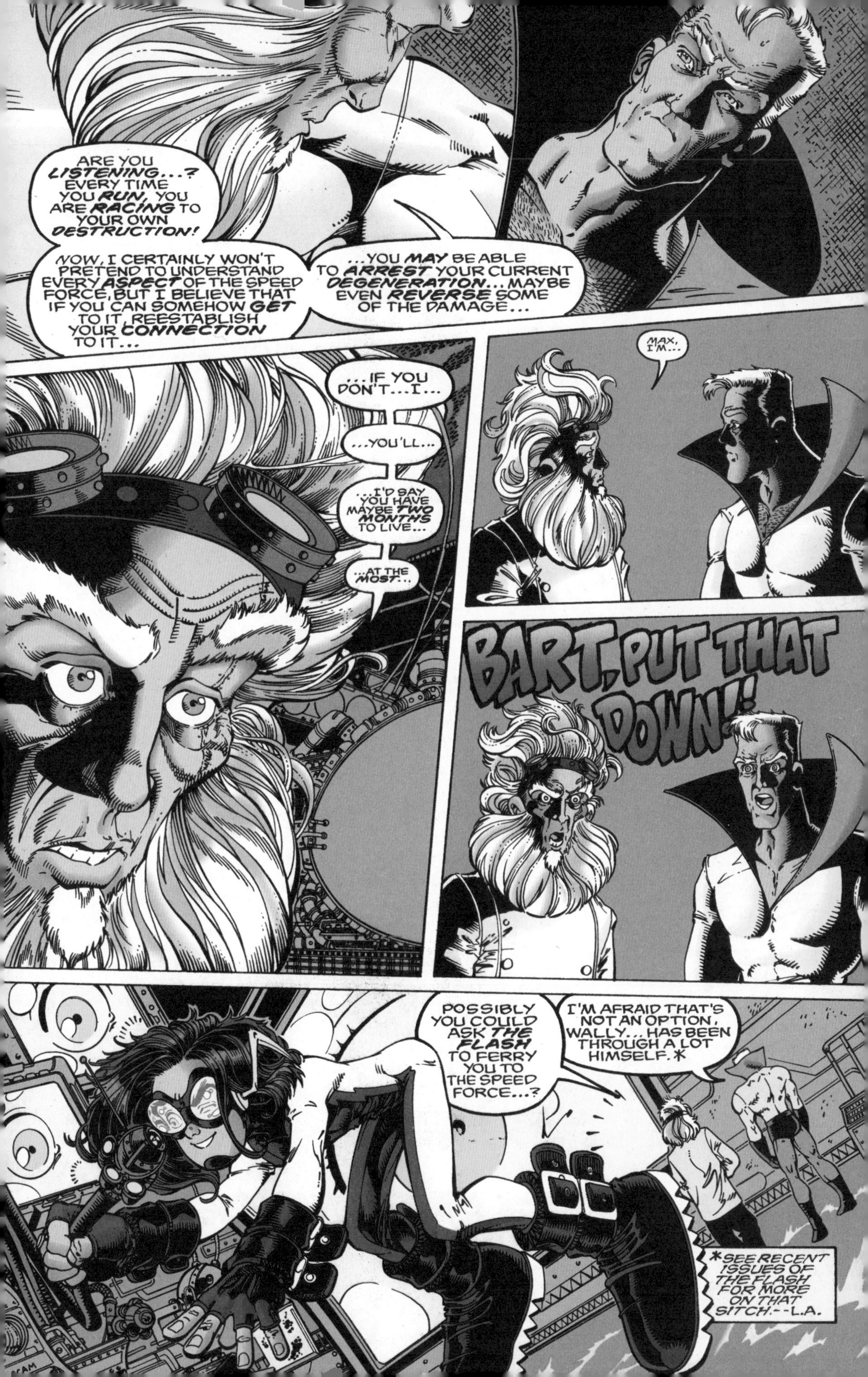
ARE YOU LISTENING...? EVERY TIME YOU RUN, YOU ARE RACING TO YOUR OWN DESTRUCTION!
NOW, I CERTAINLY WON'T PRETEND TO UNDERSTAND EVERY ASPECT OF THE SPEED FORCE, BUT I BELIEVE THAT IF YOU CAN SOMEHOW GET TO IT, REESTABLISH YOUR CONNECTION TO IT...
...YOU MAY BE ABLE TO ARREST YOUR CURRENT DEGENERATION... MAYBE EVEN REVERSE SOME OF THE DAMAGE...
...IF YOU DON'T...I...
...YOU'LL...
...I'D SAY YOU HAVE MAYBE TWO MONTHS TO LIVE...
...AT THE MOST...
MAX, I'M...
BART, PUT THAT DOWN!!
POSSIBLY YOU COULD ASK THE FLASH TO FERRY YOU TO THE SPEED FORCE...?
I'M AFRAID THAT'S NOT AN OPTION, WALLY... HAS BEEN THROUGH A LOT HIMSELF.*
*SEE RECENT ISSUES OF THE FLASH FOR MORE ON THAT SITCH.--L.A.

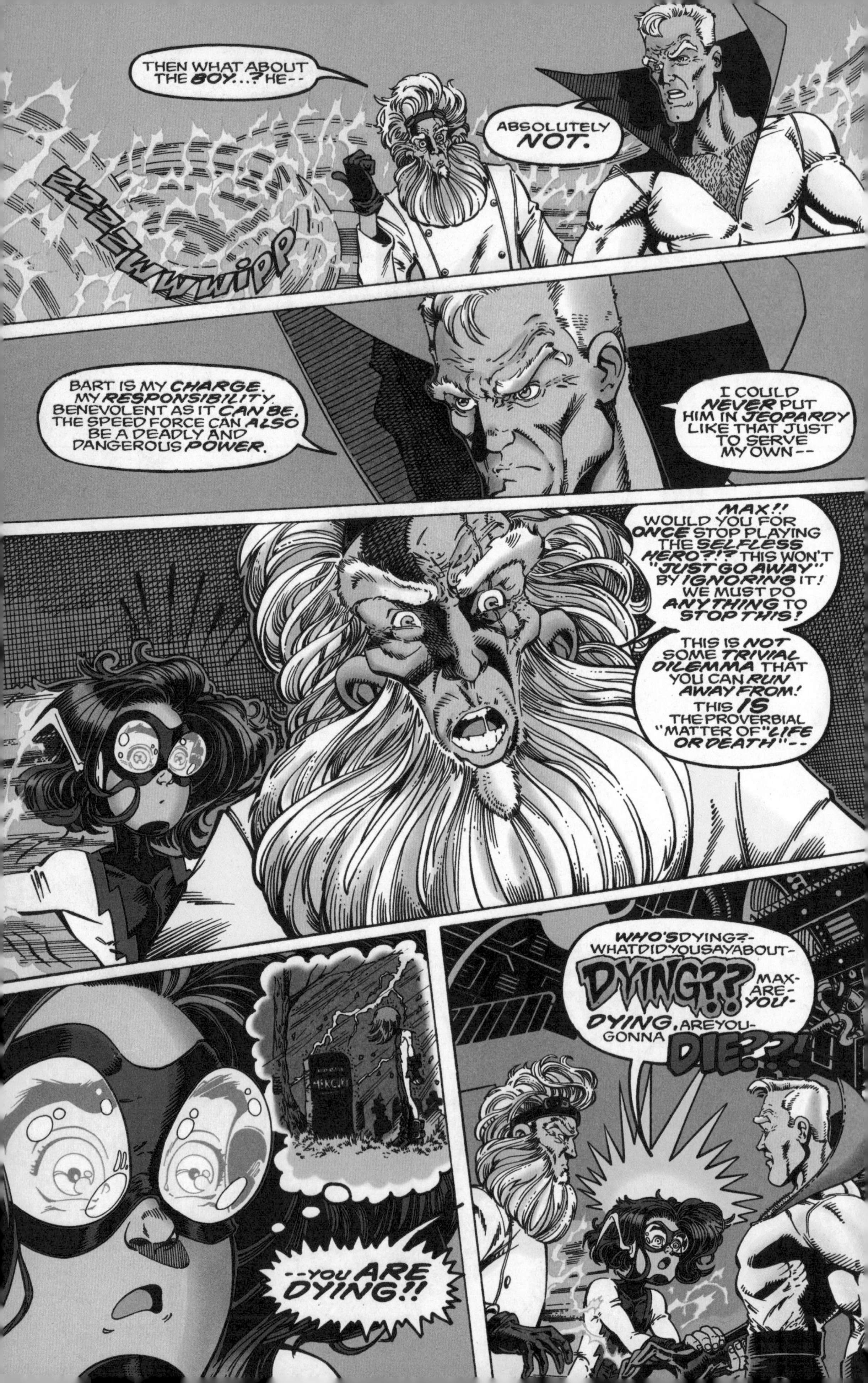
THEN WHAT ABOUT THE BOY...? HE--
ABSOLUTELY NOT.
ZZZZWWWIPP
BART IS MY CHARGE. MY RESPONSIBILITY. BENEVOLENT AS IT CAN BE, THE SPEED FORCE CAN ALSO BE A DEADLY AND DANGEROUS POWER.
I COULD NEVER PUT HIM IN JEOPARDY LIKE THAT JUST TO SERVE MY OWN--
MAX!! WOULD YOU FOR ONCE STOP PLAYING THE SELFLESS HERO?!? THIS WON'T "JUST GO AWAY" BY IGNORING IT! WE MUST DO ANYTHING TO STOP THIS!
THIS IS NOT SOME TRIVIAL DILEMMA THAT YOU CAN RUN AWAY FROM! THIS IS THE PROVERBIAL "MATTER OF" LIFE OR DEATH"--
--YOU ARE DYING?!!
WHO'S DYING?-WHATDIDYOUSAYABOUT-DYING?? MAX-ARE-YOU-DYING, AREYOU-GONNA DIE???!!

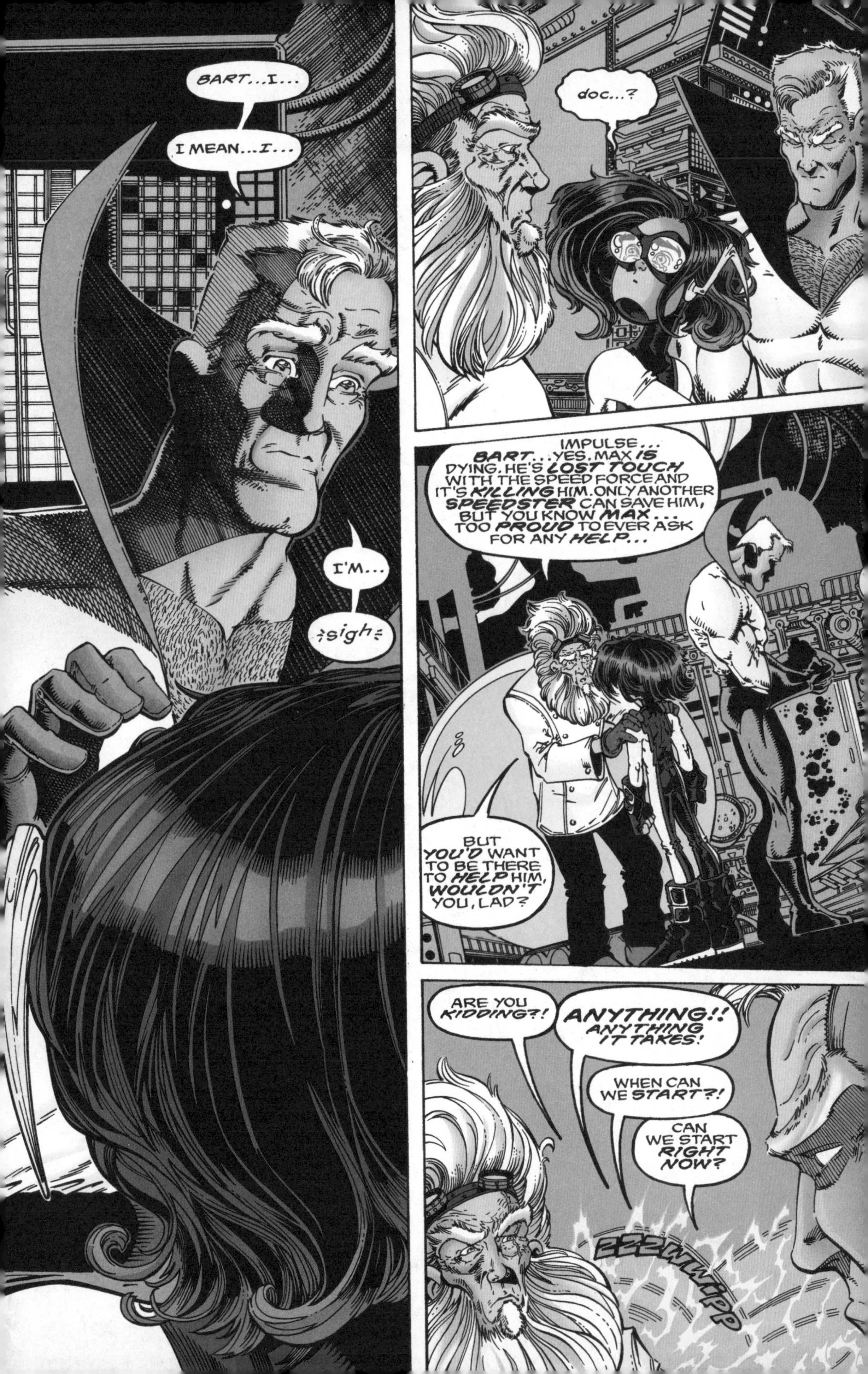
BART...I...
I MEAN...I...
I'M...
sigh
doc...?
IMPULSE... BART...YES. MAX IS DYING. HE'S LOST TOUCH WITH THE SPEED FORCE AND IT'S KILLING HIM. ONLY ANOTHER SPEEDSTER CAN SAVE HIM, BUT YOU KNOW MAX... TOO PROUD TO EVER ASK FOR ANY HELP...
BUT YOU'D WANT TO BE THERE TO HELP HIM, WOULDN'T YOU, LAD?
ARE YOU KIDDING?!
ANYTHING!! ANYTHING IT TAKES!
WHEN CAN WE START?!
CAN WE START RIGHT NOW?
ZZZWWHIPP

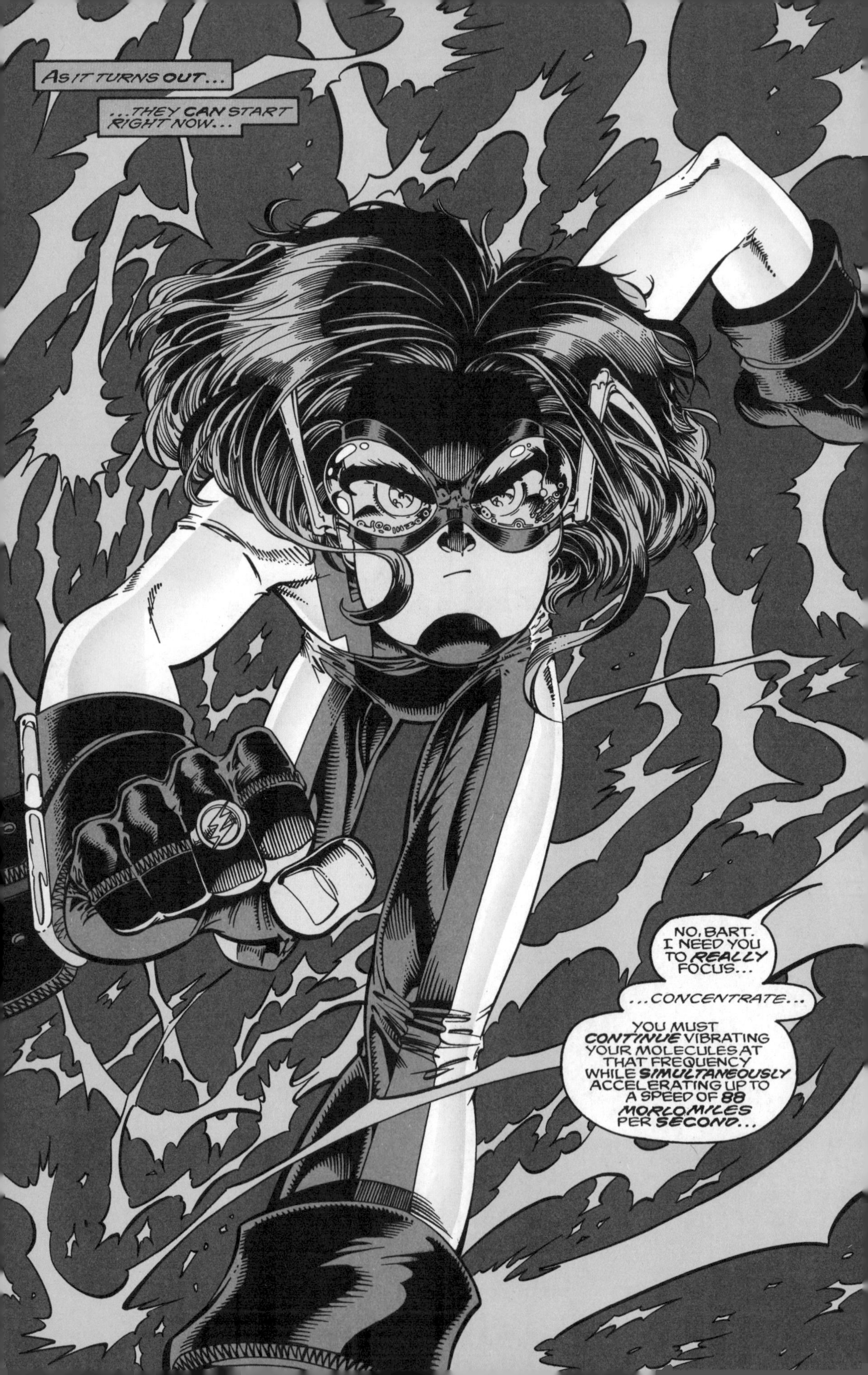

AS IT TURNS OUT...
...THEY CAN START RIGHT NOW...
NO, BART. I NEED YOU TO REALLY FOCUS...
...CONCENTRATE...
YOU MUST CONTINUE VIBRATING YOUR MOLECULES AT THAT FREQUENCY WHILE SIMULTANEOUSLY ACCELERATING UP TO A SPEED OF 88 MORLOMILES PER SECOND...

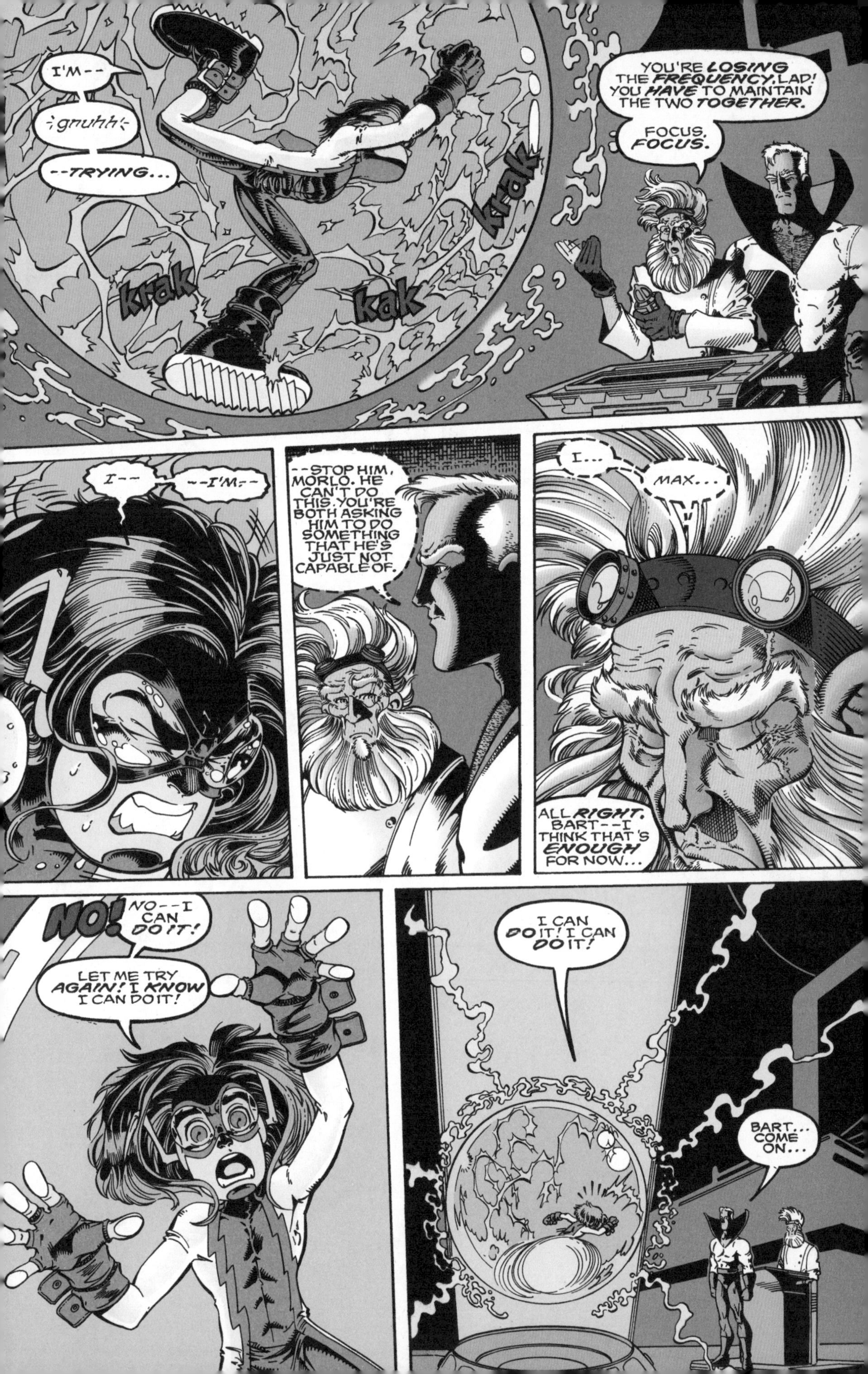

I'M--
gnuhh
--TRYING...
krak
kak
krak
YOU'RE LOSING THE FREQUENCY, LAD! YOU HAVE TO MAINTAIN THE TWO TOGETHER.
FOCUS. FOCUS.
I--
--I'M--
--STOP HIM, MORLO. HE CAN'T DO THIS. YOU'RE BOTH ASKING HIM TO DO SOMETHING THAT HE'S JUST NOT CAPABLE OF.
I...
MAX...
ALL RIGHT. BART--I THINK THAT'S ENOUGH FOR NOW...
NO!
NO--I CAN DO IT!
LET ME TRY AGAIN! I KNOW I CAN DO IT!
I CAN DO IT! I CAN DO IT!
BART... COME ON...

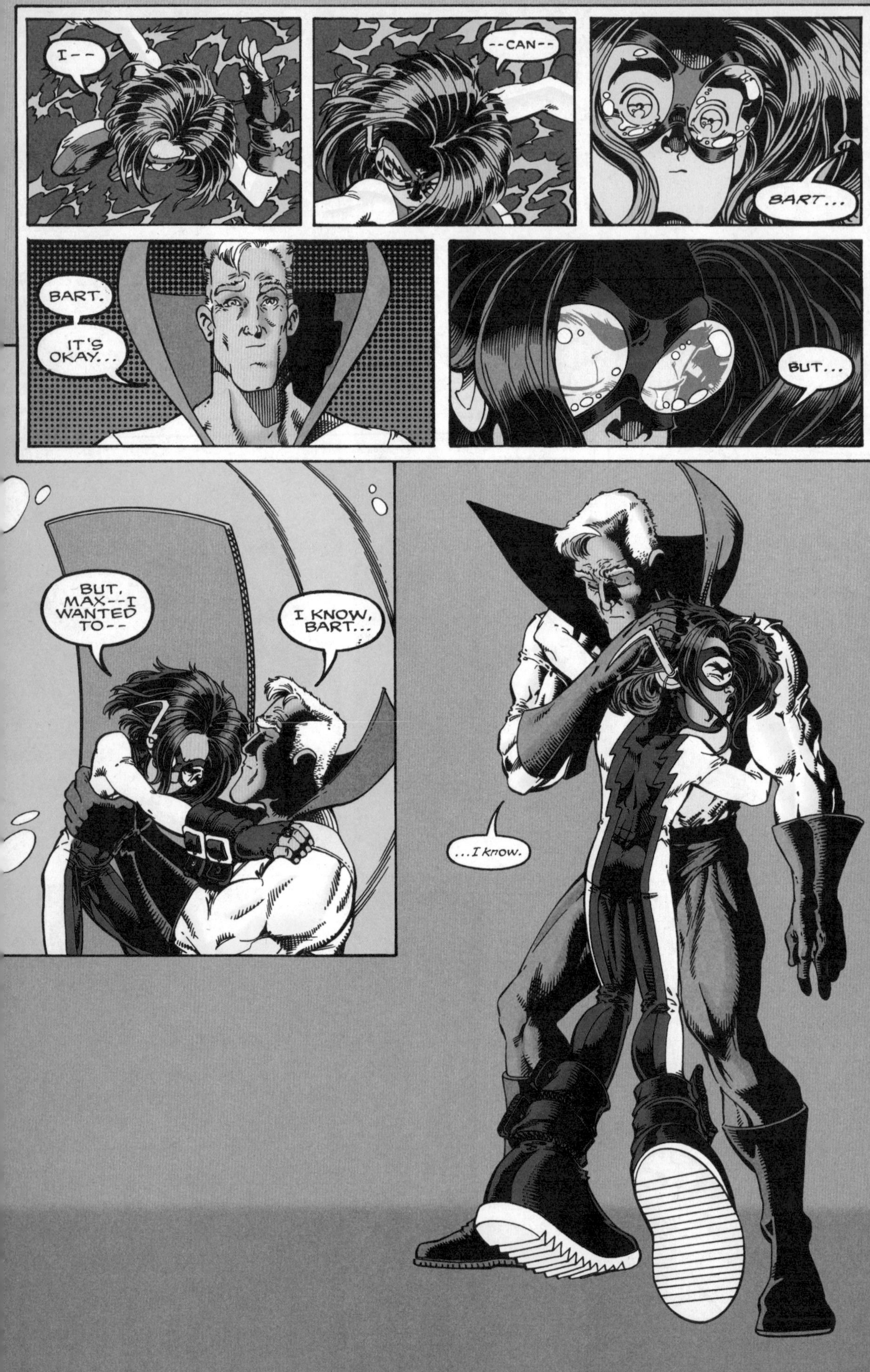
I--
--CAN--
BART...
BART.
IT'S OKAY...
BUT...
BUT, MAX--I WANTED TO--
I KNOW, BART...
...I know.

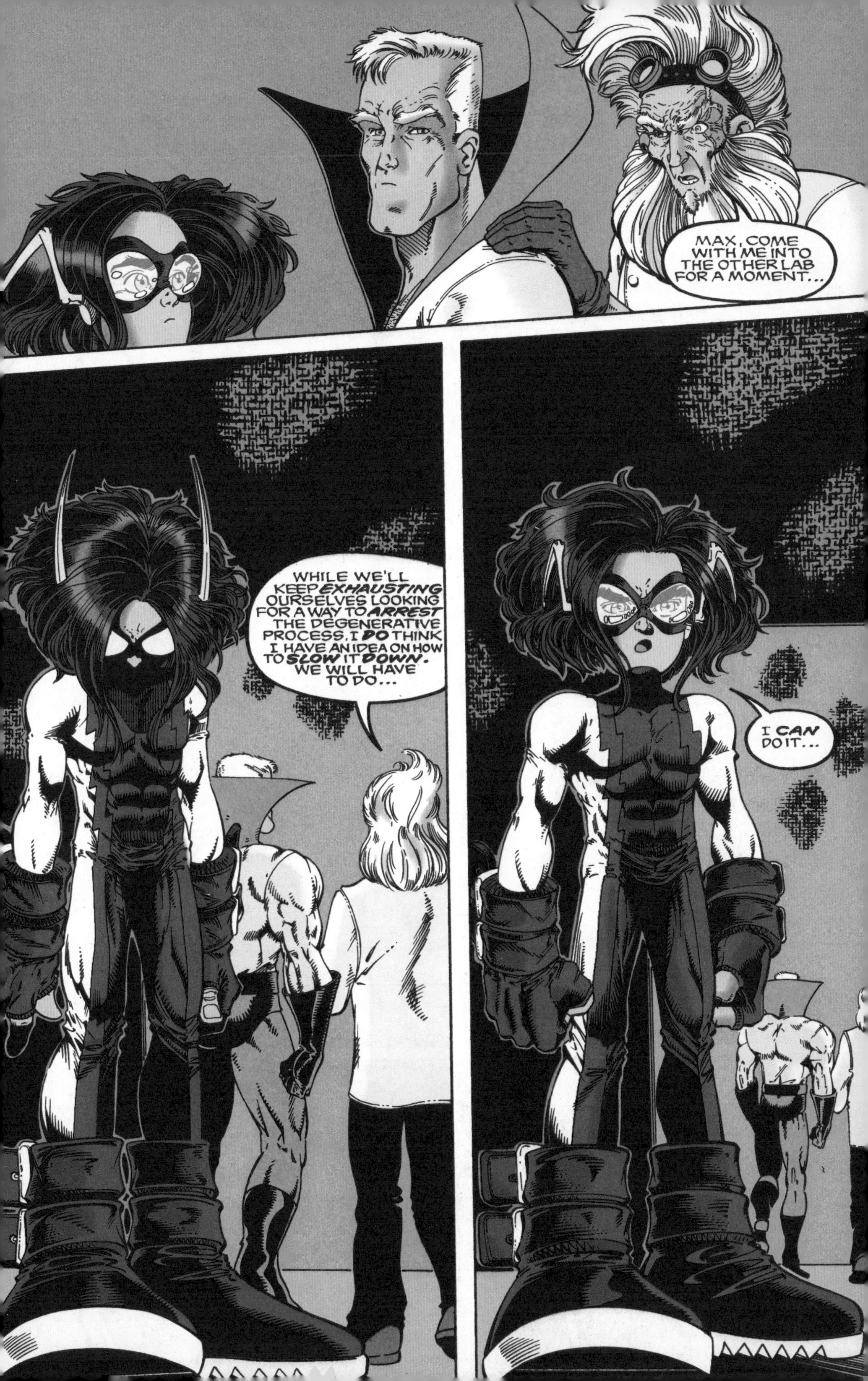
MAX, COME WITH ME INTO THE OTHER LAB FOR A MOMENT...
WHILE WE'LL KEEP EXHAUSTING OURSELVES LOOKING FOR A WAY TO ARREST THE DEGENERATIVE PROCESS, I DO THINK I HAVE AN IDEA ON HOW TO SLOW IT DOWN. WE WILL HAVE TO DO...
I CAN DO IT...

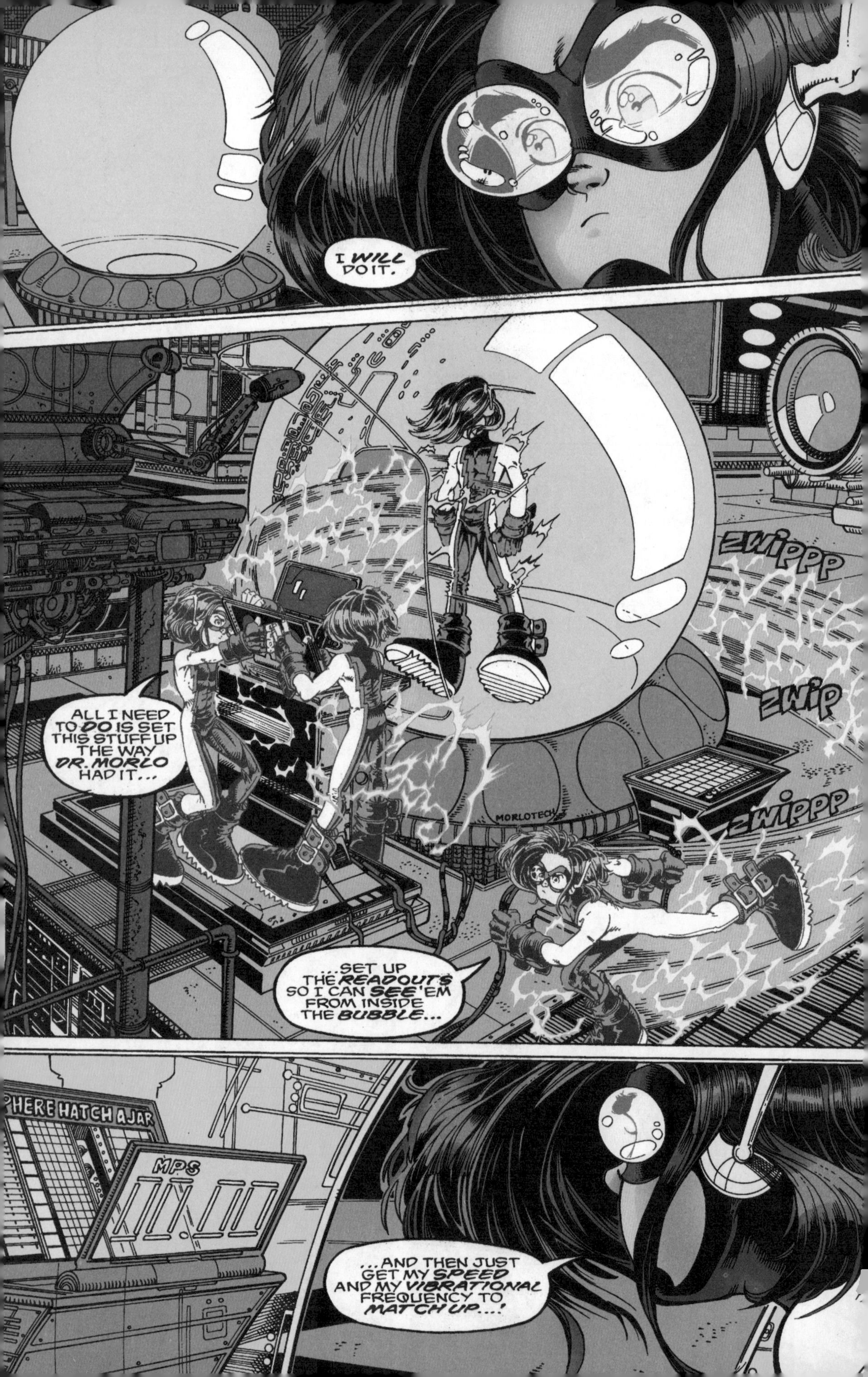
I WILL DO IT.
ZWIPPP
ZWIP
ALL I NEED TO DO IS SET THIS STUFF UP THE WAY DR. MORLO HAD IT...
MORLOTECH
ZWIPPP
...SET UP THE READOUTS SO I CAN SEE 'EM FROM INSIDE THE BUBBLE...
PHERE HATCH AJAR
MPS
...AND THEN JUST GET MY SPEED AND MY VIBRATIONAL FREQUENCY TO MATCH UP...!

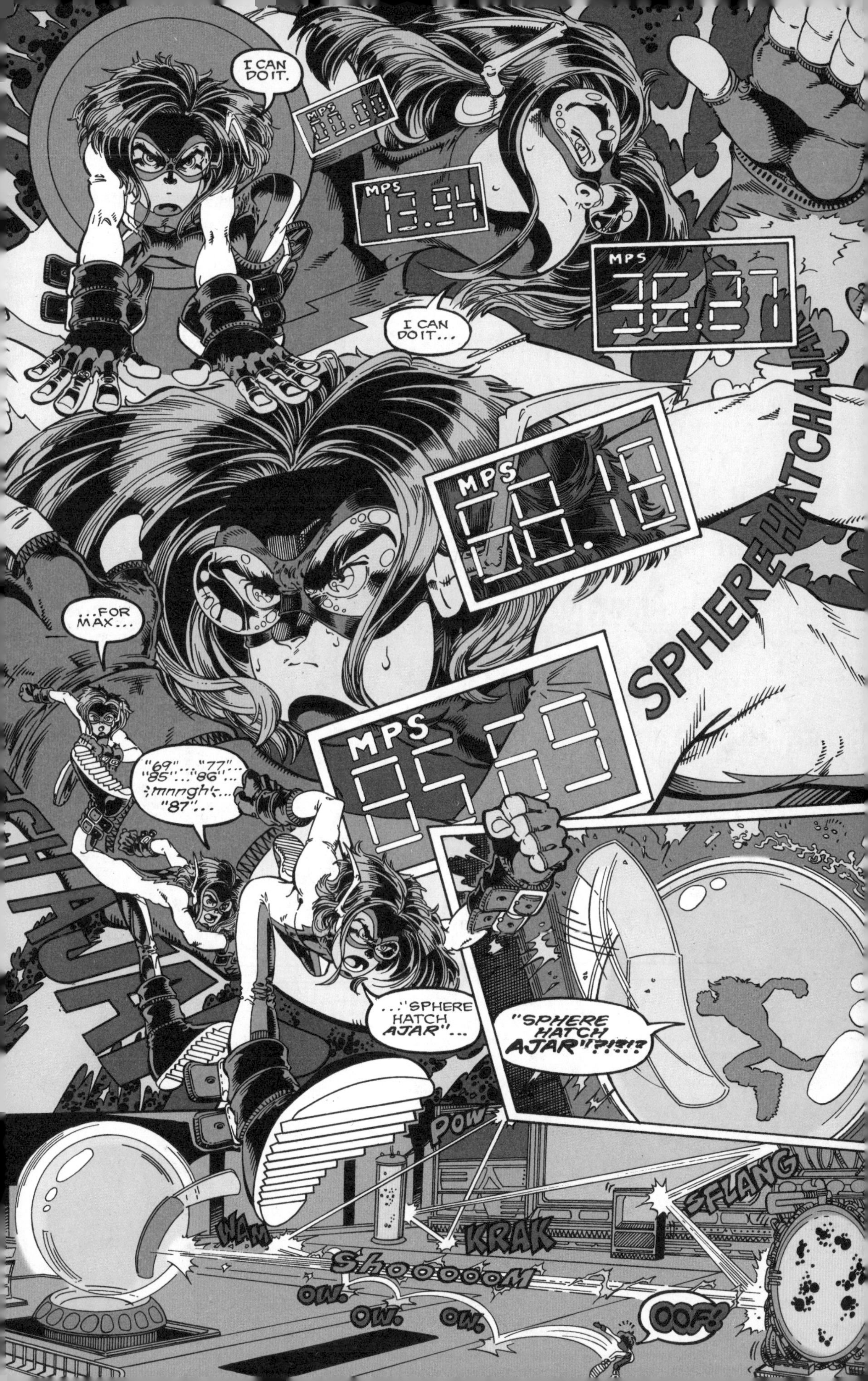
I CAN DO IT.
MPS 00.00
MPS 13.94
MPS 36.87
I CAN DO IT...
MPS 68.10
...FOR MAX...
SPHEREHATCHAJAR
MPS 95.69
"69"..."77" "85"..."86"... ;mnngh!;... "87"...
..."SPHERE HATCH AJAR"...
"SPHERE HATCH AJAR"?!?!?
POW
WAM
KRAK
SFLANG
Shoooooom
OW. OW. OW.
OOF!

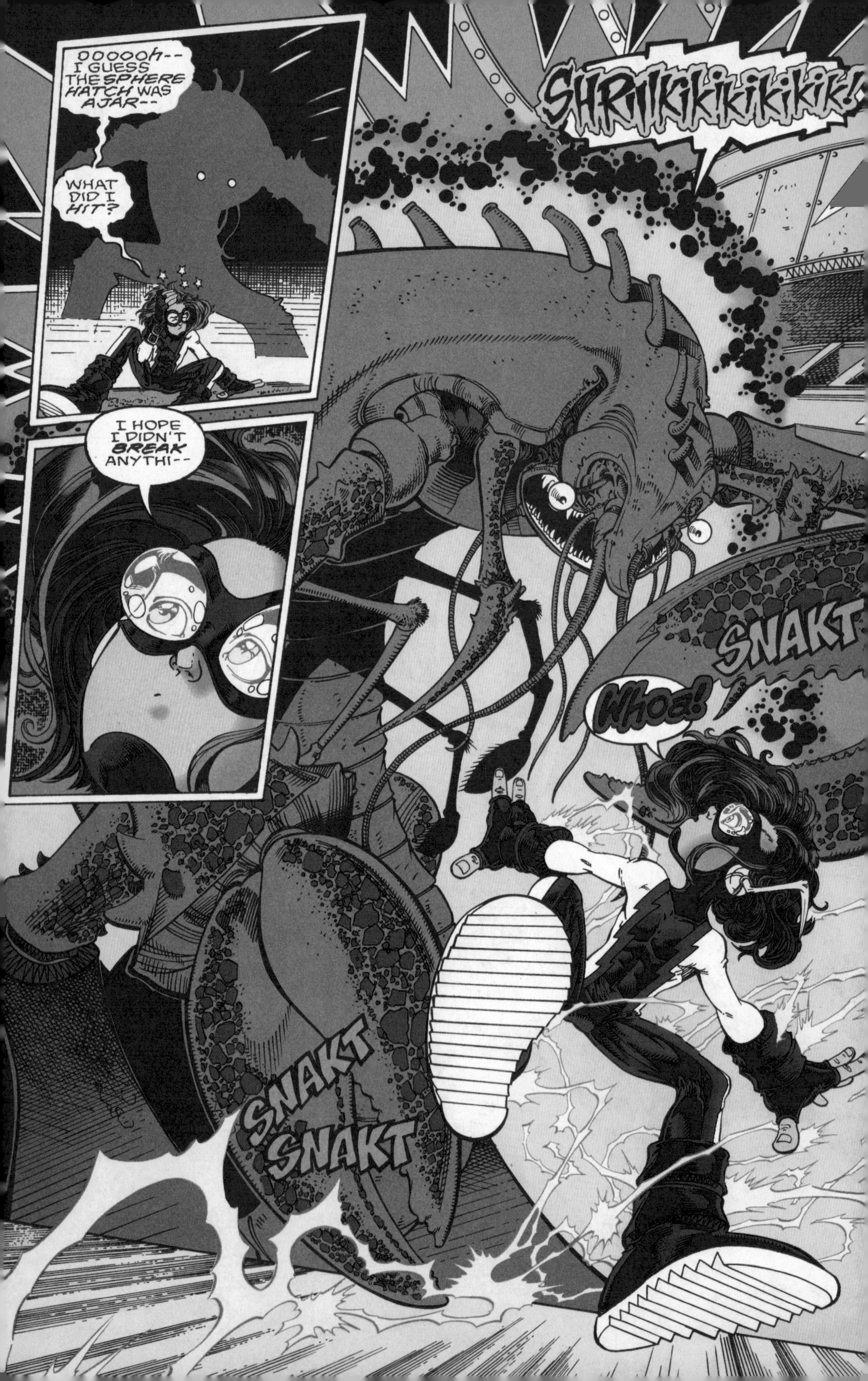
OOOOOOh-- I GUESS THE SPHERE HATCH WAS AJAR--
WHAT DID I HIT?
I HOPE I DIDN'T BREAK ANYTHI--
SHRIIIKIKIKIKIKIK!
SNAKT
WHOA!
SNAKT
SNAKT

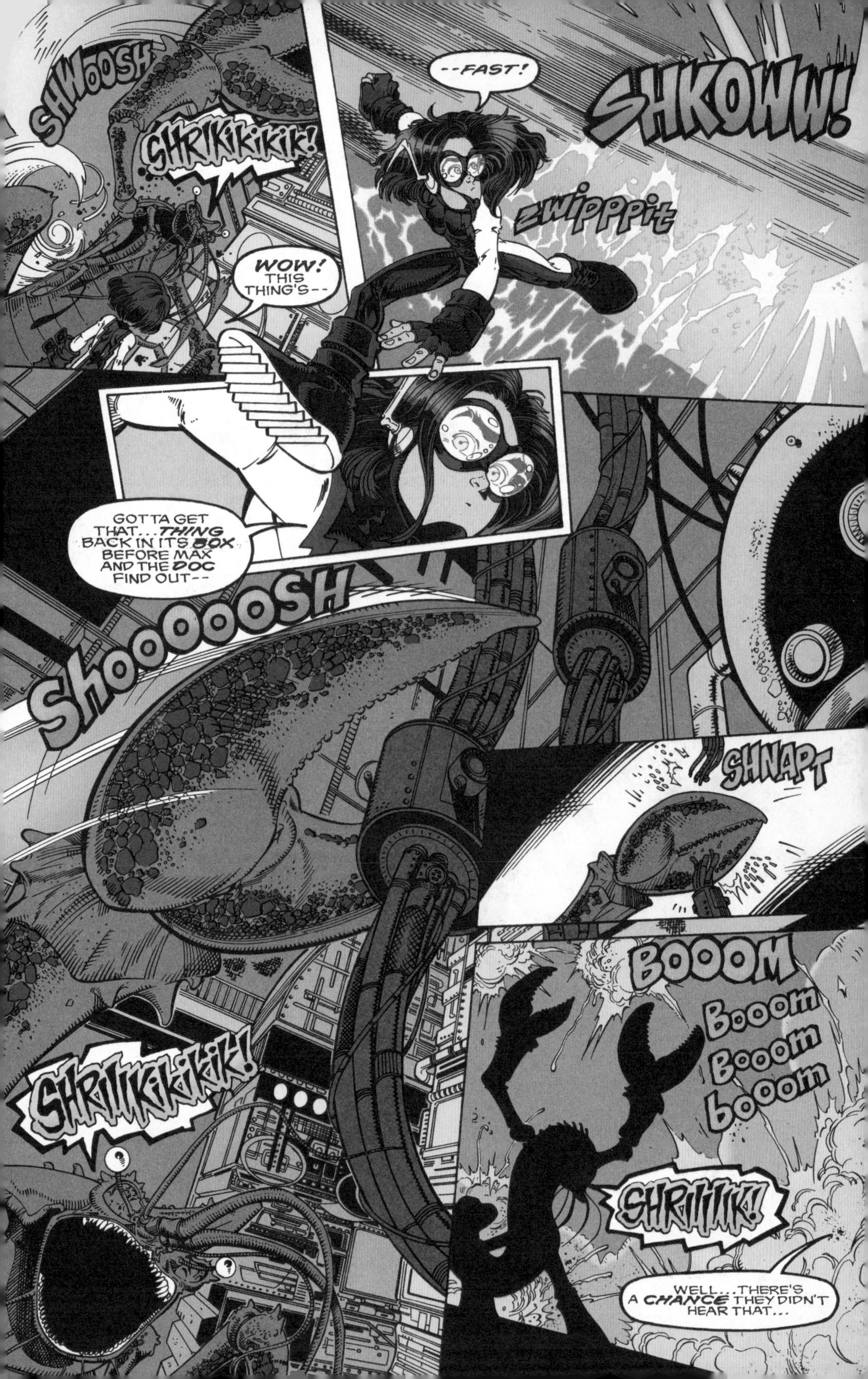
SHWOOSH
SHRIKIKIKIK!
WOW! THIS THING'S--
--FAST!
SHKOWW!
ZWIPPPIT
GOTTA GET THAT... THING BACK IN ITS BOX BEFORE MAX AND THE DOC FIND OUT--
SHOOOOOSH
SHNAPT
SHRIIIKIKIKIK!
BOOOM
Booom
Booom
booom
SHRIIIIIK!
WELL... THERE'S A CHANCE THEY DIDN'T HEAR THAT...

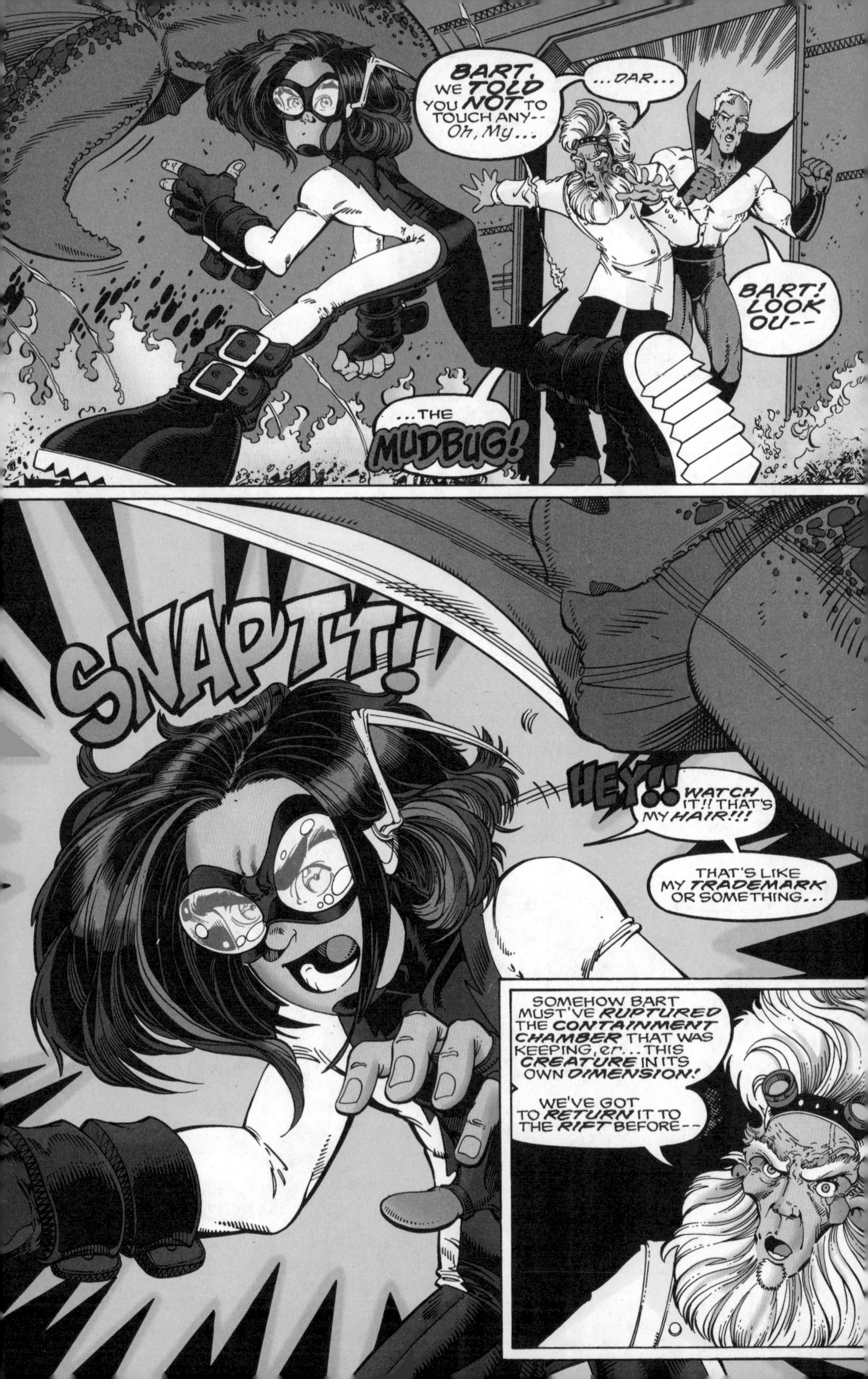
BART, WE TOLD YOU NOT TO TOUCH ANY-- Oh, My...
...DAR...
BART! LOOK OU--
...THE MUDBUG!
SNAPTT!
HEY!! WATCH IT!! THAT'S MY HAIR!!!
THAT'S LIKE MY TRADEMARK OR SOMETHING...
SOMEHOW BART MUST'VE RUPTURED THE CONTAINMENT CHAMBER THAT WAS KEEPING, er... THIS CREATURE IN ITS OWN DIMENSION!
WE'VE GOT TO RETURN IT TO THE RIFT BEFORE--

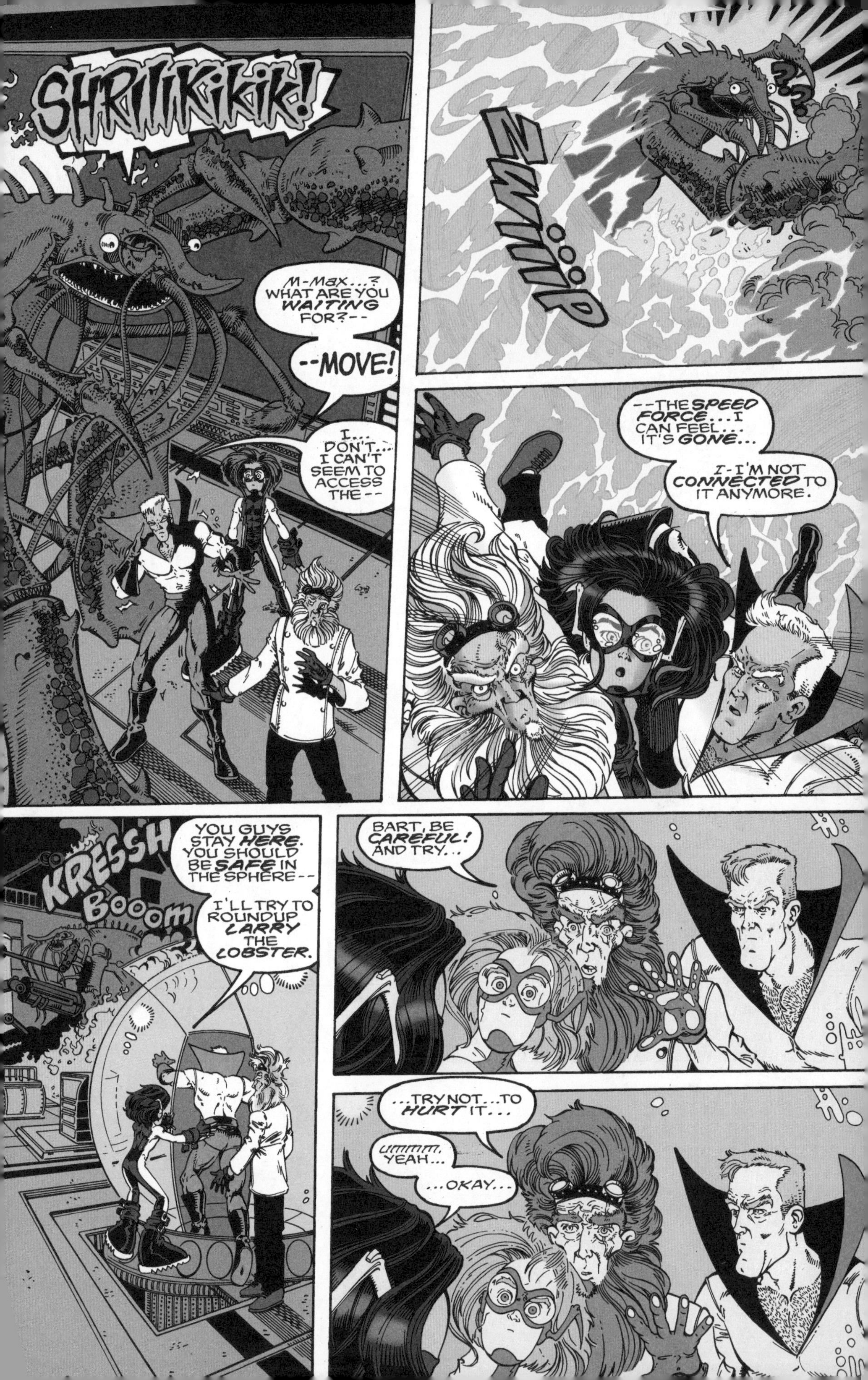
SHRIIIKIKIK!
M-MAX...? WHAT ARE YOU WAITING FOR?--
--MOVE!
I... DON'T... I CAN'T SEEM TO ACCESS THE--
ZWIIIOOOP
--THE SPEED FORCE...I CAN FEEL... IT'S GONE...
I-I'M NOT CONNECTED TO IT ANYMORE.
KRESSH
Booom
YOU GUYS STAY HERE. YOU SHOULD BE SAFE IN THE SPHERE--
I'LL TRY TO ROUNDUP LARRY THE LOBSTER.
BART, BE CAREFUL! AND TRY...
...TRY NOT...TO HURT IT...
UMMMM, YEAH...
...OKAY...

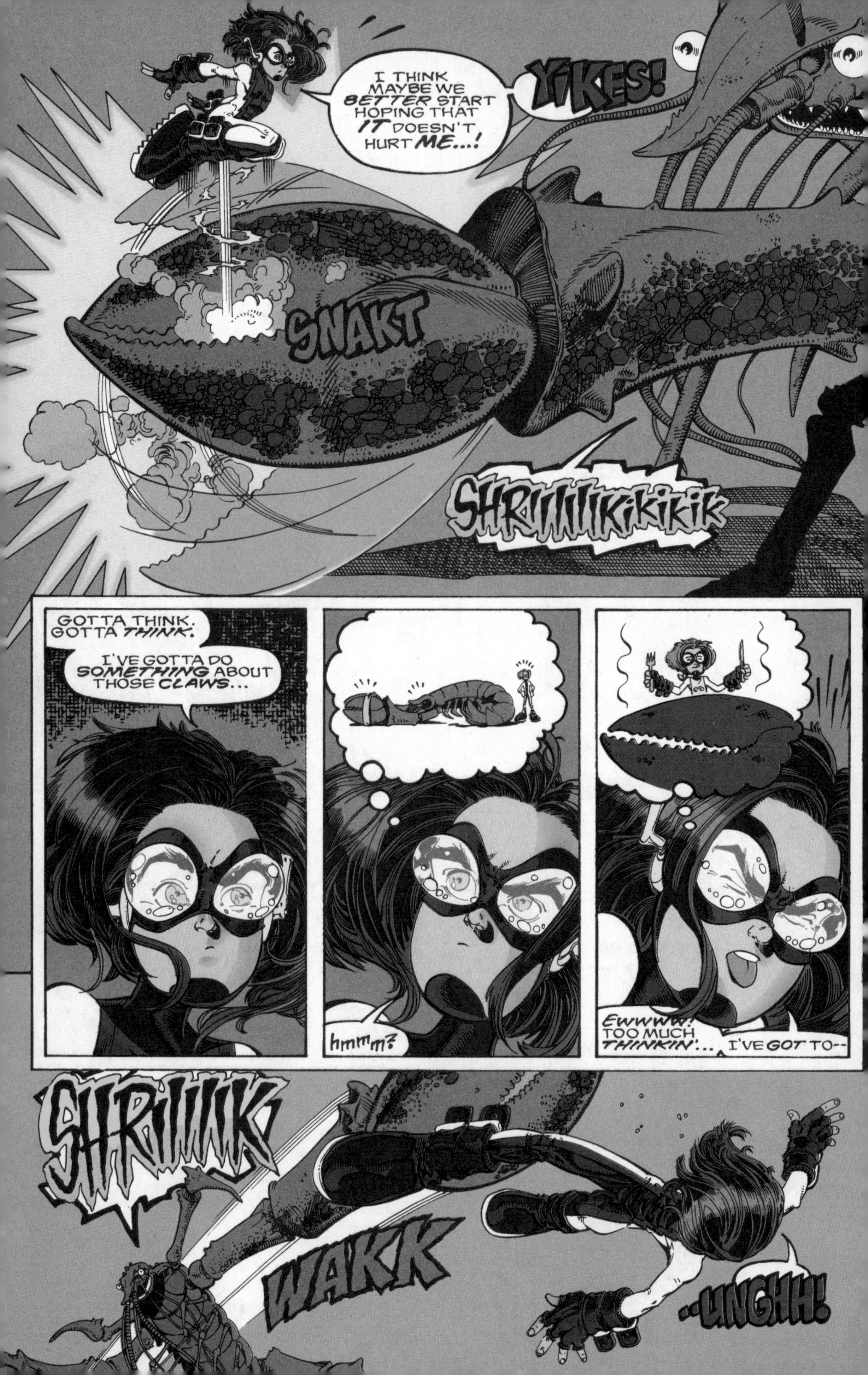

I THINK MAYBE WE BETTER START HOPING THAT IT DOESN'T HURT ME...!
YIKES!
SNAKT
SHRIIIIIKIKIKIK
GOTTA THINK. GOTTA THINK.
I'VE GOTTA DO SOMETHING ABOUT THOSE CLAWS...
hmmm?
EWWWW! TOO MUCH THINKIN'... I'VE GOT TO--
SHRIIIK
WAKK
--UNGHH!

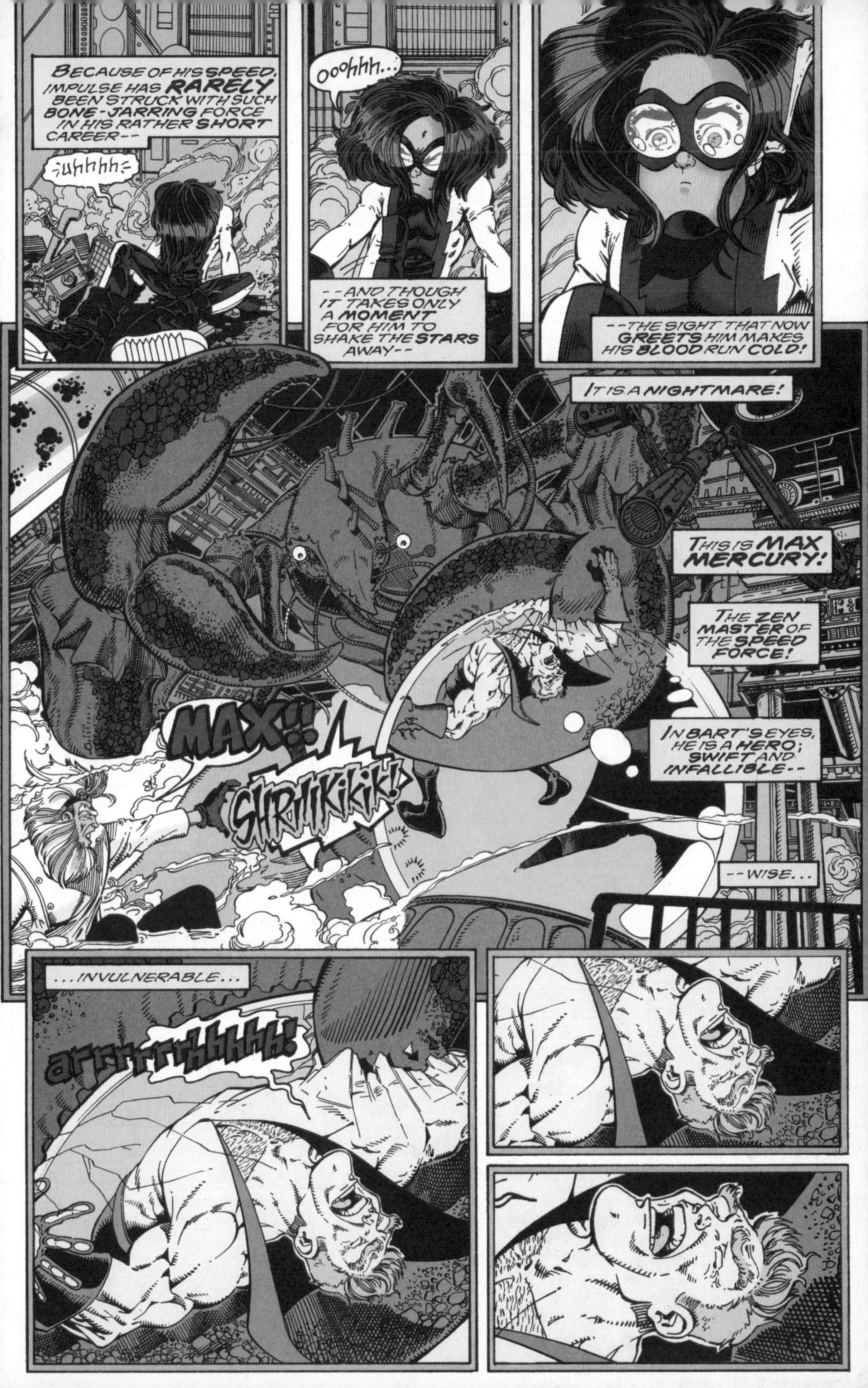
BECAUSE OF HIS SPEED, IMPULSE HAS RARELY BEEN STRUCK WITH SUCH BONE-JARRING FORCE IN HIS RATHER SHORT CAREER--
¡uhhhh¡
OOOHHH...
--AND THOUGH IT TAKES ONLY A MOMENT FOR HIM TO SHAKE THE STARS AWAY--
--THE SIGHT THAT NOW GREETS HIM MAKES HIS BLOOD RUN COLD!
IT IS A NIGHTMARE!
THIS IS MAX MERCURY!
THE ZEN MASTER OF THE SPEED FORCE!
IN BART'S EYES, HE IS A HERO; SWIFT AND INFALLIBLE--
MAX!!
SHRIIIKIKIK!
--WISE...
...INVULNERABLE...
arrrrrrhhhhh!

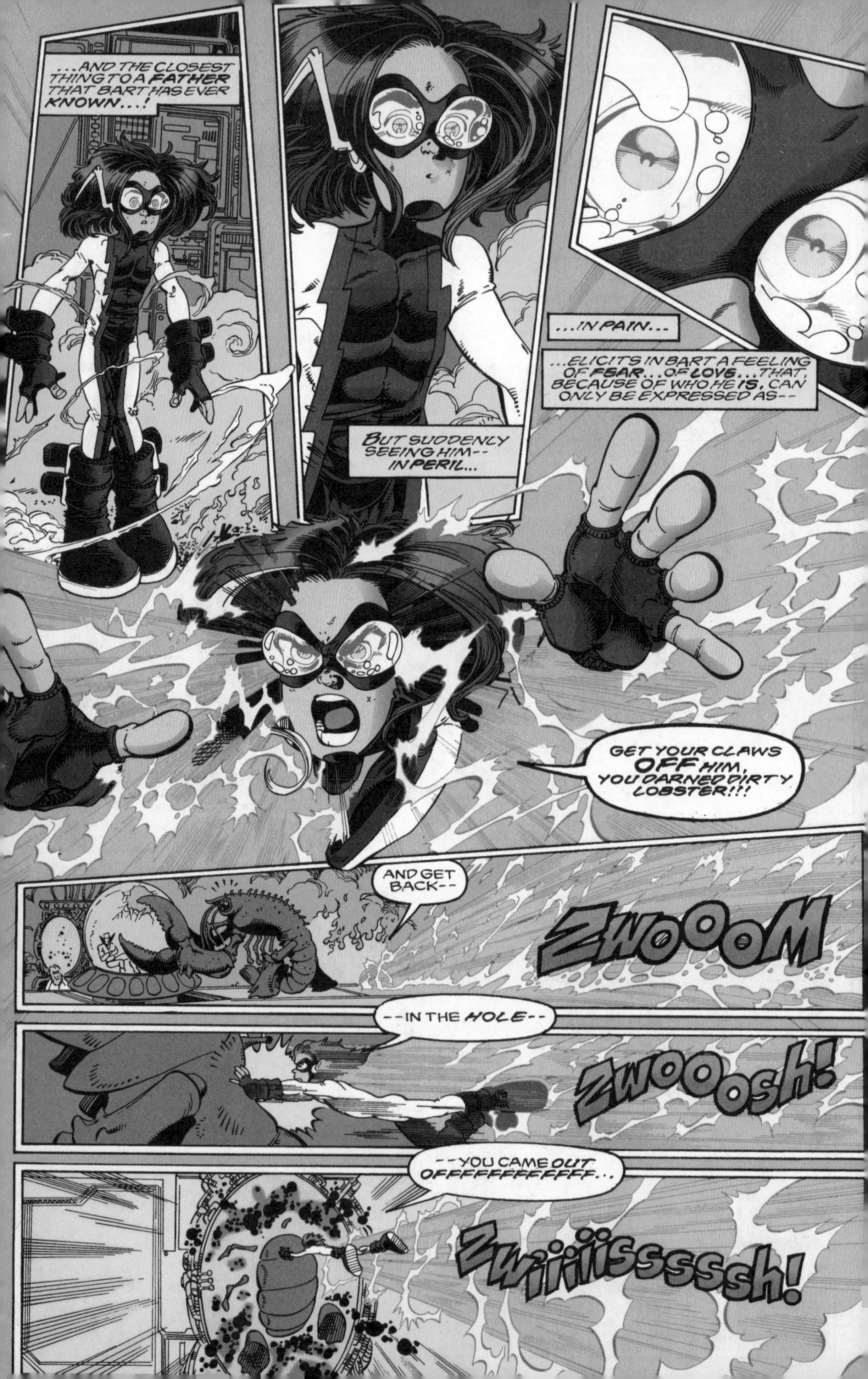
...AND THE CLOSEST THING TO A FATHER THAT BART HAS EVER KNOWN...!
BUT SUDDENLY SEEING HIM-- IN PERIL...
...IN PAIN...
...ELICITS IN BART A FEELING OF FEAR...OF LOVE...THAT, BECAUSE OF WHO HE IS, CAN ONLY BE EXPRESSED AS--
GET YOUR CLAWS OFF HIM, YOU DARNED DIRTY LOBSTER!!!
AND GET BACK--
ZWOOOOM
--IN THE HOLE--
ZWOOOOSH!
--YOU CAME OUT OFFFFFFFFFFFF...
ZWIIIIISSSSSH!

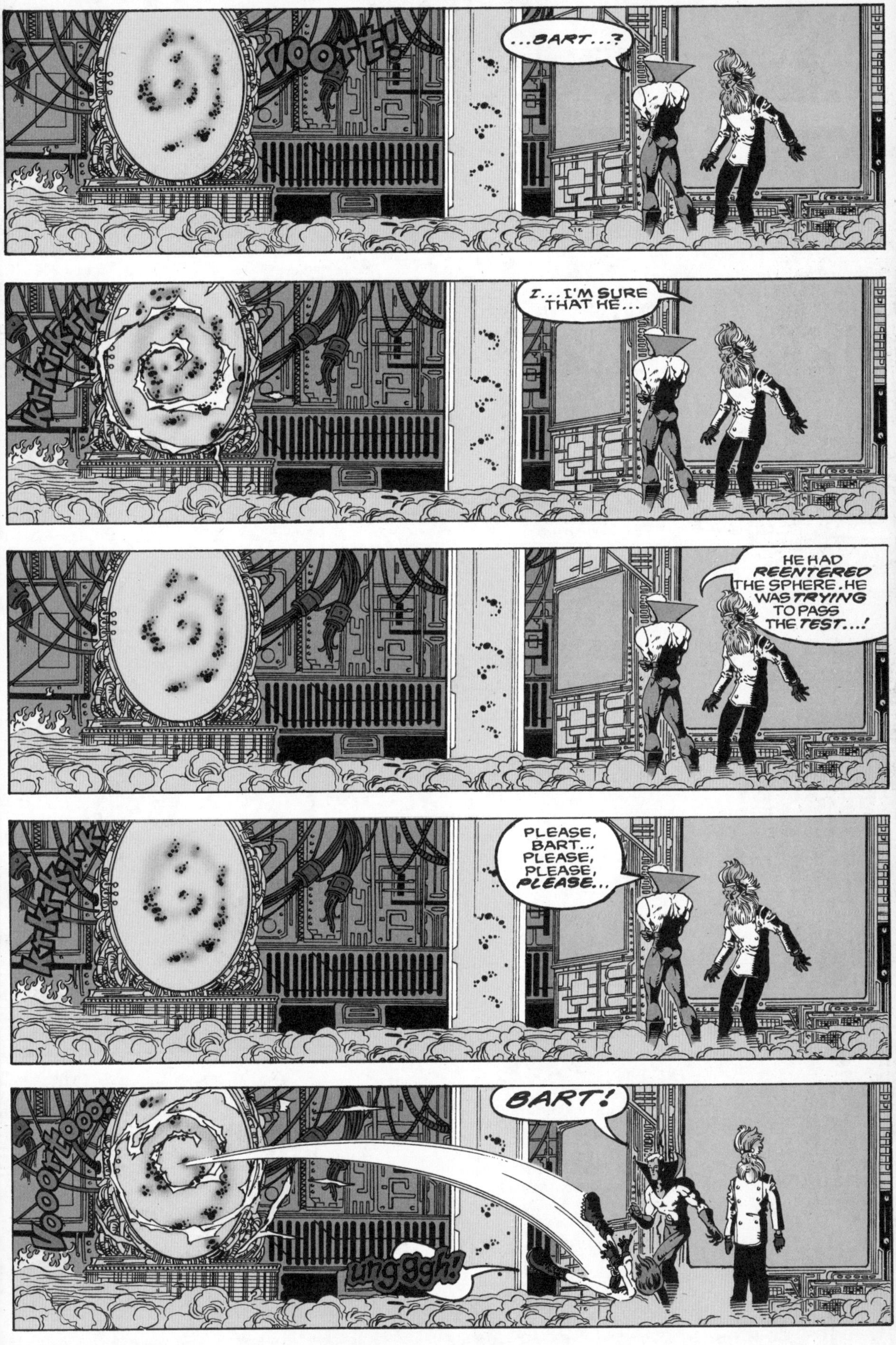
VOOrt!
...BART...?
I...I'M SURE THAT HE...
HE HAD REENTERED THE SPHERE. HE WAS TRYING TO PASS THE TEST...!
PLEASE, BART... PLEASE, PLEASE, PLEASE...
BART!
ungggh!

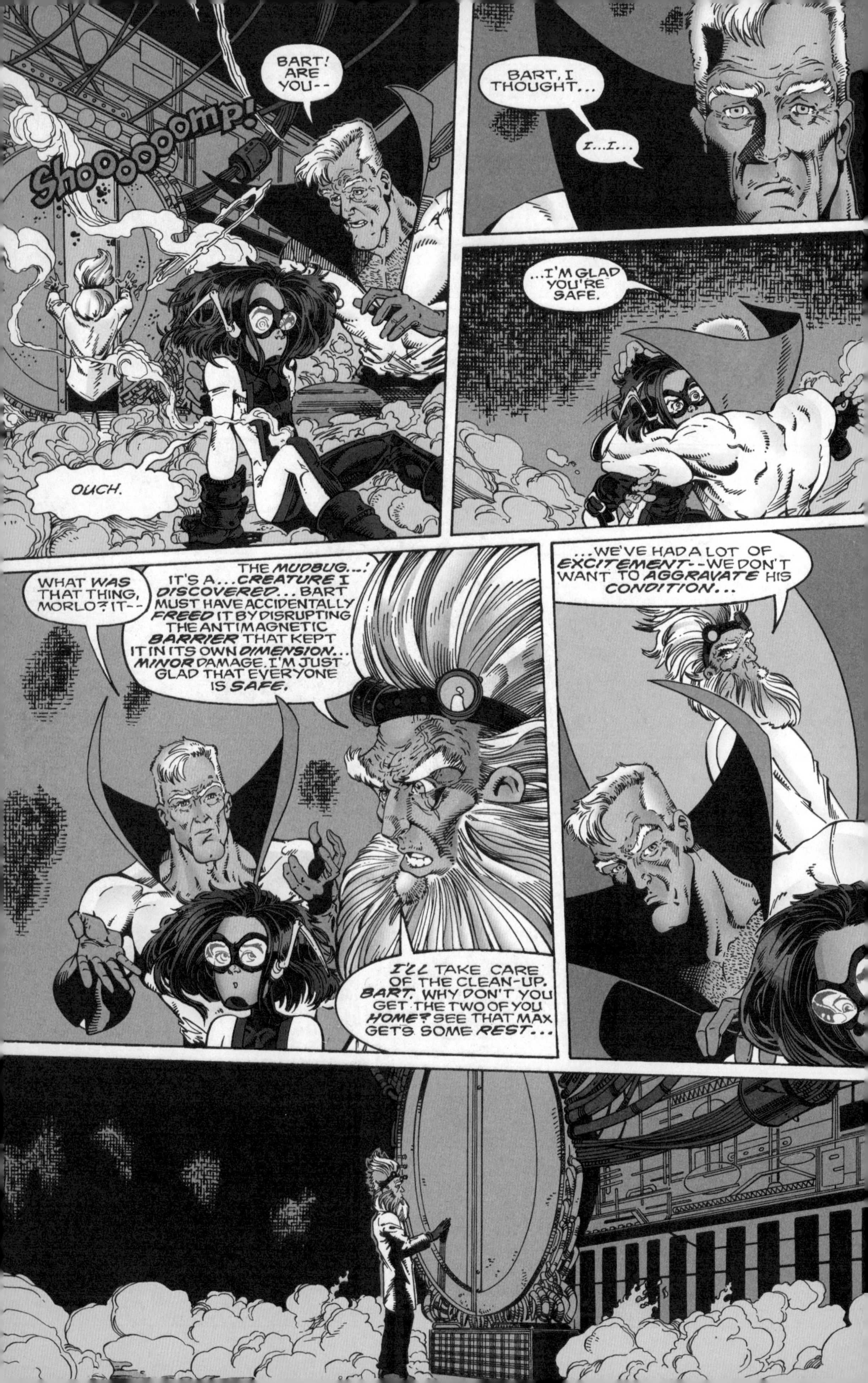
BART! ARE YOU--
SHOOOOOOOMP!
OUCH.
BART, I THOUGHT...
I...I...
...I'M GLAD YOU'RE SAFE.
WHAT WAS THAT THING, MORLO? IT--
THE MUDBUG...! IT'S A...CREATURE I DISCOVERED... BART MUST HAVE ACCIDENTALLY FREED IT BY DISRUPTING THE ANTIMAGNETIC BARRIER THAT KEPT IT IN ITS OWN DIMENSION... MINOR DAMAGE. I'M JUST GLAD THAT EVERYONE IS SAFE.
I'LL TAKE CARE OF THE CLEAN-UP. BART, WHY DON'T YOU GET THE TWO OF YOU HOME? SEE THAT MAX GETS SOME REST...
...WE'VE HAD A LOT OF EXCITEMENT--WE DON'T WANT TO AGGRAVATE HIS CONDITION...

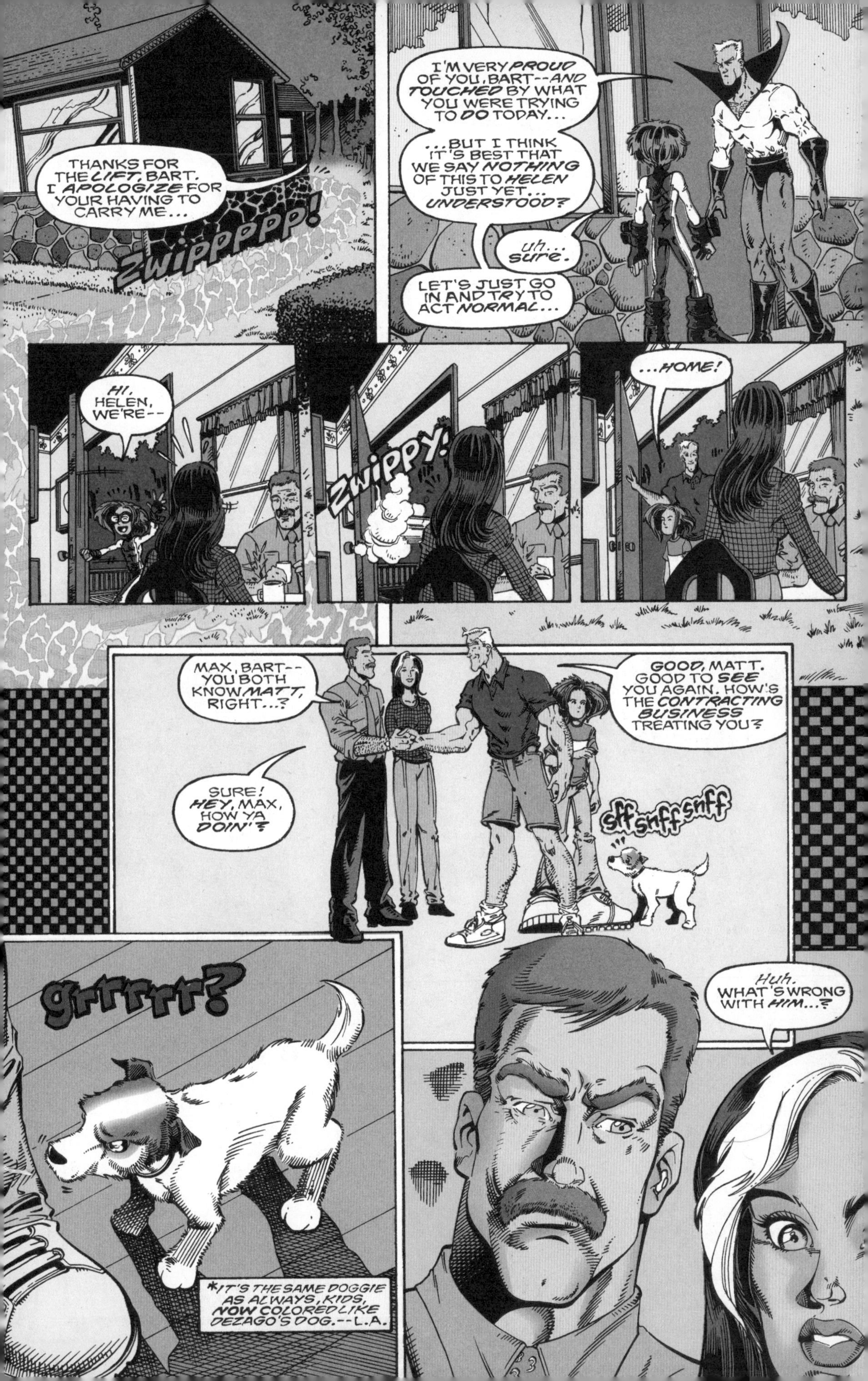
THANKS FOR THE LIFT, BART. I APOLOGIZE FOR YOUR HAVING TO CARRY ME...
ZWIPPPPPP!
I'M VERY PROUD OF YOU, BART--AND TOUCHED BY WHAT YOU WERE TRYING TO DO TODAY...
...BUT I THINK IT'S BEST THAT WE SAY NOTHING OF THIS TO HELEN JUST YET... UNDERSTOOD?
uh... sure.
LET'S JUST GO IN AND TRY TO ACT NORMAL...
HI, HELEN, WE'RE--
ZWIPPY!
...HOME!
MAX, BART--YOU BOTH KNOW MATT, RIGHT...?
GOOD, MATT. GOOD TO SEE YOU AGAIN. HOW'S THE CONTRACTING BUSINESS TREATING YOU?
SURE! HEY, MAX, HOW YA DOIN'?
sff snff snff
grrrrr?
*IT'S THE SAME DOGGIE AS ALWAYS, KIDS, NOW COLORED LIKE DEZAGO'S DOG.--L.A.
Huh. WHAT'S WRONG WITH HIM...?

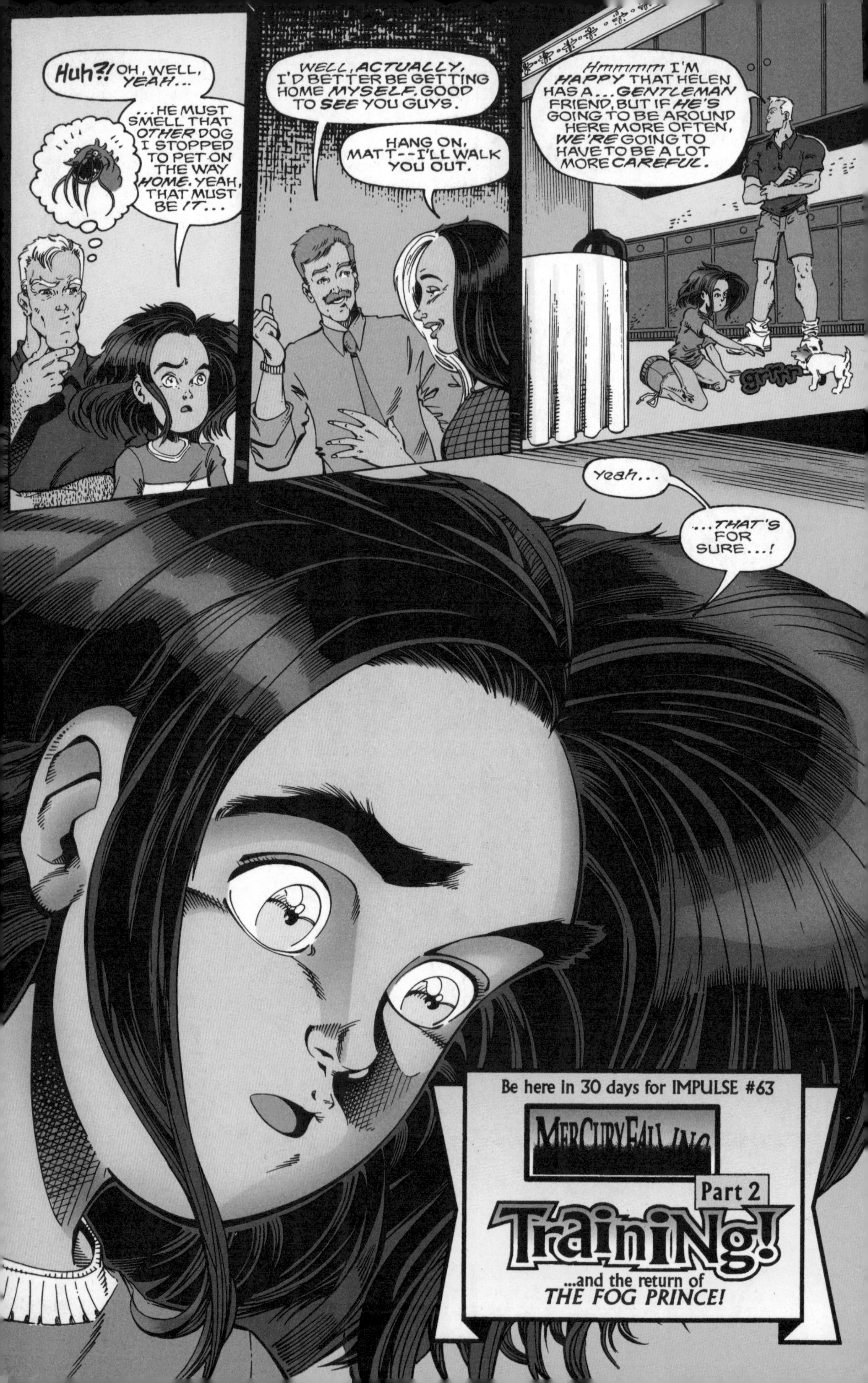
Huh?! OH, WELL, YEAH...
...HE MUST SMELL THAT OTHER DOG I STOPPED TO PET ON THE WAY HOME. YEAH, THAT MUST BE IT...
WELL, ACTUALLY, I'D BETTER BE GETTING HOME MYSELF. GOOD TO SEE YOU GUYS.
HANG ON, MATT--I'LL WALK YOU OUT.
Hmmmmm I'M HAPPY THAT HELEN HAS A... GENTLEMAN FRIEND, BUT IF HE'S GOING TO BE AROUND HERE MORE OFTEN, WE'RE GOING TO HAVE TO BE A LOT MORE CAREFUL.
grrrr
Yeah...
...THAT'S FOR SURE...!
Be here in 30 days for IMPULSE #63
MERCURY FALLING
Part 2
Training!
...and the return of THE FOG PRINCE!

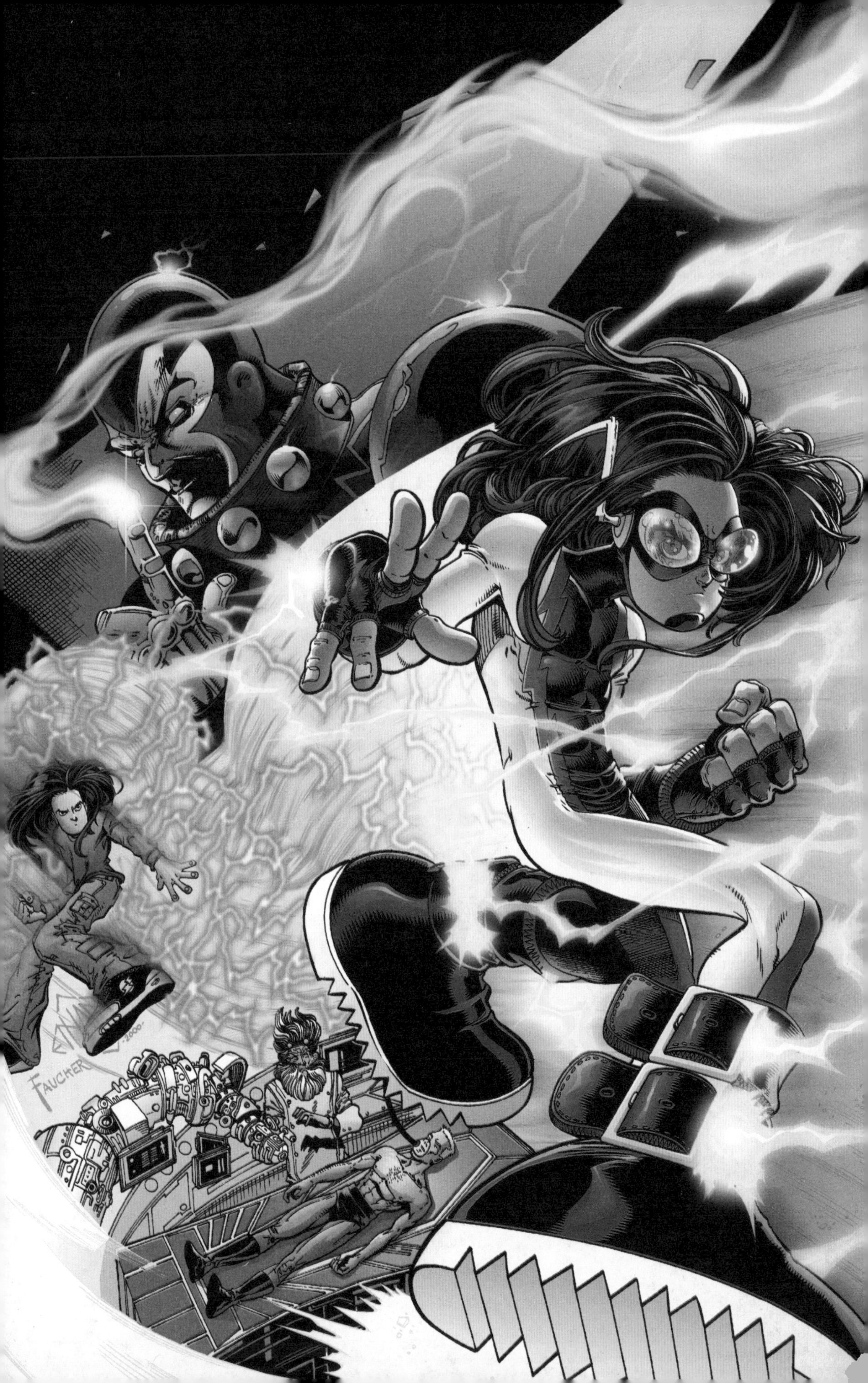
FAUCHER
-2000-

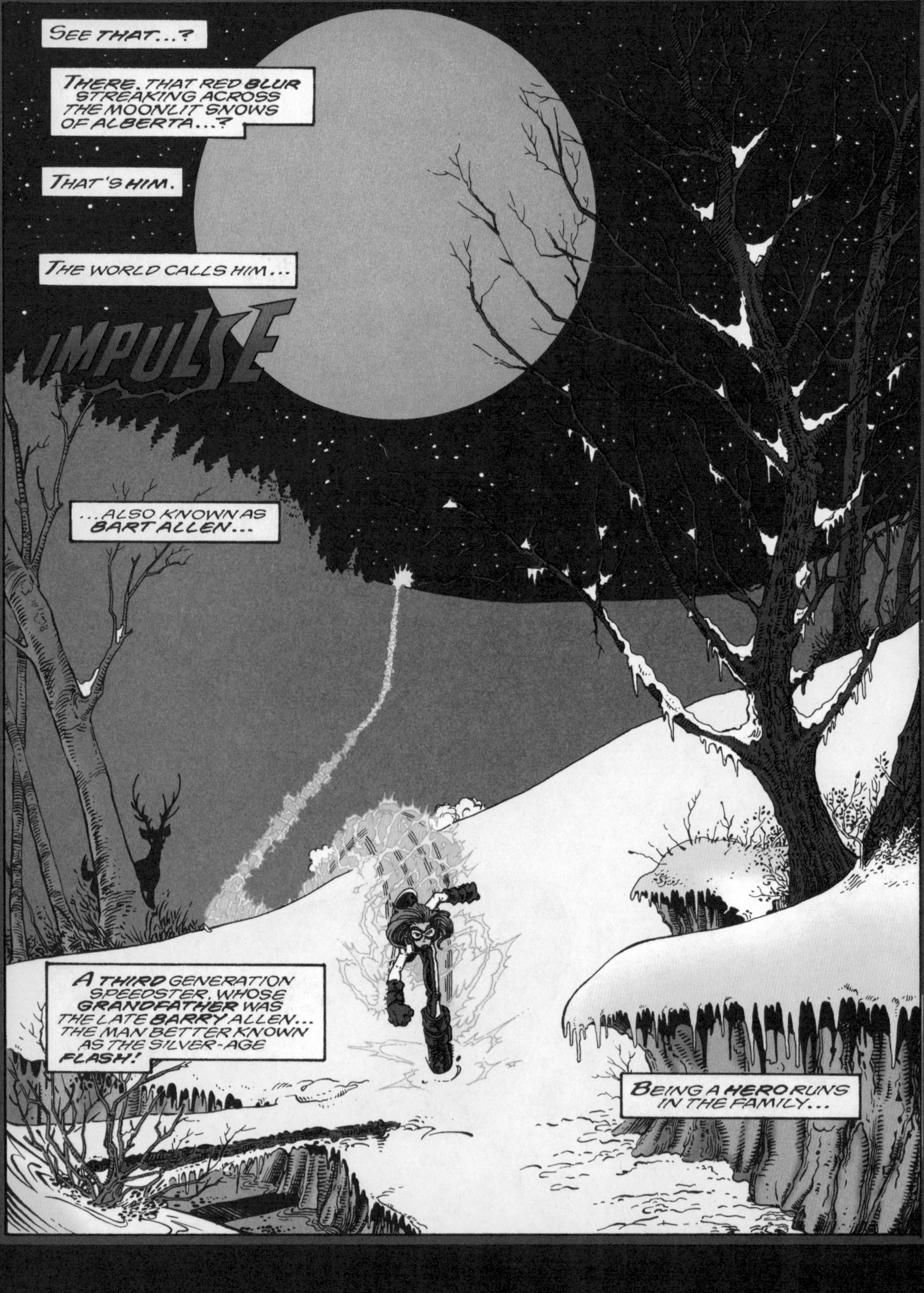
SEE THAT...?
THERE. THAT RED BLUR STREAKING ACROSS THE MOONLIT SNOWS OF ALBERTA...?
THAT'S HIM.
THE WORLD CALLS HIM...
IMPULSE
...ALSO KNOWN AS BART ALLEN...
A THIRD GENERATION SPEEDSTER, WHOSE GRANDFATHER WAS THE LATE BARRY ALLEN... THE MAN BETTER KNOWN AS THE SILVER-AGE FLASH!
BEING A HERO RUNS IN THE FAMILY...

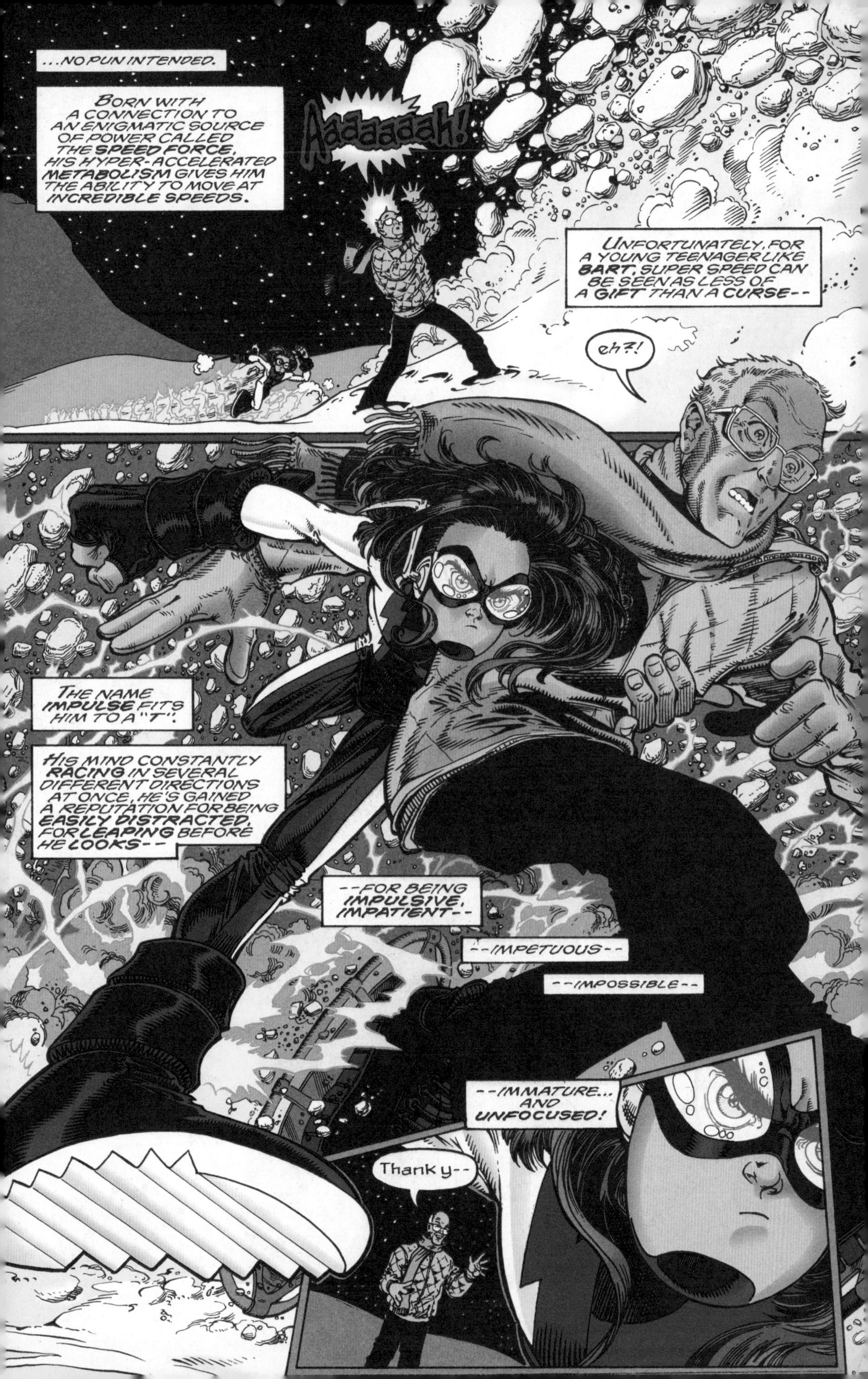

...NO PUN INTENDED.
BORN WITH A CONNECTION TO AN ENIGMATIC SOURCE OF POWER CALLED THE SPEED FORCE, HIS HYPER-ACCELERATED METABOLISM GIVES HIM THE ABILITY TO MOVE AT INCREDIBLE SPEEDS.
Aaaaaaaah!
UNFORTUNATELY, FOR A YOUNG TEENAGER LIKE BART, SUPER SPEED CAN BE SEEN AS LESS OF A GIFT THAN A CURSE--
eh?!
THE NAME IMPULSE FITS HIM TO A "T".
HIS MIND CONSTANTLY RACING IN SEVERAL DIFFERENT DIRECTIONS AT ONCE, HE'S GAINED A REPUTATION FOR BEING EASILY DISTRACTED, FOR LEAPING BEFORE HE LOOKS--
--FOR BEING IMPULSIVE, IMPATIENT--
--IMPETUOUS--
--IMPOSSIBLE--
--IMMATURE... AND UNFOCUSED!
Thank y--

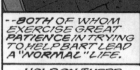

AT HOME, BART LIVES WITH HIS MENTOR AND GUARDIAN, MAX MERCURY, AND MAX'S DAUGHTER, HELEN--

HIYA, BART! HOW WAS SCHOOL TODAY, SWEETIE?

OKAY.

--BOTH OF WHOM EXERCISE GREAT PATIENCE IN TRYING TO HELP BART LEAD A "NORMAL" LIFE.

HOLD ON THERE, MISTER--NO PLAYING VIDEO GAMES UNTIL YOU COME BACK AND HANG UP YOUR--

--JACKET?!?

HE DID IT... HE ACTUALLY DID IT?! WITHOUT BEING TOLD!?

HE'S GOT TO BE UP TO SOMETHING...

BART, BEFORE YOU GO OUT TO HANG WITH YOUR FRIENDS, I WANT YOU TO BE SURE TO CLEAN UP THIS PIGS-

--ty...?

WHAT'S GOING ON HERE?! THE PLACE IS SPOTLESS!!

WHAT ARE YOU WORKING ON?

OH, JUST MY HOMEWORK. I THOUGHT I'D GET IT DONE NOW, BEFORE I GO OUT WITH THE GUYS AND THAT WAY I WON'T HAFTA WORRY ABOUT IT LATER.

HOMEWORK!! HE'S ACTUALLY DOING HIS HOMEWORK!

I TOLD MAX THAT MY WORKING WITH BART ON HIS PERSONAL SKILLS WOULD PAY OFF...!

I ROCK! YEA, ME!

*HELEN TOOK ON THIS RESPONSIBILITY BACK IN IMPULSE #52.--L.A.W.

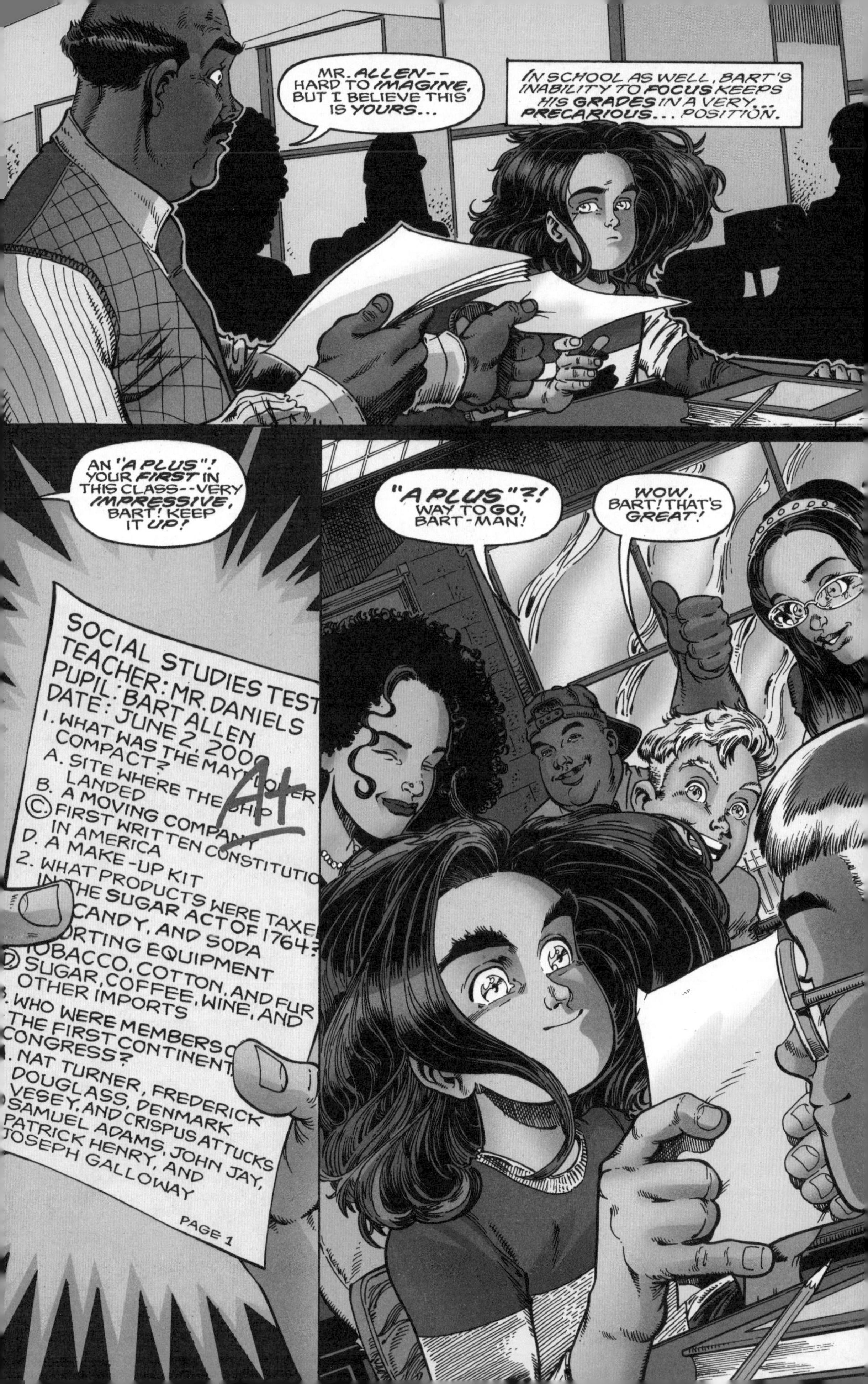
MR. ALLEN-- HARD TO IMAGINE, BUT I BELIEVE THIS IS YOURS...
IN SCHOOL AS WELL, BART'S INABILITY TO FOCUS KEEPS HIS GRADES IN A VERY... PRECARIOUS... POSITION.
AN "A PLUS"! YOUR FIRST IN THIS CLASS--VERY IMPRESSIVE, BART! KEEP IT UP!
SOCIAL STUDIES TEST
TEACHER: MR. DANIELS
PUPIL: BART ALLEN
DATE: JUNE 2, 200
1. WHAT WAS THE MAY COMPACT?
A. SITE WHERE THE SHIP LANDED
B. A MOVING COMPANY
C. FIRST WRITTEN CONSTITUTIO IN AMERICA
D. A MAKE-UP KIT
A+
2. WHAT PRODUCTS WERE TAXE THE SUGAR ACT OF 1764?
CANDY, AND SODA
ORTING EQUIPMENT
OBACCO, COTTON, AND FUR
D SUGAR, COFFEE, WINE, AND OTHER IMPORTS
WHO WERE MEMBERS THE FIRST CONTINENT CONGRESS?
NAT TURNER, FREDERICK DOUGLASS, DENMARK VESEY, AND CRISPUS ATTUCKS
SAMUEL ADAMS, JOHN JAY, PATRICK HENRY, AND JOSEPH GALLOWAY
PAGE 1
"A PLUS"?! WAY TO GO, BART-MAN!
WOW, BART! THAT'S GREAT!

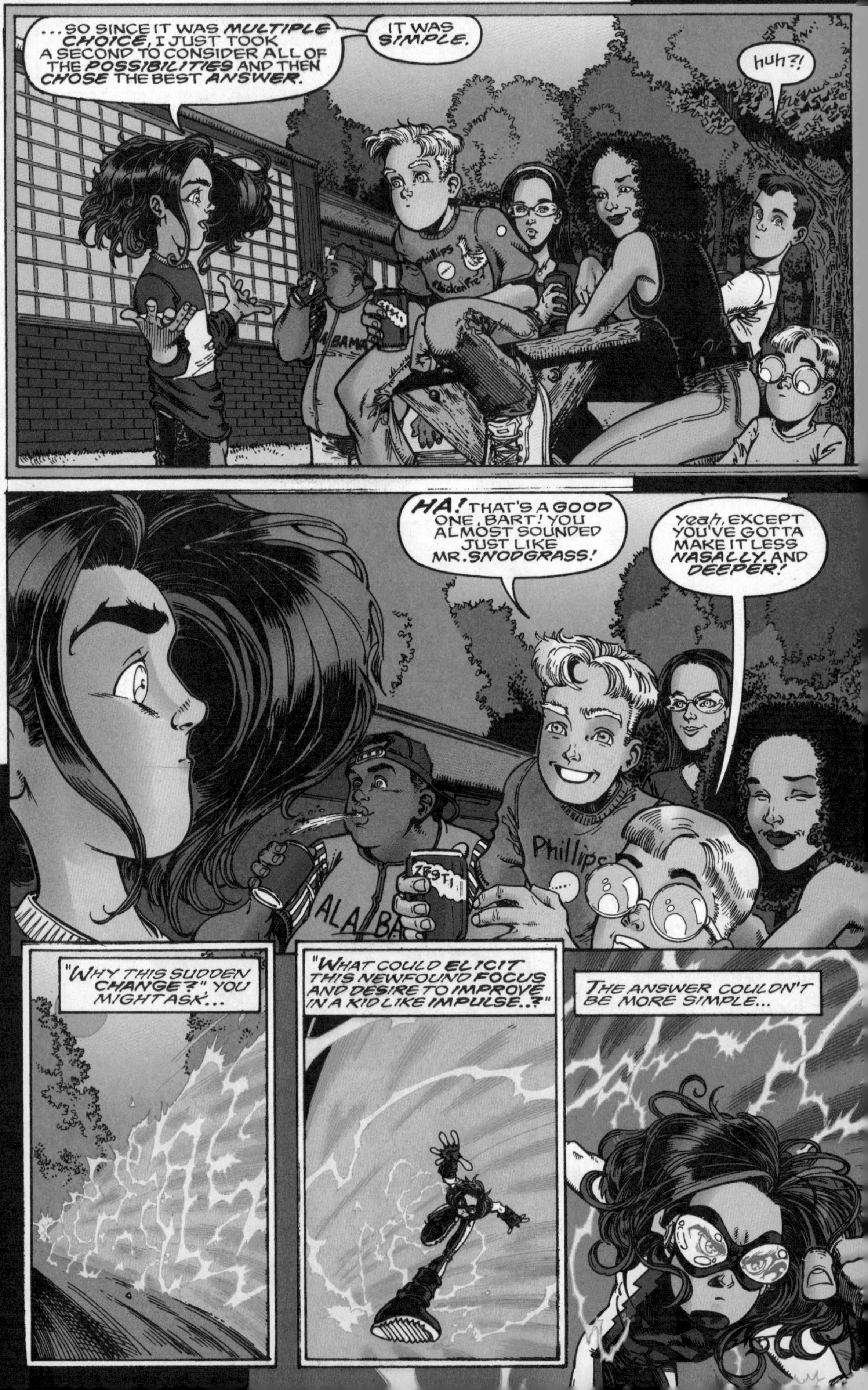
...SO SINCE IT WAS MULTIPLE CHOICE, I JUST TOOK A SECOND TO CONSIDER ALL OF THE POSSIBILITIES AND THEN CHOSE THE BEST ANSWER.
IT WAS SIMPLE.
huh?!
HA! THAT'S A GOOD ONE, BART! YOU ALMOST SOUNDED JUST LIKE MR. SNODGRASS!
Yeah, EXCEPT YOU'VE GOTTA MAKE IT LESS NASALLY. AND DEEPER!
...
"WHY THIS SUDDEN CHANGE?" YOU MIGHT ASK...
"WHAT COULD ELICIT THIS NEWFOUND FOCUS AND DESIRE TO IMPROVE IN A KID LIKE IMPULSE..?"
THE ANSWER COULDN'T BE MORE SIMPLE...

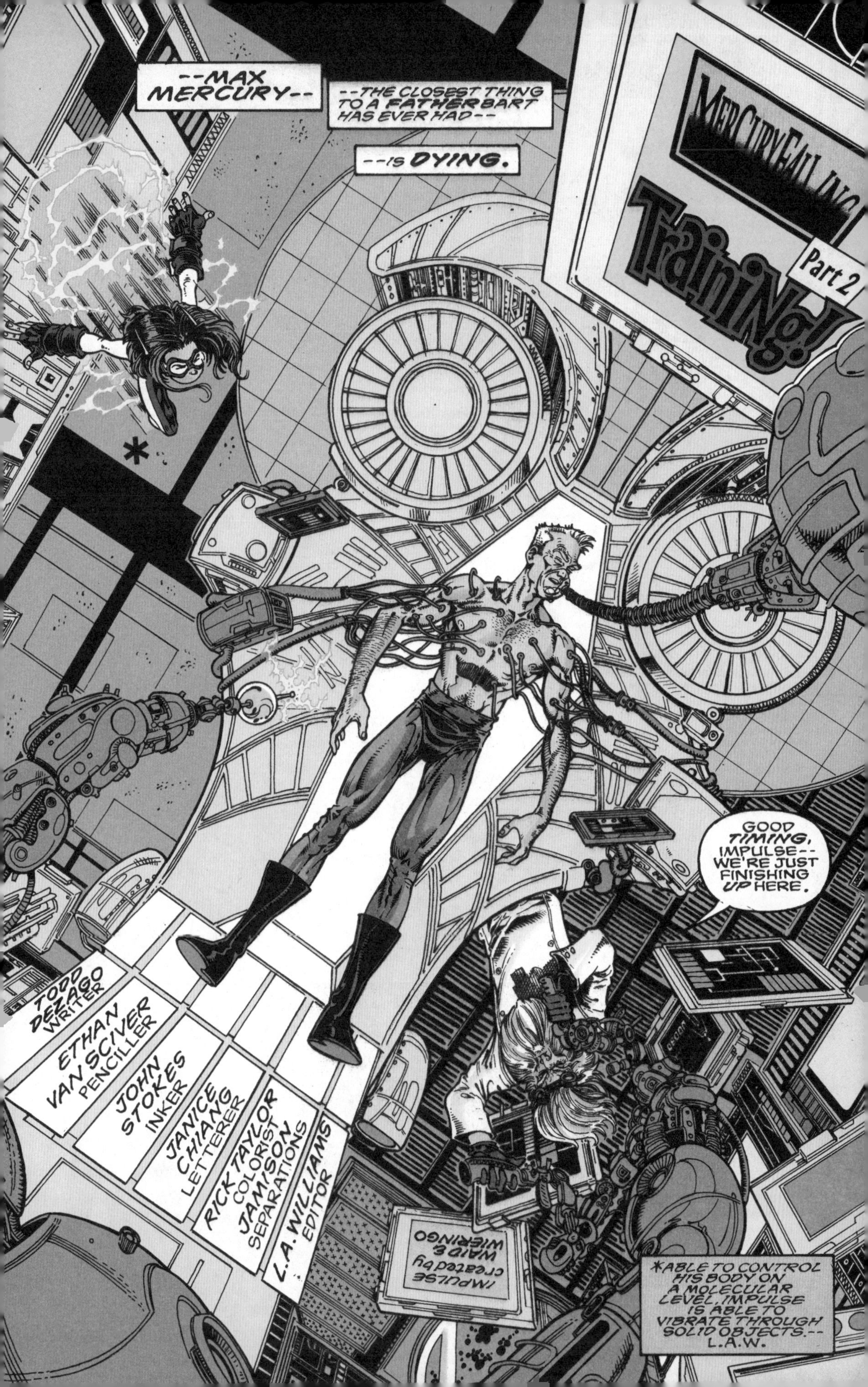
--MAX MERCURY--
--THE CLOSEST THING TO A FATHER BART HAS EVER HAD--
--IS DYING.
MERCURY FALLING
Training!
Part 2
GOOD TIMING, IMPULSE--WE'RE JUST FINISHING UP HERE.
*ABLE TO CONTROL HIS BODY ON A MOLECULAR LEVEL, IMPULSE IS ABLE TO VIBRATE THROUGH SOLID OBJECTS.--L.A.W.
TODD DEZAGO WRITER
ETHAN VAN SCIVER PENCILLER
JOHN STOKES INKER
JANICE CHIANG LETTERER
RICK TAYLOR COLORIST
JAMISON SEPARATIONS
L.A. WILLIAMS EDITOR
IMPULSE created by WAID & WIERINGO

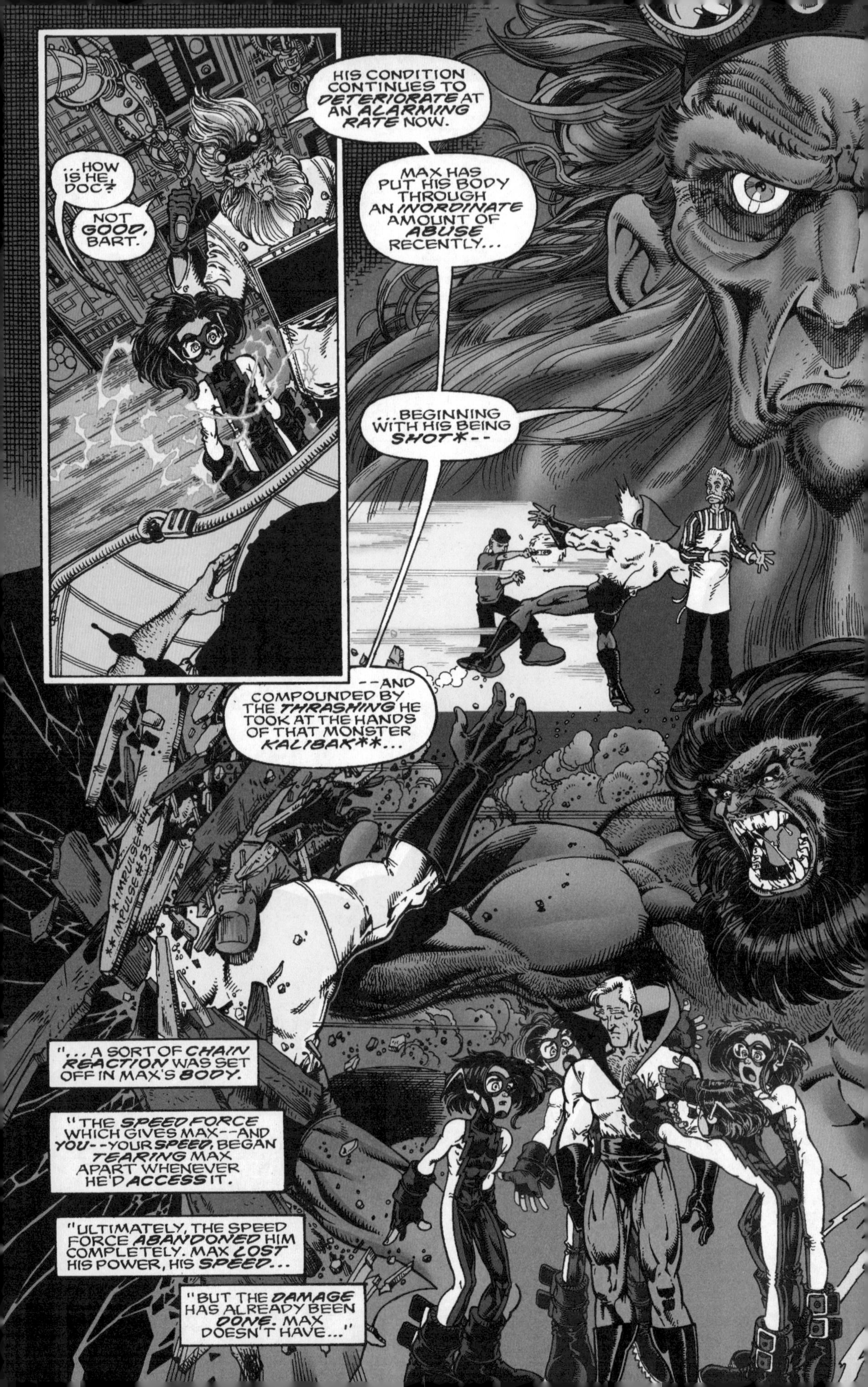
...HOW IS HE, DOC?
NOT GOOD, BART.
HIS CONDITION CONTINUES TO DETERIORATE AT AN ALARMING RATE NOW.
MAX HAS PUT HIS BODY THROUGH AN INORDINATE AMOUNT OF ABUSE RECENTLY...
...BEGINNING WITH HIS BEING SHOT*--
--AND COMPOUNDED BY THE THRASHING HE TOOK AT THE HANDS OF THAT MONSTER KALIBAK**...
*IMPULSE #44
**IMPULSE #53
"...A SORT OF CHAIN REACTION WAS SET OFF IN MAX'S BODY.
"THE SPEED FORCE WHICH GIVES MAX--AND YOU--YOUR SPEED, BEGAN TEARING MAX APART WHENEVER HE'D ACCESS IT.
"ULTIMATELY, THE SPEED FORCE ABANDONED HIM COMPLETELY. MAX LOST HIS POWER, HIS SPEED...
"BUT THE DAMAGE HAS ALREADY BEEN DONE. MAX DOESN'T HAVE..."

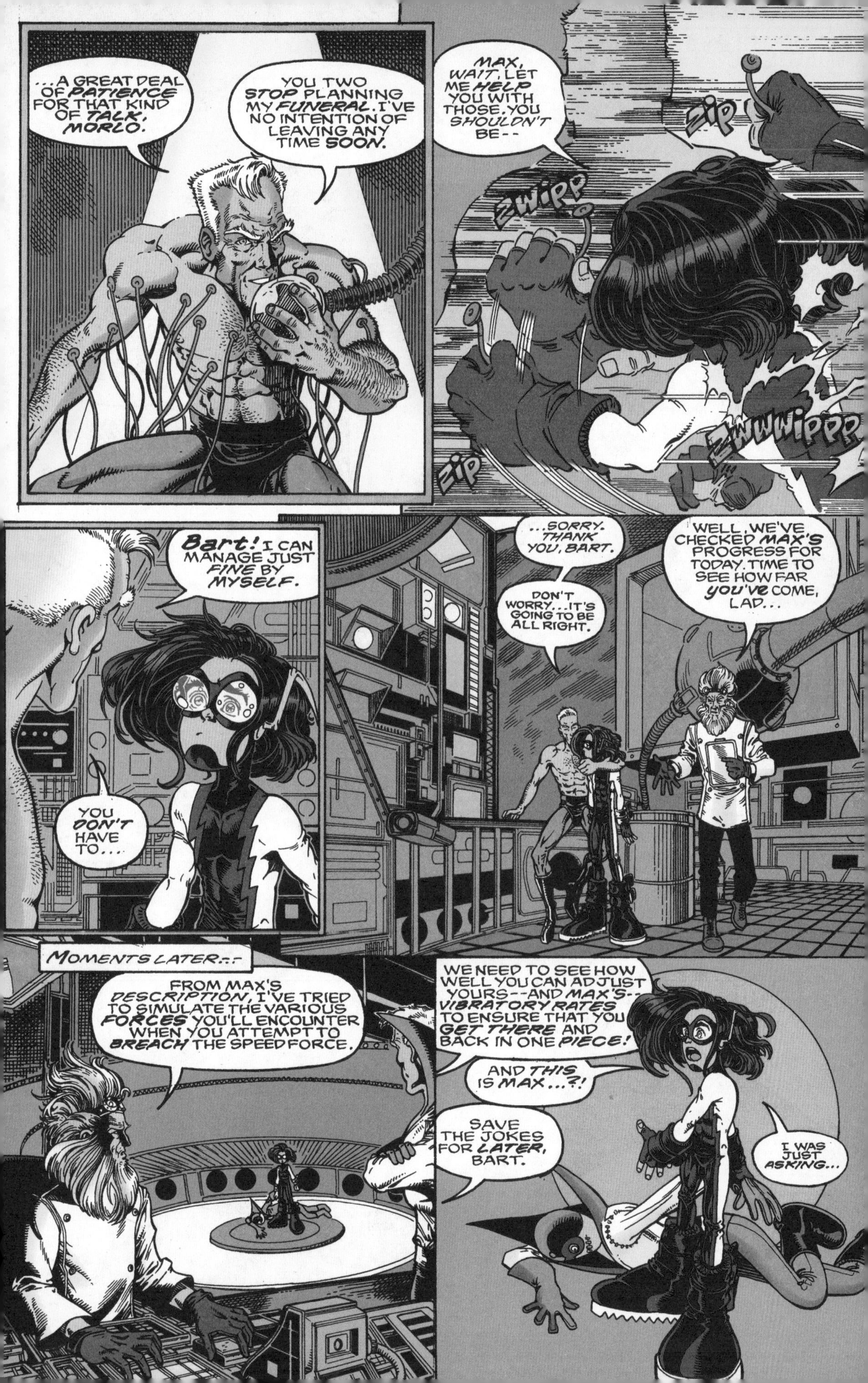
...A GREAT DEAL OF PATIENCE FOR THAT KIND OF TALK, MORLO.
YOU TWO STOP PLANNING MY FUNERAL. I'VE NO INTENTION OF LEAVING ANY TIME SOON.
MAX, WAIT, LET ME HELP YOU WITH THOSE. YOU SHOULDN'T BE--
ZIP
ZWIPP
ZWWWIPPP
ZIP
Bart! I CAN MANAGE JUST FINE BY MYSELF.
YOU DON'T HAVE TO...
...SORRY. THANK YOU, BART.
DON'T WORRY...IT'S GOING TO BE ALL RIGHT.
WELL, WE'VE CHECKED MAX'S PROGRESS FOR TODAY. TIME TO SEE HOW FAR YOU'VE COME, LAD...
MOMENTS LATER...
FROM MAX'S DESCRIPTION, I'VE TRIED TO SIMULATE THE VARIOUS FORCES YOU'LL ENCOUNTER WHEN YOU ATTEMPT TO BREACH THE SPEED FORCE.
WE NEED TO SEE HOW WELL YOU CAN ADJUST YOURS--AND MAX'S--VIBRATORY RATES TO ENSURE THAT YOU GET THERE AND BACK IN ONE PIECE!
AND THIS IS MAX...?!
SAVE THE JOKES FOR LATER, BART.
I WAS JUST ASKING...

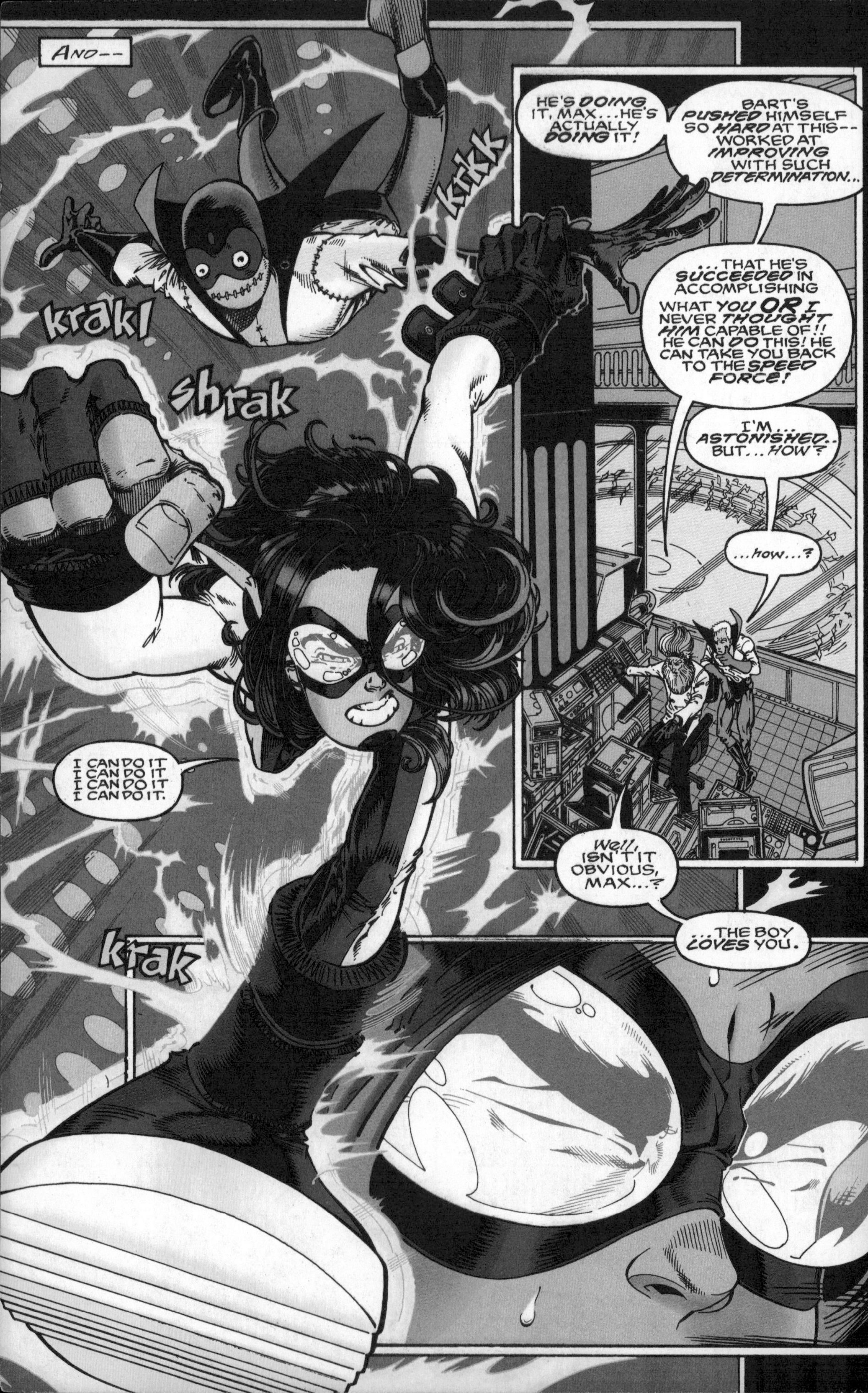
AND--
krkk
krak!
shrak
HE'S DOING IT, MAX... HE'S ACTUALLY DOING IT!
BART'S PUSHED HIMSELF SO HARD AT THIS-- WORKED AT IMPROVING WITH SUCH DETERMINATION...
...THAT HE'S SUCCEEDED IN ACCOMPLISHING WHAT YOU OR I NEVER THOUGHT HIM CAPABLE OF!! HE CAN DO THIS! HE CAN TAKE YOU BACK TO THE SPEED FORCE!
I'M... ASTONISHED... BUT... HOW?
...how...?
I CAN DO IT I CAN DO IT I CAN DO IT I CAN DO IT.
Well, ISN'T IT OBVIOUS, MAX...?
...THE BOY LOVES YOU.
krak

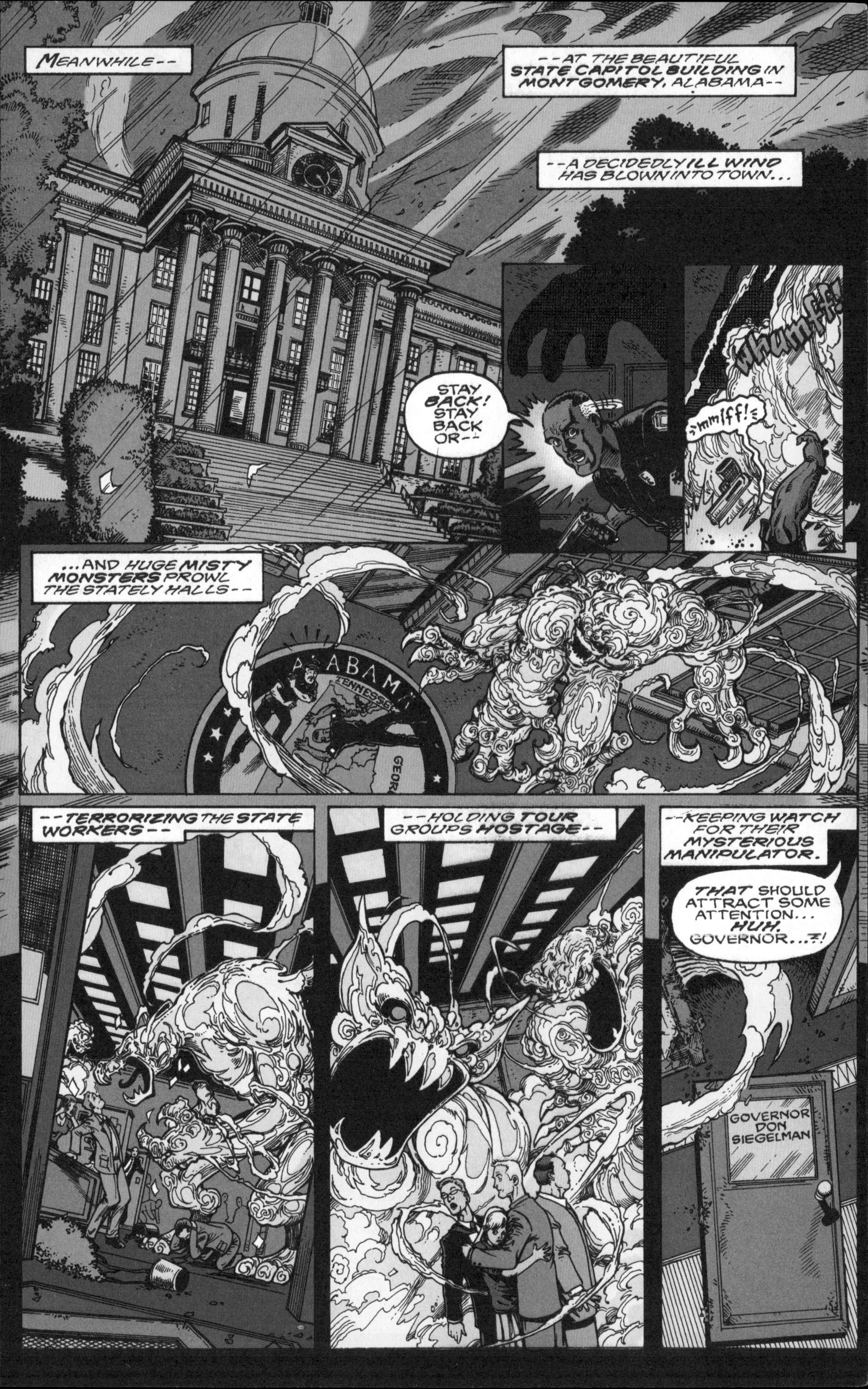
MEANWHILE--
--AT THE BEAUTIFUL STATE CAPITOL BUILDING IN MONTGOMERY, ALABAMA--
--A DECIDEDLY ILL WIND HAS BLOWN INTO TOWN...
STAY BACK! STAY BACK OR--
WHUMFF!
MMIFF!
...AND HUGE MISTY MONSTERS PROWL THE STATELY HALLS--
ALABAMA
TENNESSEE
GEORGIA
--TERRORIZING THE STATE WORKERS--
--HOLDING TOUR GROUPS HOSTAGE--
--KEEPING WATCH FOR THEIR MYSTERIOUS MANIPULATOR.
THAT SHOULD ATTRACT SOME ATTENTION... HUH, GOVERNOR...?!
GOVERNOR DON SIEGELMAN

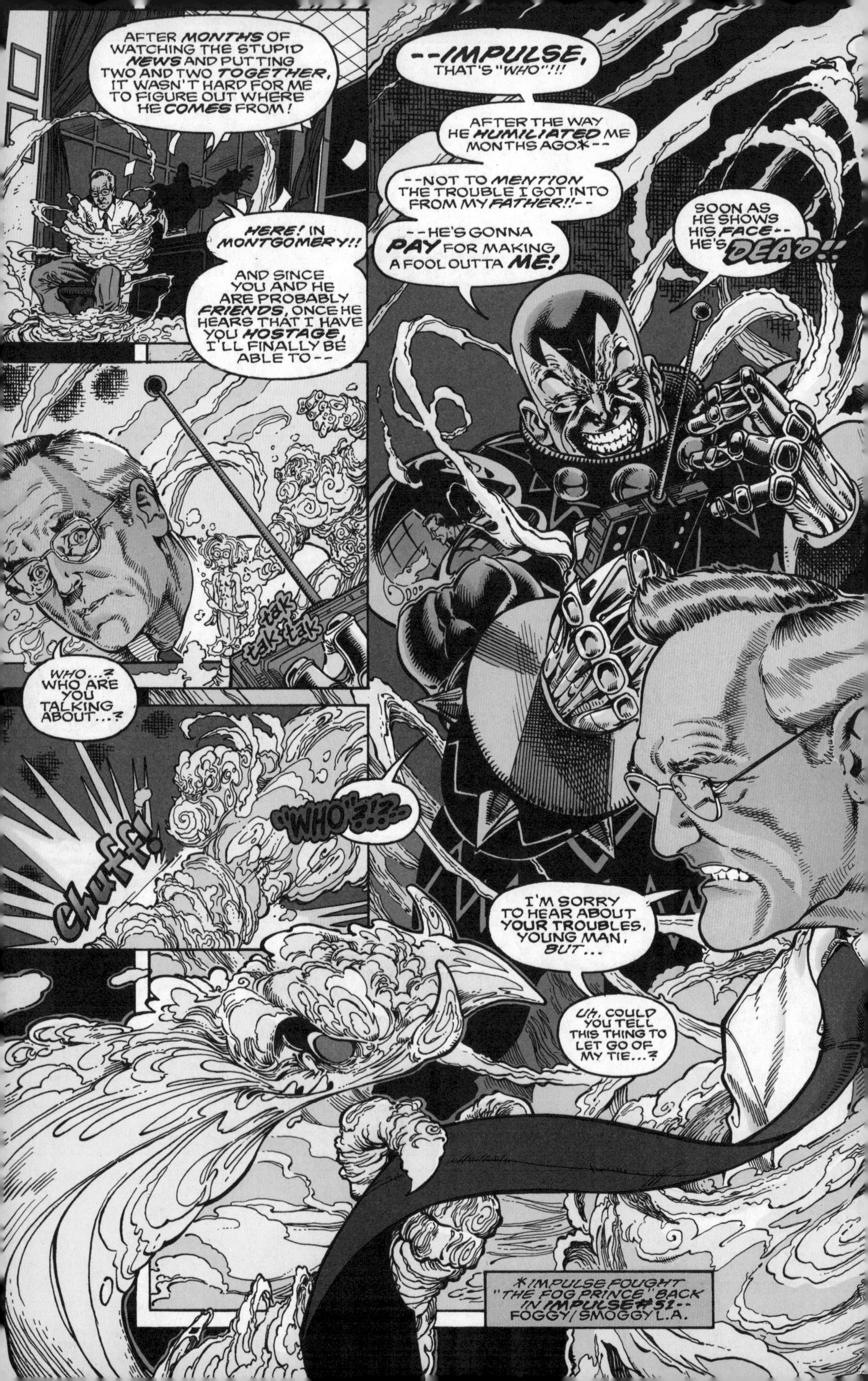

AFTER MONTHS OF WATCHING THE STUPID NEWS AND PUTTING TWO AND TWO TOGETHER, IT WASN'T HARD FOR ME TO FIGURE OUT WHERE HE COMES FROM!
HERE! IN MONTGOMERY!!
AND SINCE YOU AND HE ARE PROBABLY FRIENDS, ONCE HE HEARS THAT I HAVE YOU HOSTAGE, I'LL FINALLY BE ABLE TO--
tak tak tak
WHO...? WHO ARE YOU TALKING ABOUT...?
chuff!
"WHO"?!?--
--IMPULSE, THAT'S "WHO"!!!
AFTER THE WAY HE HUMILIATED ME MONTHS AGO*--
--NOT TO MENTION THE TROUBLE I GOT INTO FROM MY FATHER!!--
--HE'S GONNA PAY FOR MAKING A FOOL OUTTA ME!
SOON AS HE SHOWS HIS FACE--HE'S DEAD!!
I'M SORRY TO HEAR ABOUT YOUR TROUBLES, YOUNG MAN, BUT...
UH, COULD YOU TELL THIS THING TO LET GO OF MY TIE...?
*IMPULSE FOUGHT "THE FOG PRINCE" BACK IN IMPULSE #51--FOGGY/SMOGGY L.A.

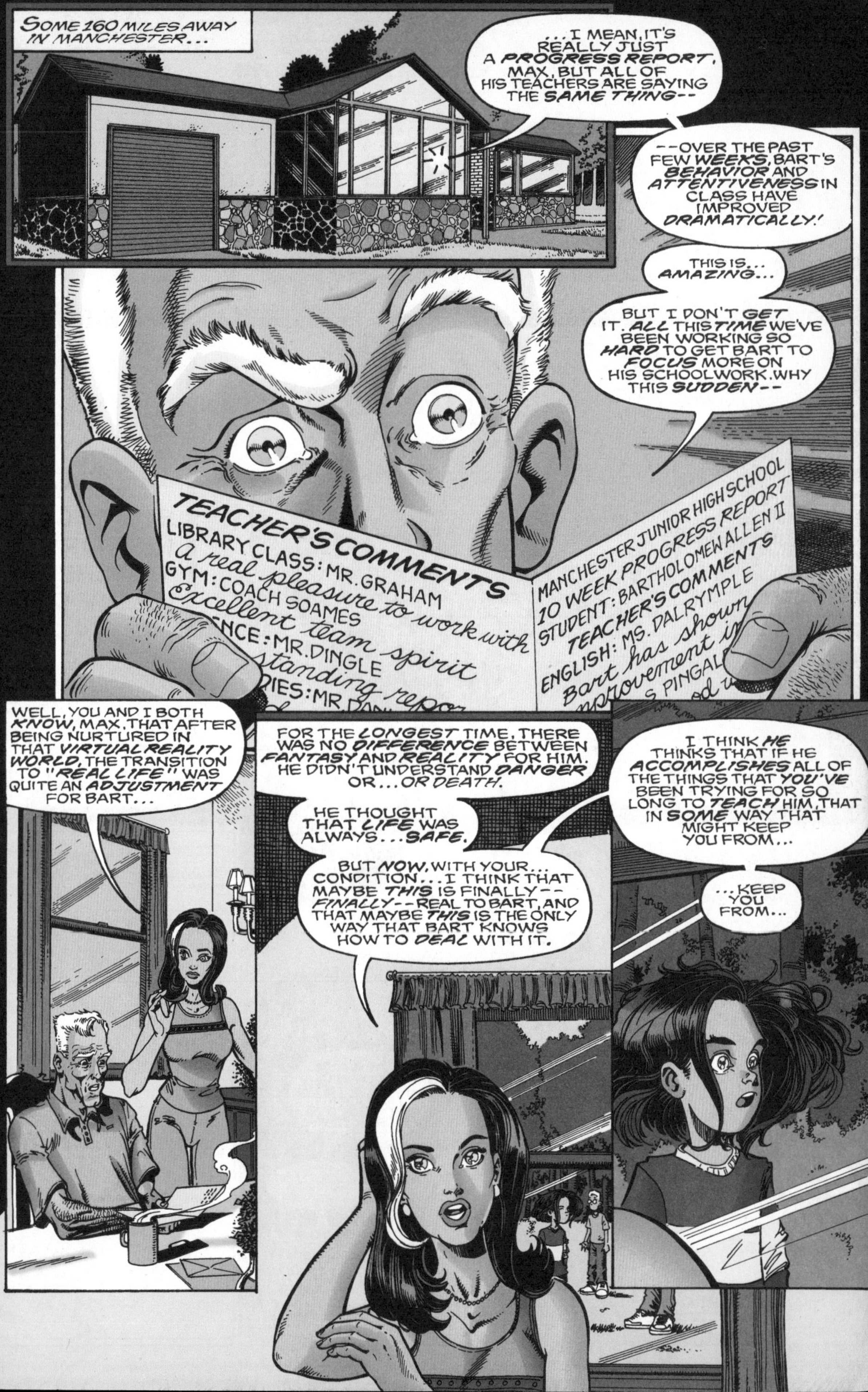

SOME 160 MILES AWAY IN MANCHESTER...
...I MEAN, IT'S REALLY JUST A PROGRESS REPORT, MAX, BUT ALL OF HIS TEACHERS ARE SAYING THE SAME THING--
--OVER THE PAST FEW WEEKS, BART'S BEHAVIOR AND ATTENTIVENESS IN CLASS HAVE IMPROVED DRAMATICALLY!
THIS IS... AMAZING...
BUT I DON'T GET IT. ALL THIS TIME WE'VE BEEN WORKING SO HARD TO GET BART TO FOCUS MORE ON HIS SCHOOLWORK. WHY THIS SUDDEN--
MANCHESTER JUNIOR HIGH SCHOOL
10 WEEK PROGRESS REPORT
STUDENT: BARTHOLOMEW ALLEN II
TEACHER'S COMMENTS
ENGLISH: MS. DALRYMPLE
Bart has shown
TEACHER'S COMMENTS
LIBRARY CLASS: MR. GRAHAM
A real pleasure to work with
GYM: COACH SOAMES
Excellent team spirit
NCE: MR. DINGLE
WELL, YOU AND I BOTH KNOW, MAX, THAT AFTER BEING NURTURED IN THAT VIRTUAL REALITY WORLD, THE TRANSITION TO "REAL LIFE" WAS QUITE AN ADJUSTMENT FOR BART...
FOR THE LONGEST TIME, THERE WAS NO DIFFERENCE BETWEEN FANTASY AND REALITY FOR HIM. HE DIDN'T UNDERSTAND DANGER OR... OR DEATH.
HE THOUGHT THAT LIFE WAS ALWAYS... SAFE.
BUT NOW, WITH YOUR... CONDITION... I THINK THAT MAYBE THIS IS FINALLY--FINALLY--REAL TO BART, AND THAT MAYBE THIS IS THE ONLY WAY THAT BART KNOWS HOW TO DEAL WITH IT.
I THINK HE THINKS THAT IF HE ACCOMPLISHES ALL OF THE THINGS THAT YOU'VE BEEN TRYING FOR SO LONG TO TEACH HIM, THAT IN SOME WAY THAT MIGHT KEEP YOU FROM...
...KEEP YOU FROM...

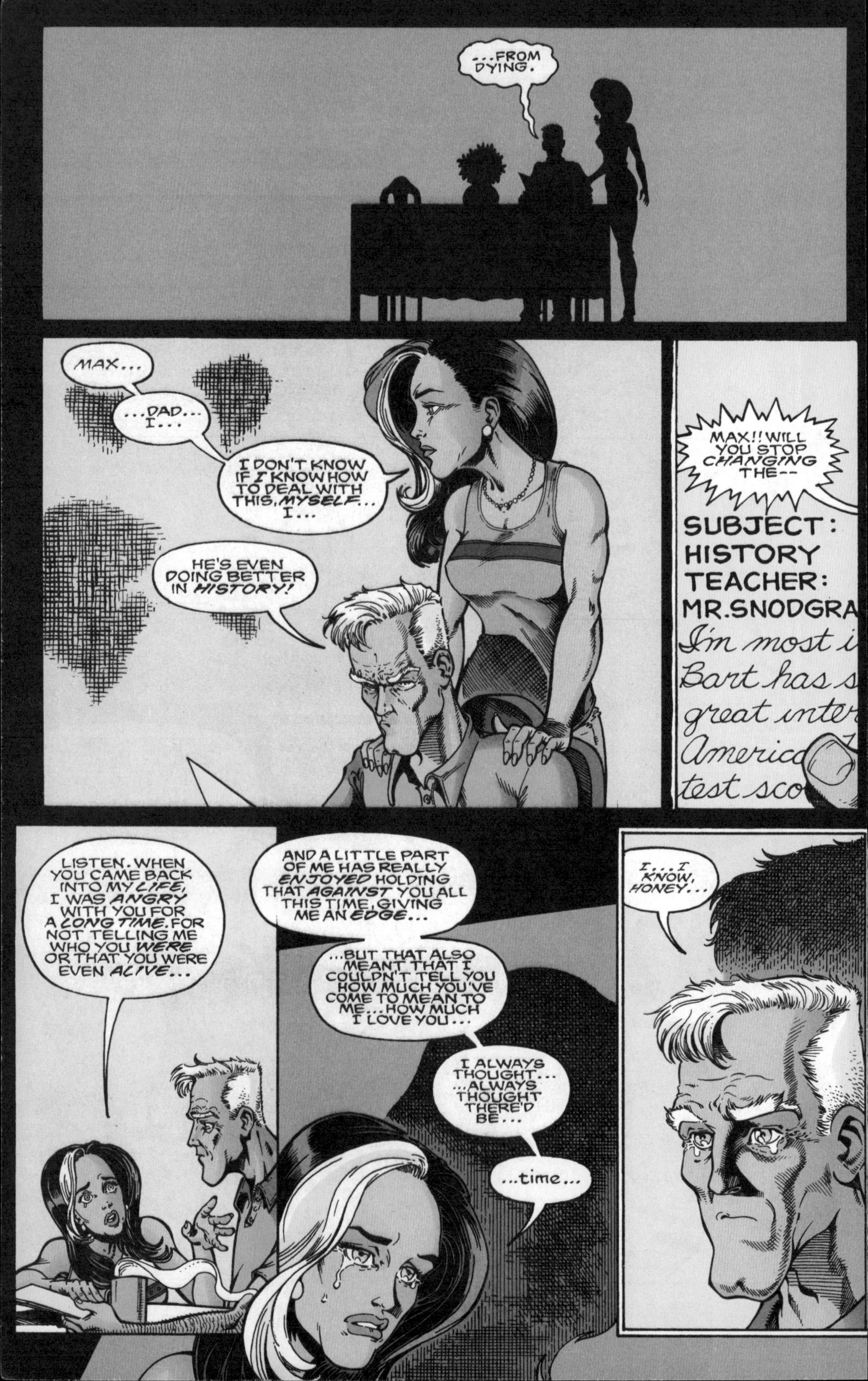
...FROM DYING.
MAX...
...DAD... I...
I DON'T KNOW IF I KNOW HOW TO DEAL WITH THIS, MYSELF... I...
HE'S EVEN DOING BETTER IN HISTORY!
MAX!! WILL YOU STOP CHANGING THE--
SUBJECT: HISTORY
TEACHER: MR.SNODGRA
I'm most i
Bart has s
great inter
America
test sco
LISTEN. WHEN YOU CAME BACK INTO MY LIFE, I WAS ANGRY WITH YOU FOR A LONG TIME. FOR NOT TELLING ME WHO YOU WERE OR THAT YOU WERE EVEN ALIVE...
AND A LITTLE PART OF ME HAS REALLY ENJOYED HOLDING THAT AGAINST YOU ALL THIS TIME, GIVING ME AN EDGE...
...BUT THAT ALSO MEANT THAT I COULDN'T TELL YOU HOW MUCH YOU'VE COME TO MEAN TO ME... HOW MUCH I LOVE YOU...
I ALWAYS THOUGHT... ...ALWAYS THOUGHT THERE'D BE...
...time...
I... I KNOW, HONEY...

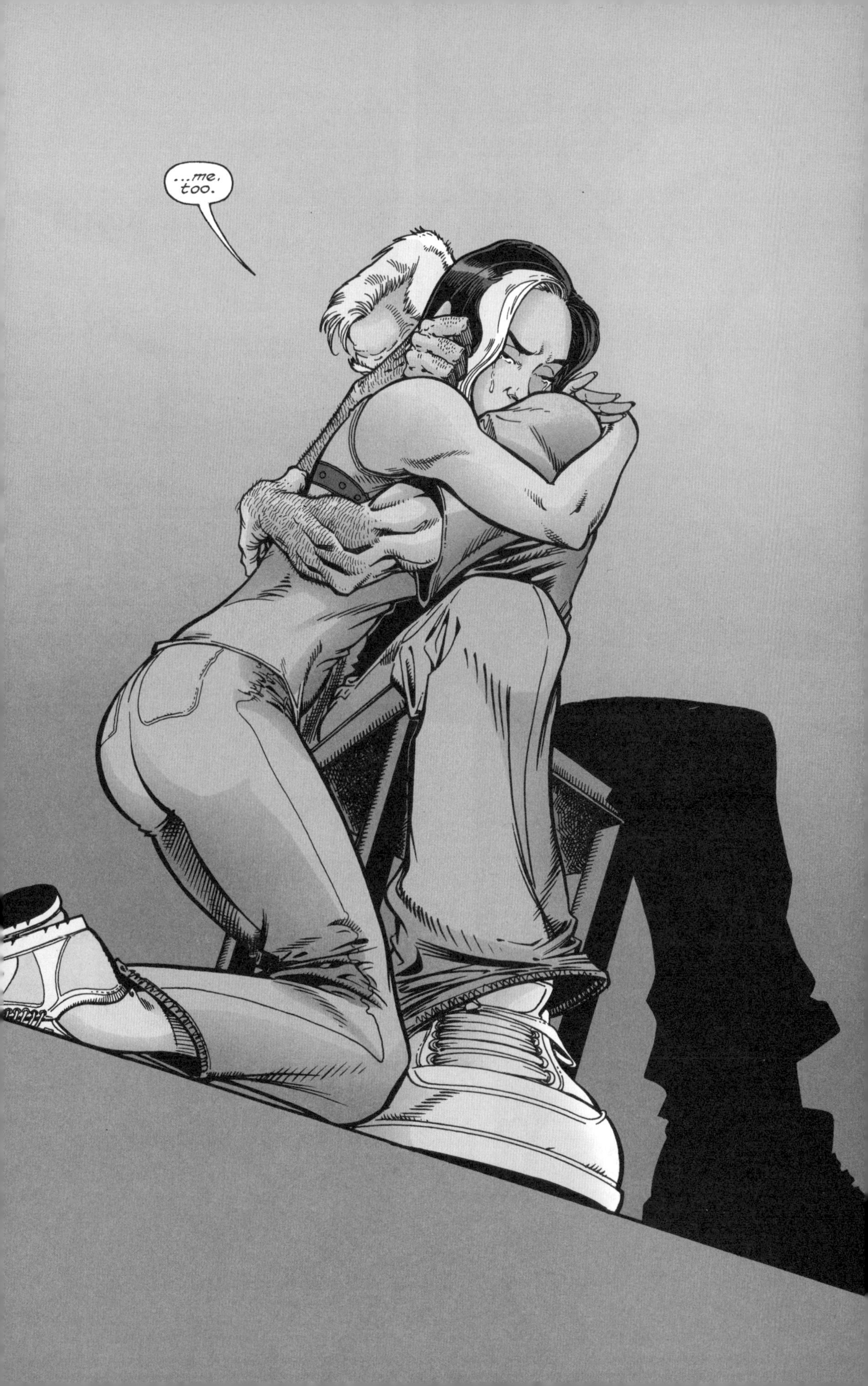
...me, too.

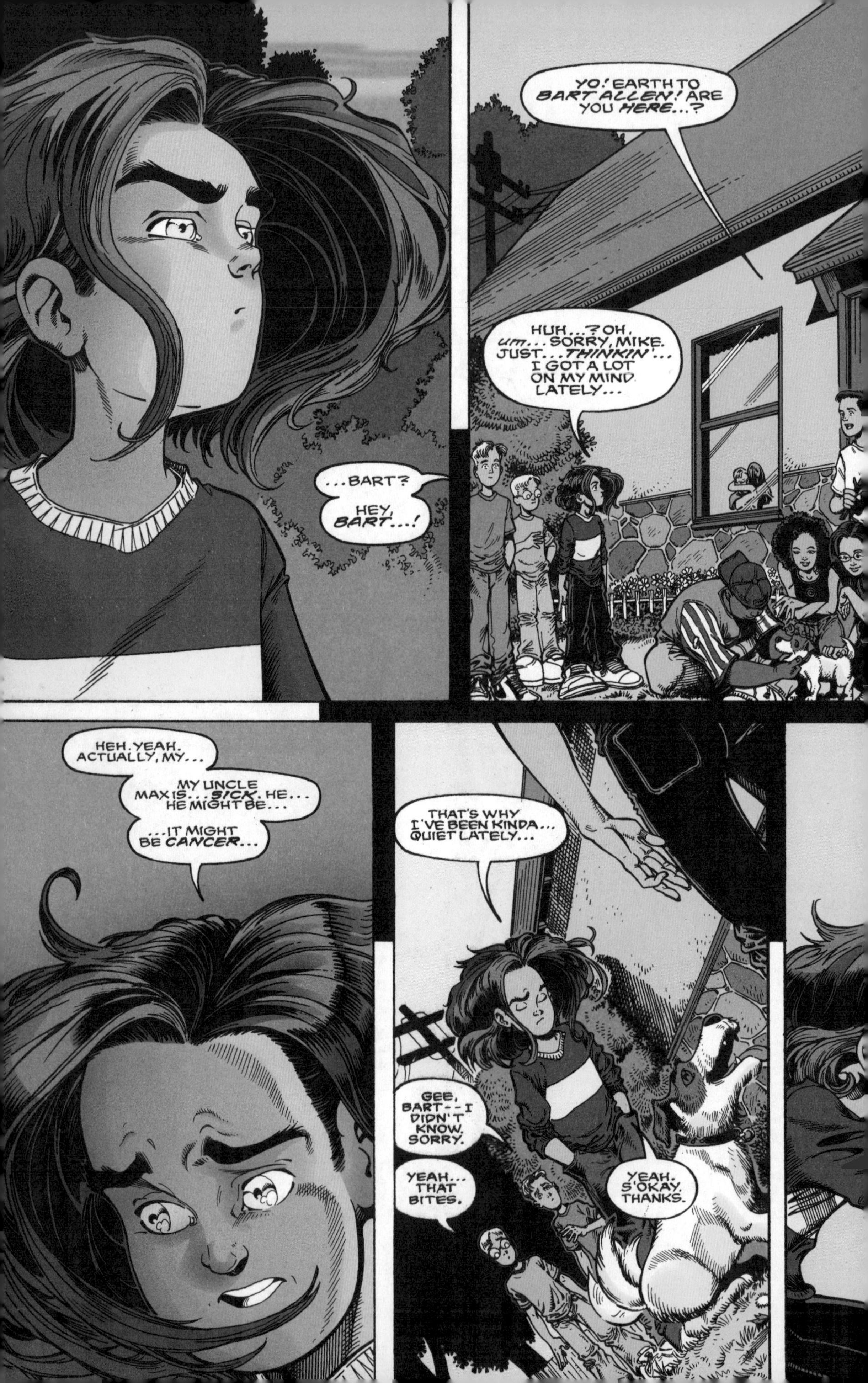
...BART?
HEY, BART...!
YO! EARTH TO BART ALLEN! ARE YOU HERE...?
HUH...? OH, UM... SORRY, MIKE. JUST...THINKIN'... I GOT A LOT ON MY MIND LATELY...
HEH. YEAH. ACTUALLY, MY...
MY UNCLE MAX IS... SICK. HE... HE MIGHT BE...
...IT MIGHT BE CANCER...
THAT'S WHY I'VE BEEN KINDA... QUIET LATELY...
GEE, BART--I DIDN'T KNOW. SORRY.
YEAH... THAT BITES.
YEAH. S'OKAY. THANKS.

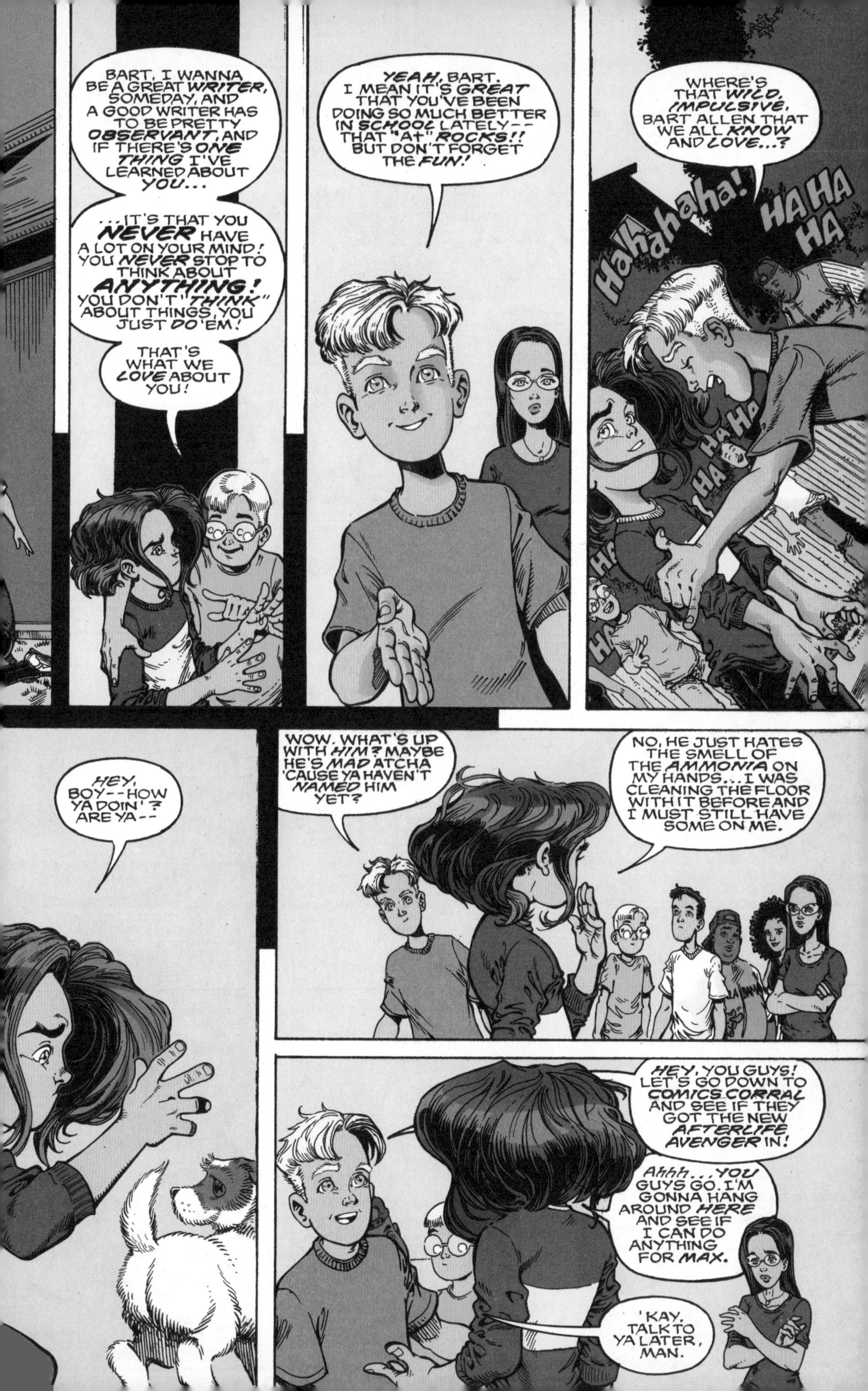

BART, I WANNA BE A GREAT WRITER, SOMEDAY, AND A GOOD WRITER HAS TO BE PRETTY OBSERVANT, AND IF THERE'S ONE THING I'VE LEARNED ABOUT YOU...
...IT'S THAT YOU NEVER HAVE A LOT ON YOUR MIND! YOU NEVER STOP TO THINK ABOUT ANYTHING! YOU DON'T "THINK" ABOUT THINGS, YOU JUST DO 'EM!
THAT'S WHAT WE LOVE ABOUT YOU!
YEAH, BART. I MEAN IT'S GREAT THAT YOU'VE BEEN DOING SO MUCH BETTER IN SCHOOL LATELY-- THAT "A+" ROCKS!! BUT DON'T FORGET THE FUN!
WHERE'S THAT WILD, IMPULSIVE, BART ALLEN THAT WE ALL KNOW AND LOVE...?
HaHahaha!
HA HA HA
HA HA HA
HA
HA
HEY, BOY--HOW YA DOIN'? ARE YA--
WOW. WHAT'S UP WITH HIM? MAYBE HE'S MAD ATCHA 'CAUSE YA HAVEN'T NAMED HIM YET?
NO, HE JUST HATES THE SMELL OF THE AMMONIA ON MY HANDS...I WAS CLEANING THE FLOOR WITH IT BEFORE AND I MUST STILL HAVE SOME ON ME.
HEY, YOU GUYS! LET'S GO DOWN TO COMICS CORRAL AND SEE IF THEY GOT THE NEW AFTERLIFE AVENGER IN!
Ahhh...YOU GUYS GO. I'M GONNA HANG AROUND HERE AND SEE IF I CAN DO ANYTHING FOR MAX.
'KAY. TALK TO YA LATER, MAN.

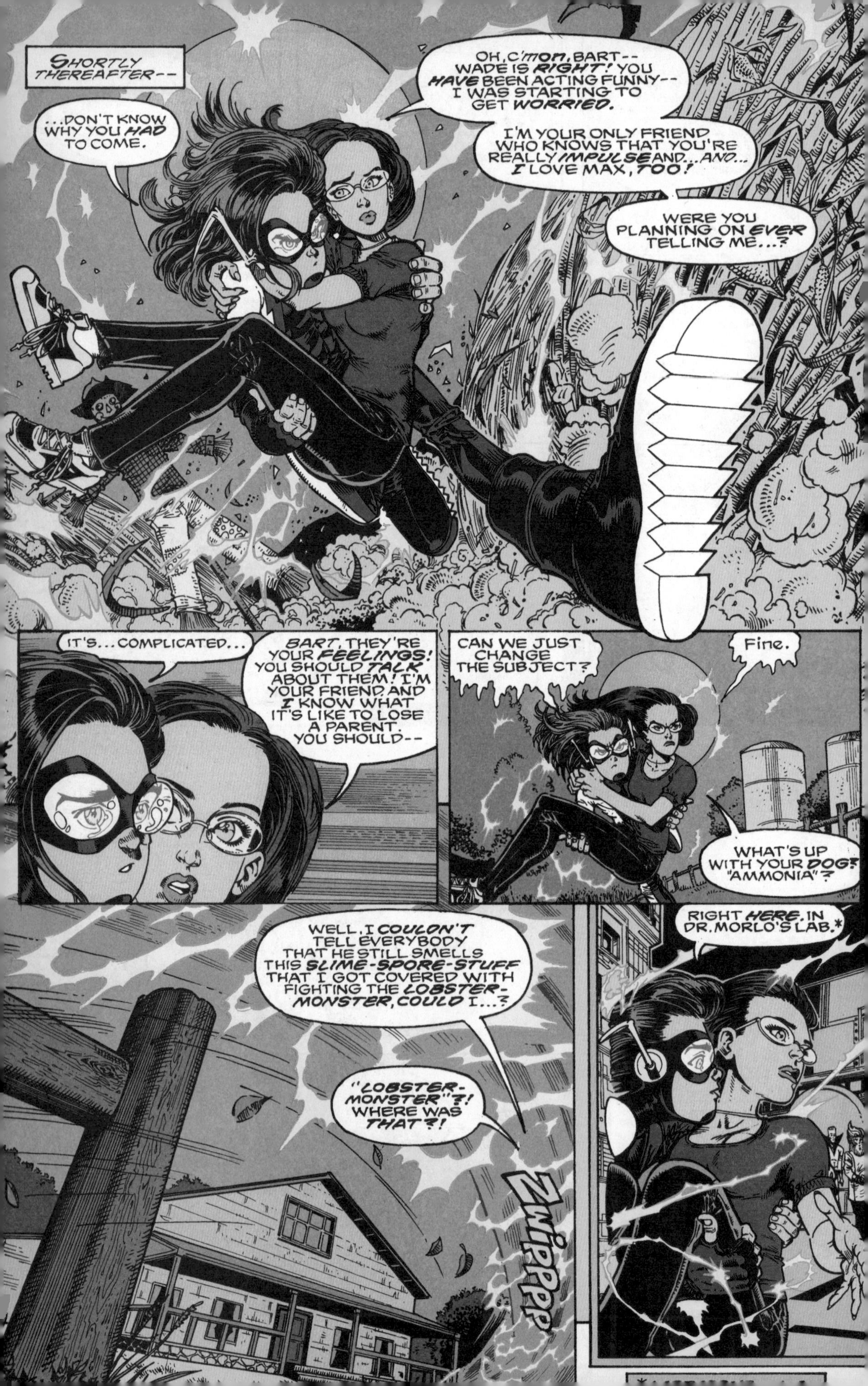

SHORTLY THEREAFTER--
...DON'T KNOW WHY YOU HAD TO COME.
OH, C'MON, BART-- WADE IS RIGHT! YOU HAVE BEEN ACTING FUNNY-- I WAS STARTING TO GET WORRIED.
I'M YOUR ONLY FRIEND WHO KNOWS THAT YOU'RE REALLY IMPULSE AND... AND... I LOVE MAX, TOO!
WERE YOU PLANNING ON EVER TELLING ME...?
IT'S... COMPLICATED...
BART, THEY'RE YOUR FEELINGS! YOU SHOULD TALK ABOUT THEM! I'M YOUR FRIEND, AND I KNOW WHAT IT'S LIKE TO LOSE A PARENT. YOU SHOULD--
CAN WE JUST CHANGE THE SUBJECT?
Fine.
WHAT'S UP WITH YOUR DOG? "AMMONIA"?
WELL, I COULDN'T TELL EVERYBODY THAT HE STILL SMELLS THIS SLIME-SPORE-STUFF THAT I GOT COVERED WITH FIGHTING THE LOBSTER-MONSTER, COULD I...?
"LOBSTER-MONSTER"?! WHERE WAS THAT?!
ZWIPPPP
RIGHT HERE, IN DR. MORLO'S LAB.*

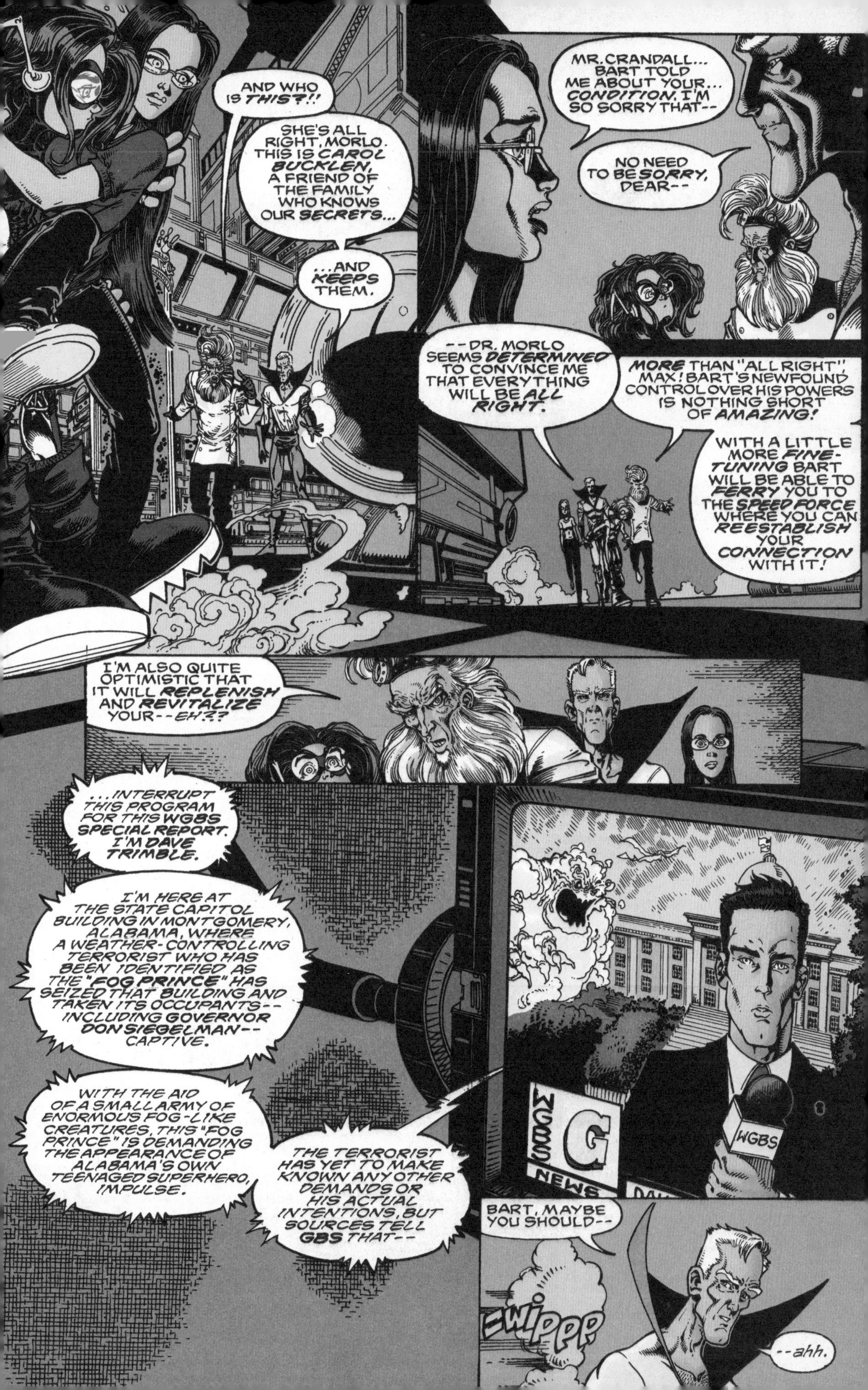
AND WHO IS THIS?!!
SHE'S ALL RIGHT, MORLO. THIS IS CAROL BUCKLEN, A FRIEND OF THE FAMILY WHO KNOWS OUR SECRETS...
...AND KEEPS THEM.
MR. CRANDALL... BART TOLD ME ABOUT YOUR... CONDITION. I'M SO SORRY THAT--
NO NEED TO BE SORRY, DEAR--
--DR. MORLO SEEMS DETERMINED TO CONVINCE ME THAT EVERYTHING WILL BE ALL RIGHT.
MORE THAN "ALL RIGHT" MAX! BART'S NEWFOUND CONTROL OVER HIS POWERS IS NOTHING SHORT OF AMAZING!
WITH A LITTLE MORE FINE-TUNING BART WILL BE ABLE TO FERRY YOU TO THE SPEED FORCE WHERE YOU CAN REESTABLISH YOUR CONNECTION WITH IT!
I'M ALSO QUITE OPTIMISTIC THAT IT WILL REPLENISH AND REVITALIZE YOUR--EH??
...INTERRUPT THIS PROGRAM FOR THIS WGBS SPECIAL REPORT. I'M DAVE TRIMBLE.
I'M HERE AT THE STATE CAPITOL BUILDING IN MONTGOMERY, ALABAMA, WHERE A WEATHER-CONTROLLING TERRORIST WHO HAS BEEN IDENTIFIED AS THE "FOG PRINCE" HAS SEIZED THAT BUILDING AND TAKEN ITS OCCUPANTS--INCLUDING GOVERNOR DON SIEGELMAN--CAPTIVE.
WITH THE AID OF A SMALL ARMY OF ENORMOUS FOG-LIKE CREATURES, THIS "FOG PRINCE" IS DEMANDING THE APPEARANCE OF ALABAMA'S OWN TEENAGED SUPERHERO, IMPULSE.
THE TERRORIST HAS YET TO MAKE KNOWN ANY OTHER DEMANDS OR HIS ACTUAL INTENTIONS, BUT SOURCES TELL GBS THAT--
WGBS
G
NEWS
WGBS
BART, MAYBE YOU SHOULD--
WIPPP
--ahh.

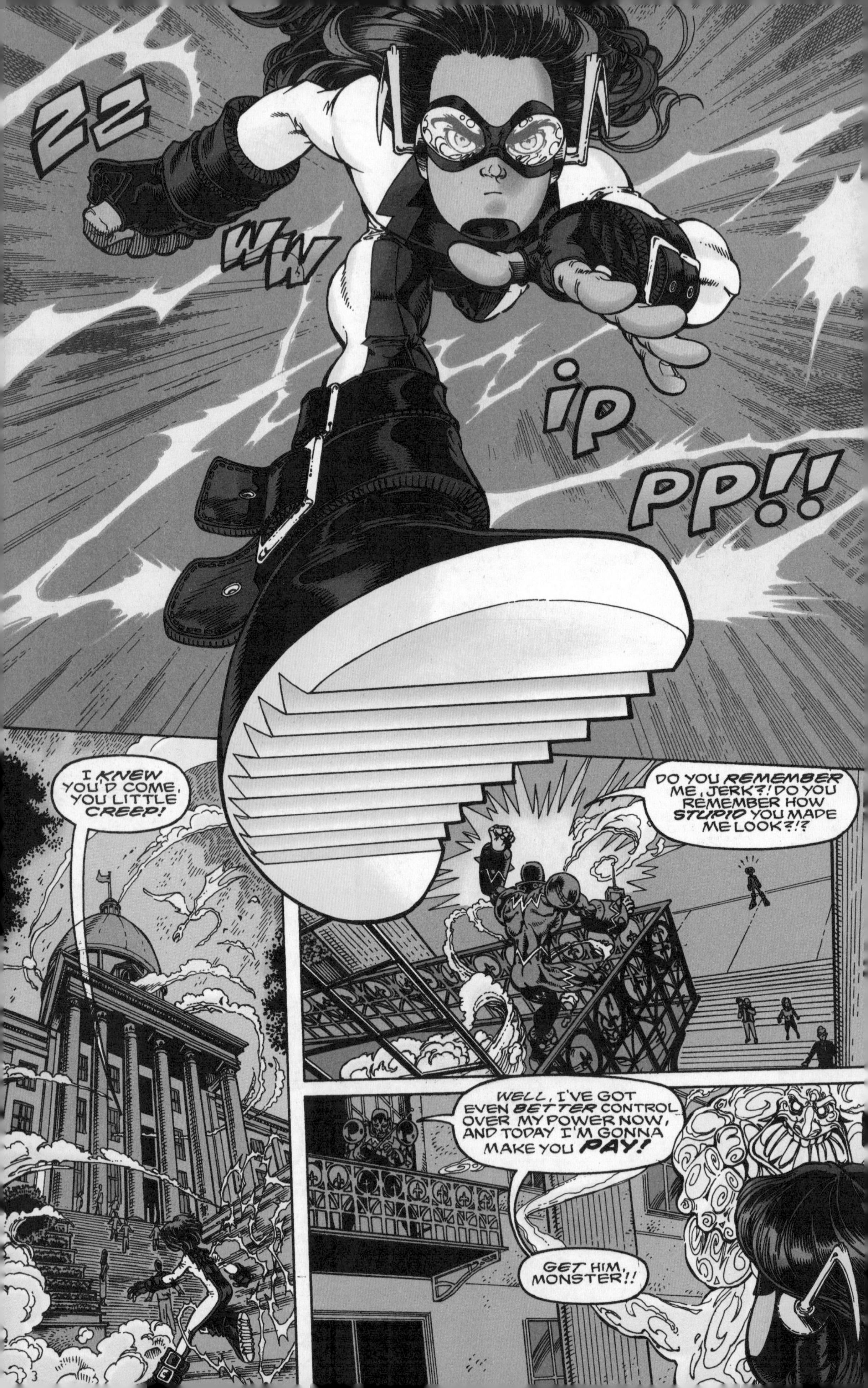
ZZ
WW
ip
PP!!
I KNEW YOU'D COME, YOU LITTLE CREEP!
DO YOU REMEMBER ME, JERK?! DO YOU REMEMBER HOW STUPID YOU MADE ME LOOK?!?
WELL, I'VE GOT EVEN BETTER CONTROL OVER MY POWER NOW, AND TODAY I'M GONNA MAKE YOU PAY!
GET HIM, MONSTER!!

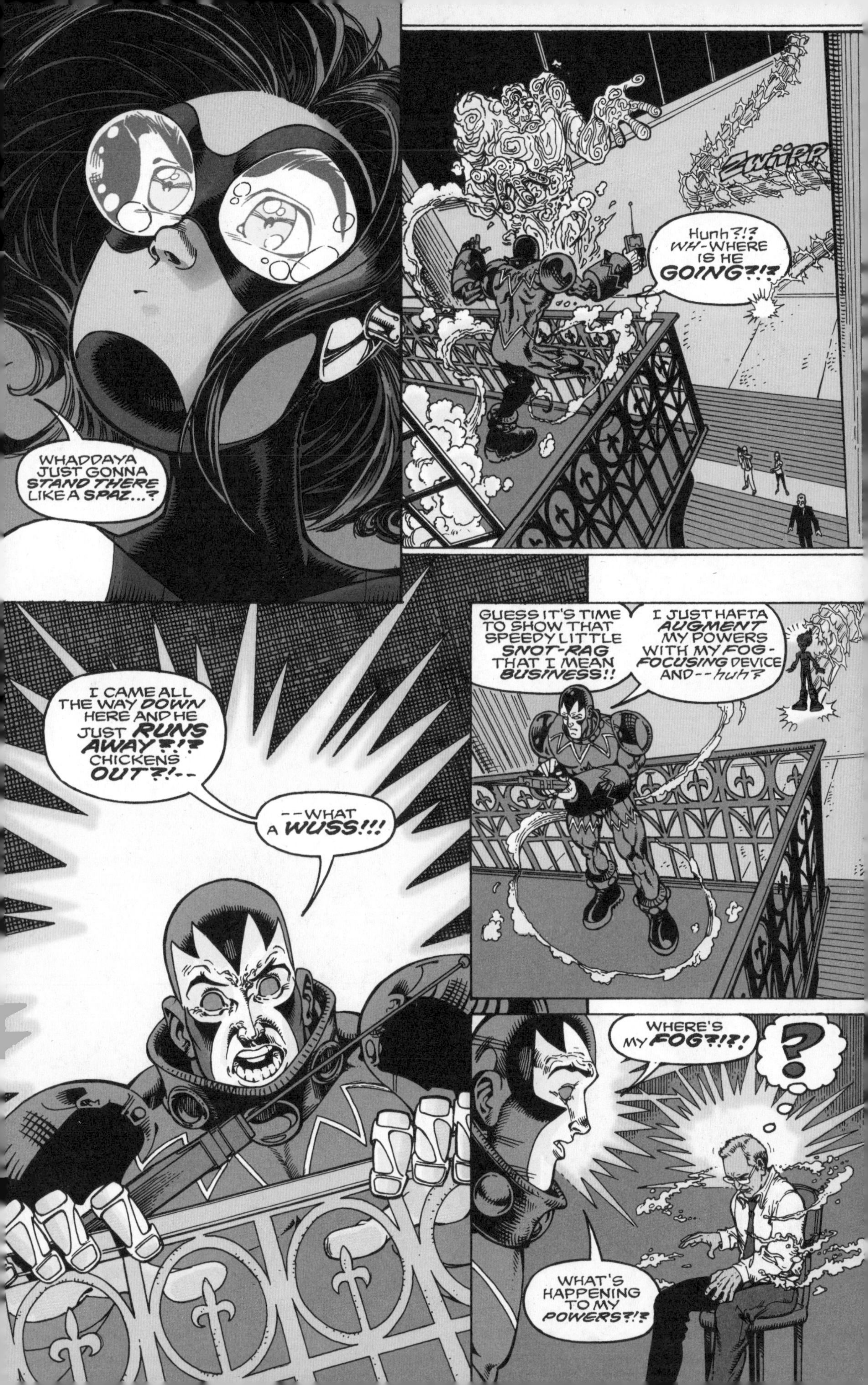
WHADDAYA JUST GONNA STAND THERE LIKE A SPAZ...?
ZWIIPP
Hunh?!? WH-WHERE IS HE GOING?!?
I CAME ALL THE WAY DOWN HERE AND HE JUST RUNS AWAY?!? CHICKENS OUT?!--
--WHAT A WUSS!!!
GUESS IT'S TIME TO SHOW THAT SPEEDY LITTLE SNOT-RAG THAT I MEAN BUSINESS!!
I JUST HAFTA AUGMENT MY POWERS WITH MY FOG-FOCUSING DEVICE AND--huh?
WHERE'S MY FOG?!?!
?
WHAT'S HAPPENING TO MY POWERS?!?

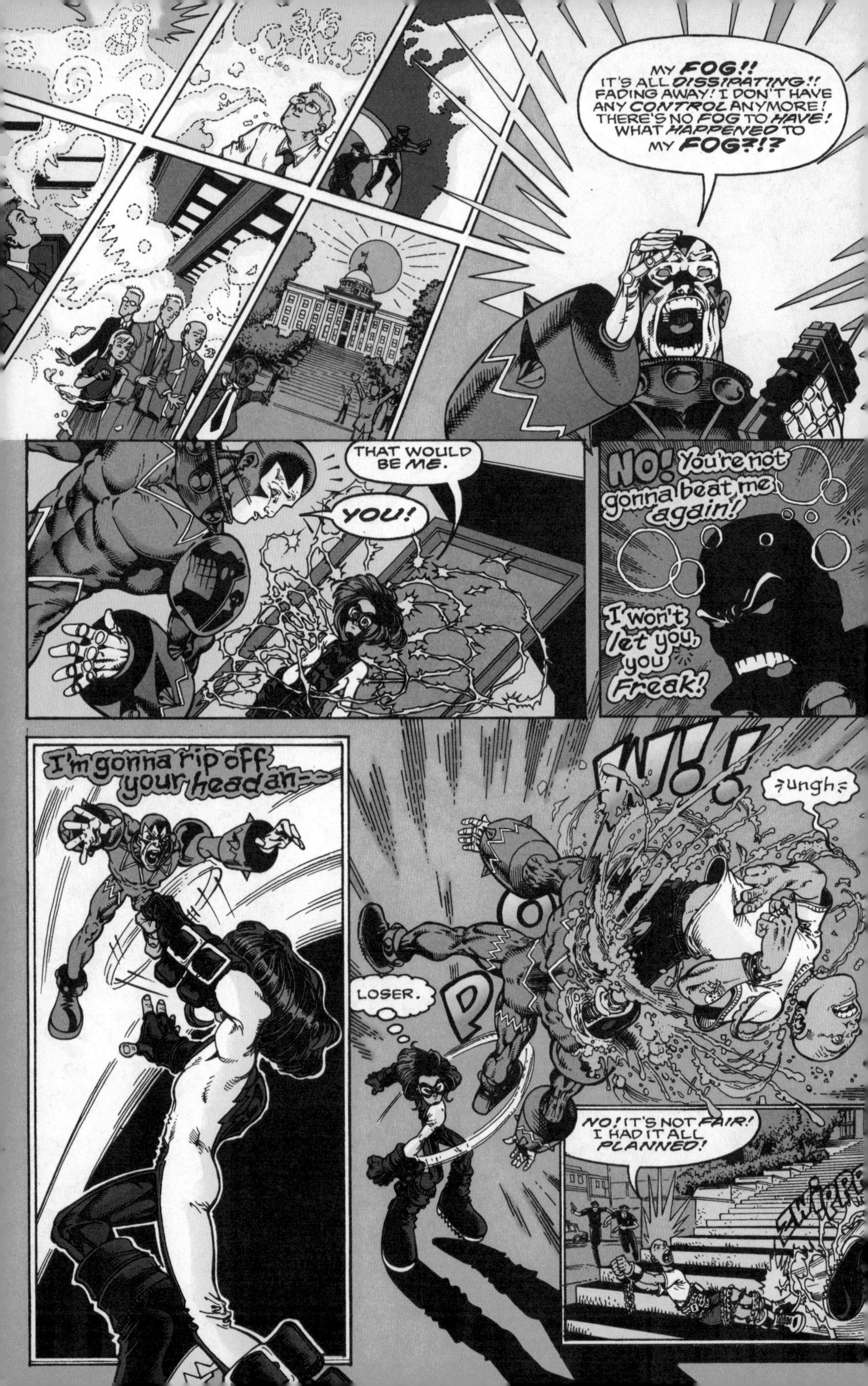
MY FOG!! IT'S ALL DISSIPATING!! FADING AWAY! I DON'T HAVE ANY CONTROL ANYMORE! THERE'S NO FOG TO HAVE! WHAT HAPPENED TO MY FOG?!?
THAT WOULD BE ME.
YOU!
NO! You're not gonna beat me again!
I won't let you, you Freak!
I'm gonna rip off your head an--
ungh
LOSER.
NO! IT'S NOT FAIR! I HAD IT ALL PLANNED!

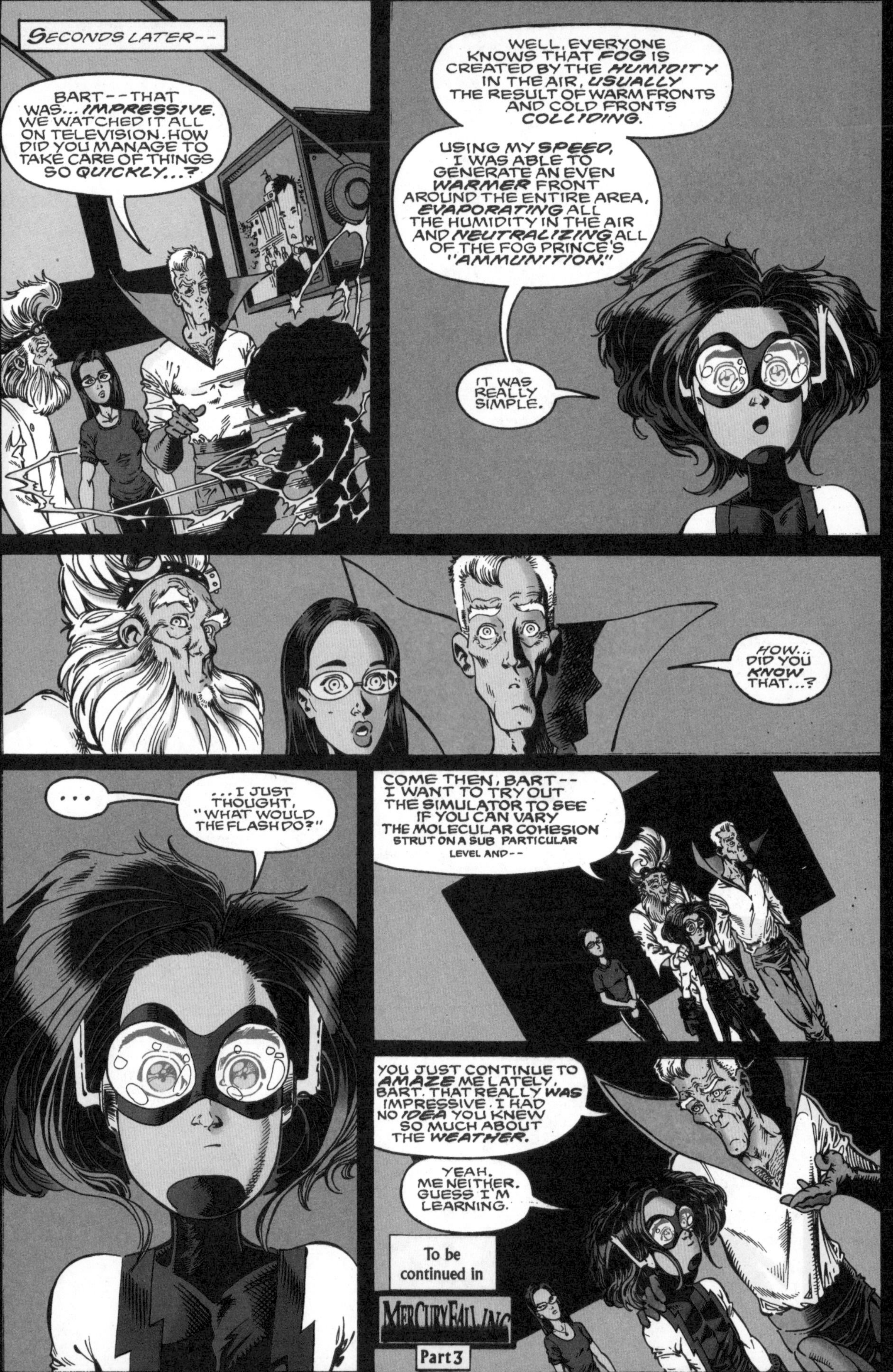

SECONDS LATER--
BART--THAT WAS... IMPRESSIVE. WE WATCHED IT ALL ON TELEVISION. HOW DID YOU MANAGE TO TAKE CARE OF THINGS SO QUICKLY...?
WELL, EVERYONE KNOWS THAT FOG IS CREATED BY THE HUMIDITY IN THE AIR, USUALLY THE RESULT OF WARM FRONTS AND COLD FRONTS COLLIDING.
USING MY SPEED, I WAS ABLE TO GENERATE AN EVEN WARMER FRONT AROUND THE ENTIRE AREA, EVAPORATING ALL THE HUMIDITY IN THE AIR AND NEUTRALIZING ALL OF THE FOG PRINCE'S "AMMUNITION."
IT WAS REALLY SIMPLE.
HOW... DID YOU KNOW THAT...?
...
...I JUST THOUGHT, "WHAT WOULD THE FLASH DO?"
COME THEN, BART-- I WANT TO TRY OUT THE SIMULATOR TO SEE IF YOU CAN VARY THE MOLECULAR COHESION STRUT ON A SUB PARTICULAR LEVEL AND--
YOU JUST CONTINUE TO AMAZE ME LATELY, BART. THAT REALLY WAS IMPRESSIVE. I HAD NO IDEA YOU KNEW SO MUCH ABOUT THE WEATHER.
YEAH. ME NEITHER. GUESS I'M LEARNING.
To be continued in
MERCURY FALLING
Part 3

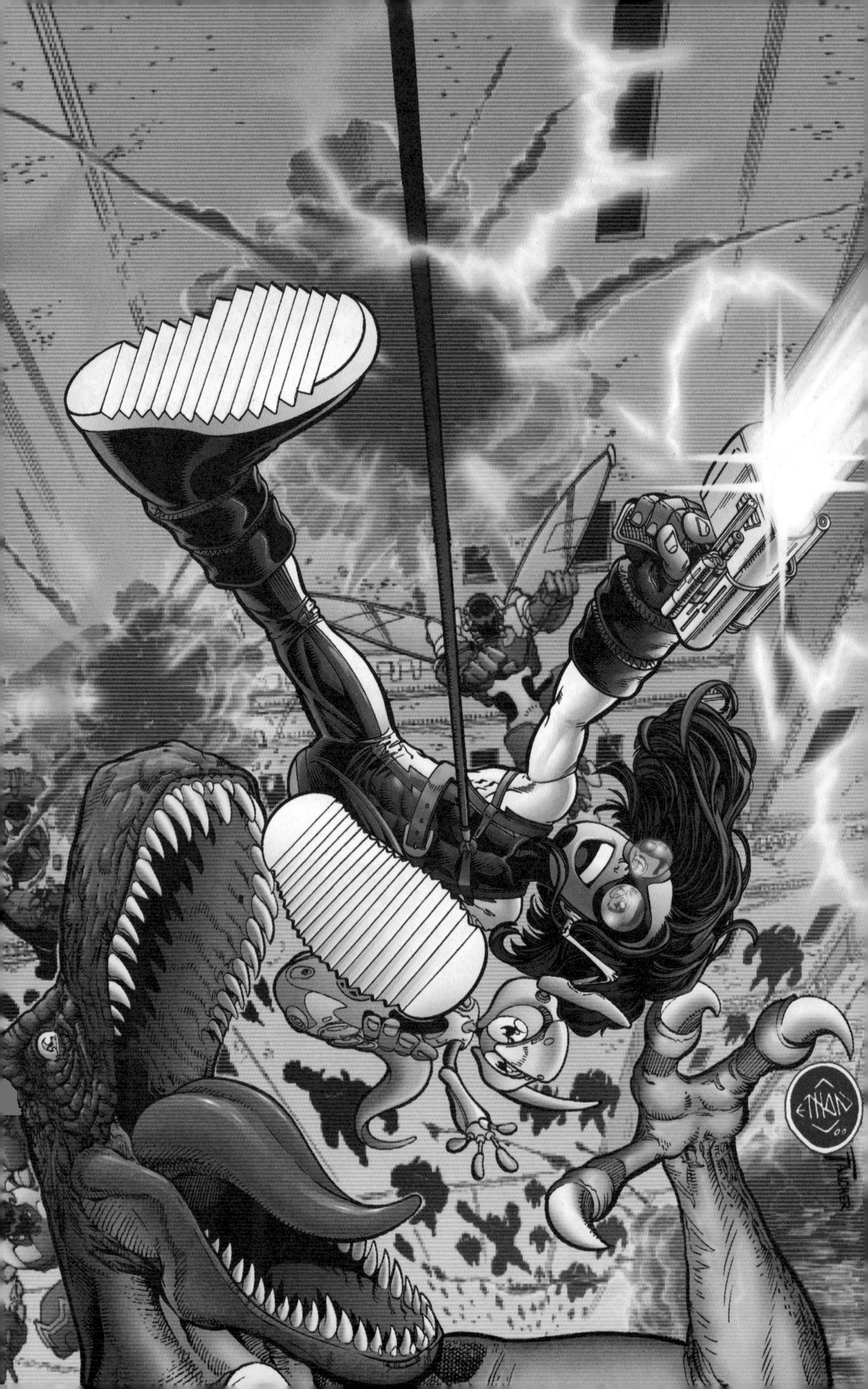

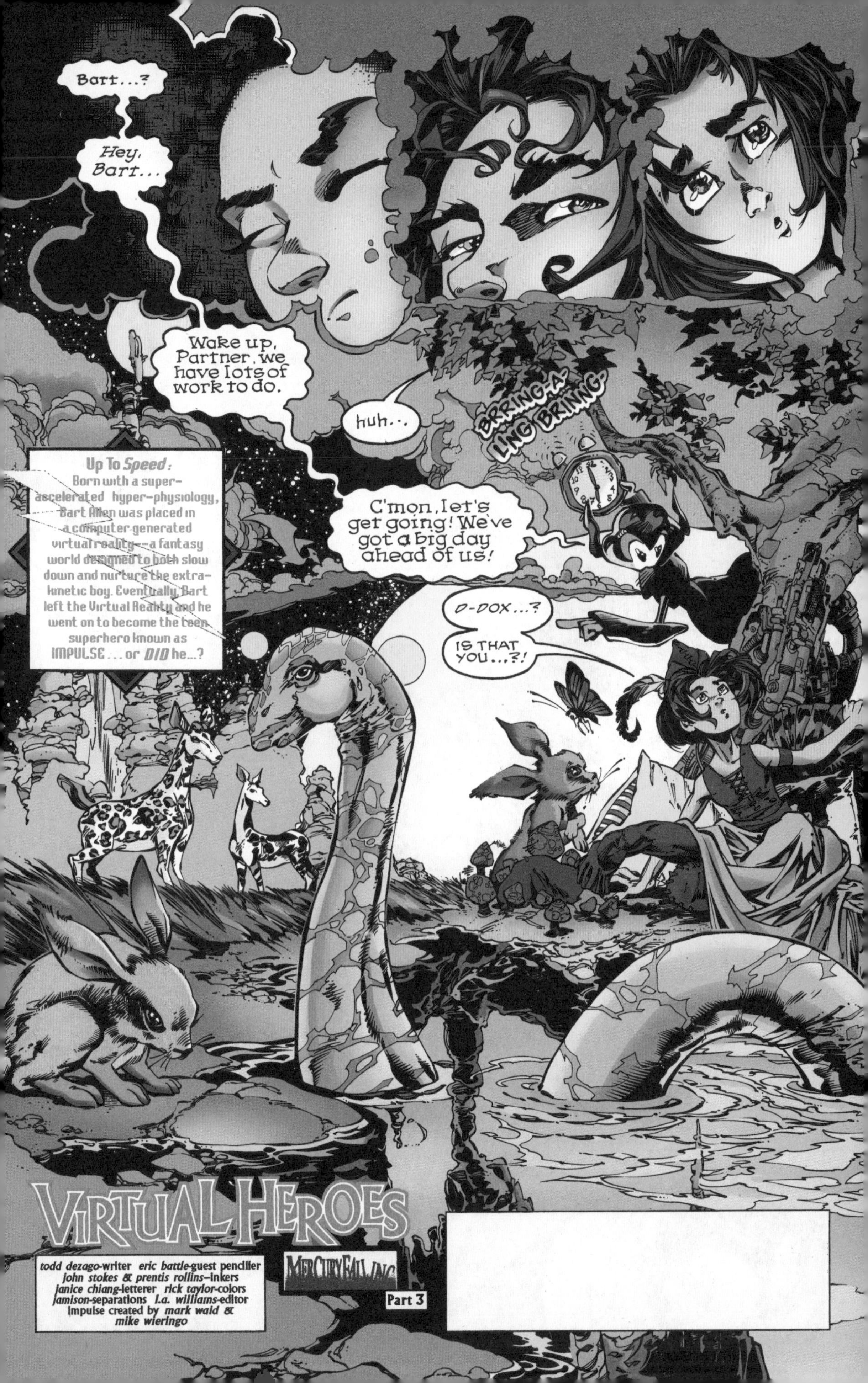
Bart...?
Hey, Bart...
Wake up, Partner, we have lots of work to do.
huh...
BRRING-A-LING BRINNG
Up To Speed: Born with a super-accelerated hyper-physiology, Bart Allen was placed in a computer-generated virtual reality--a fantasy world designed to both slow down and nurture the extra-kinetic boy. Eventually, Bart left the Virtual Reality and he went on to become the teen superhero known as IMPULSE... or DID he...?
C'mon, let's get going! We've got a big day ahead of us!
D-DOX...?
IS THAT YOU...?!
VIRTUAL HEROES
MERCURY FALLING Part 3
todd dezago-writer eric battle-guest penciller john stokes & prentis rollins-inkers janice chiang-letterer rick taylor-colors jamison-separations l.a. williams-editor impulse created by mark waid & mike wieringo

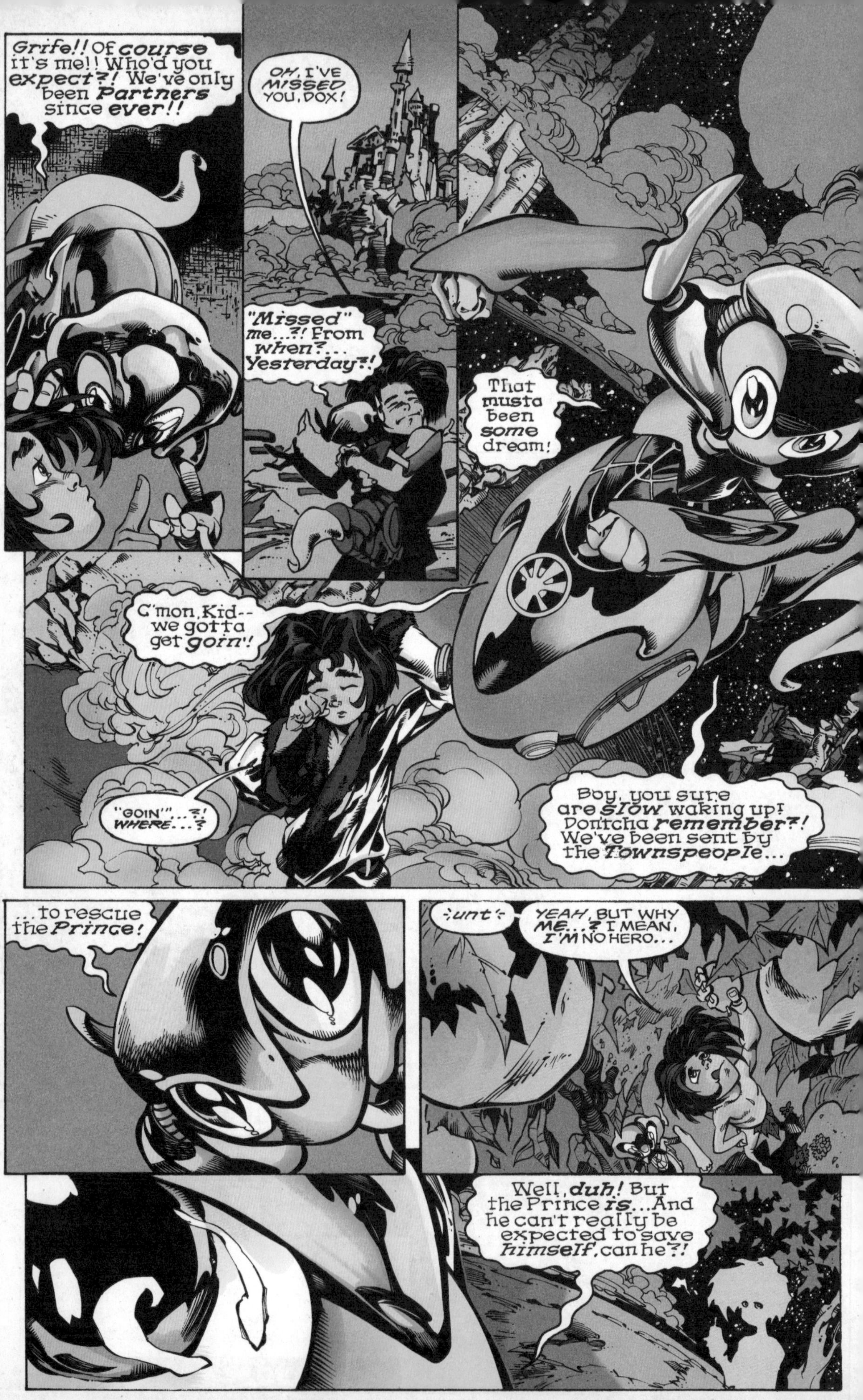
Grife!! Of course it's me!! Who'd you expect?! We've only been Partners since ever!!
OH, I'VE MISSED YOU, DOX!
"Missed" me...?! From when?... Yesterday?!
That musta been some dream!
C'mon, Kid-- we gotta get goin'!
"GOIN'"...?! WHERE...?
Boy, you sure are slow waking up! Dontcha remember?! We've been sent by the Townspeople...
...to rescue the Prince!
:unt:
YEAH, BUT WHY ME...? I MEAN, I'M NO HERO...
Well, duh! But the Prince is...And he can't really be expected to save himself, can he?!

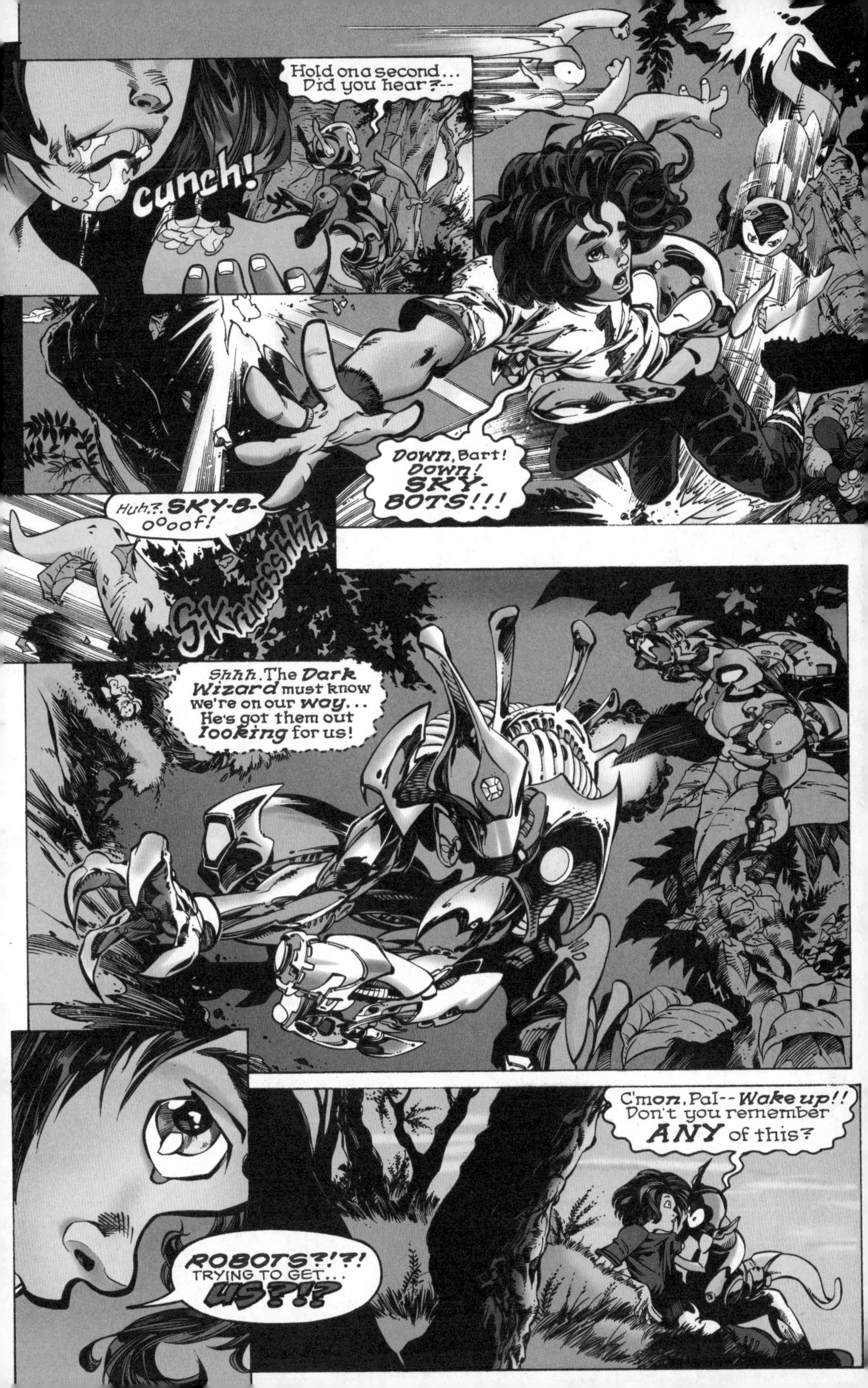

Hold on a second... Did you hear?--
CUNCH!
Down, Bart! Down! SKY-BOTS!!!
Huh?. SKY-B- ooooF!
S-KRUNSSSHHH
Shhh. The Dark Wizard must know we're on our way... He's got them out looking for us!
C'mon, Pal-- Wake up!! Don't you remember ANY of this?
ROBOTS?!?! TRYING TO GET... US?!?

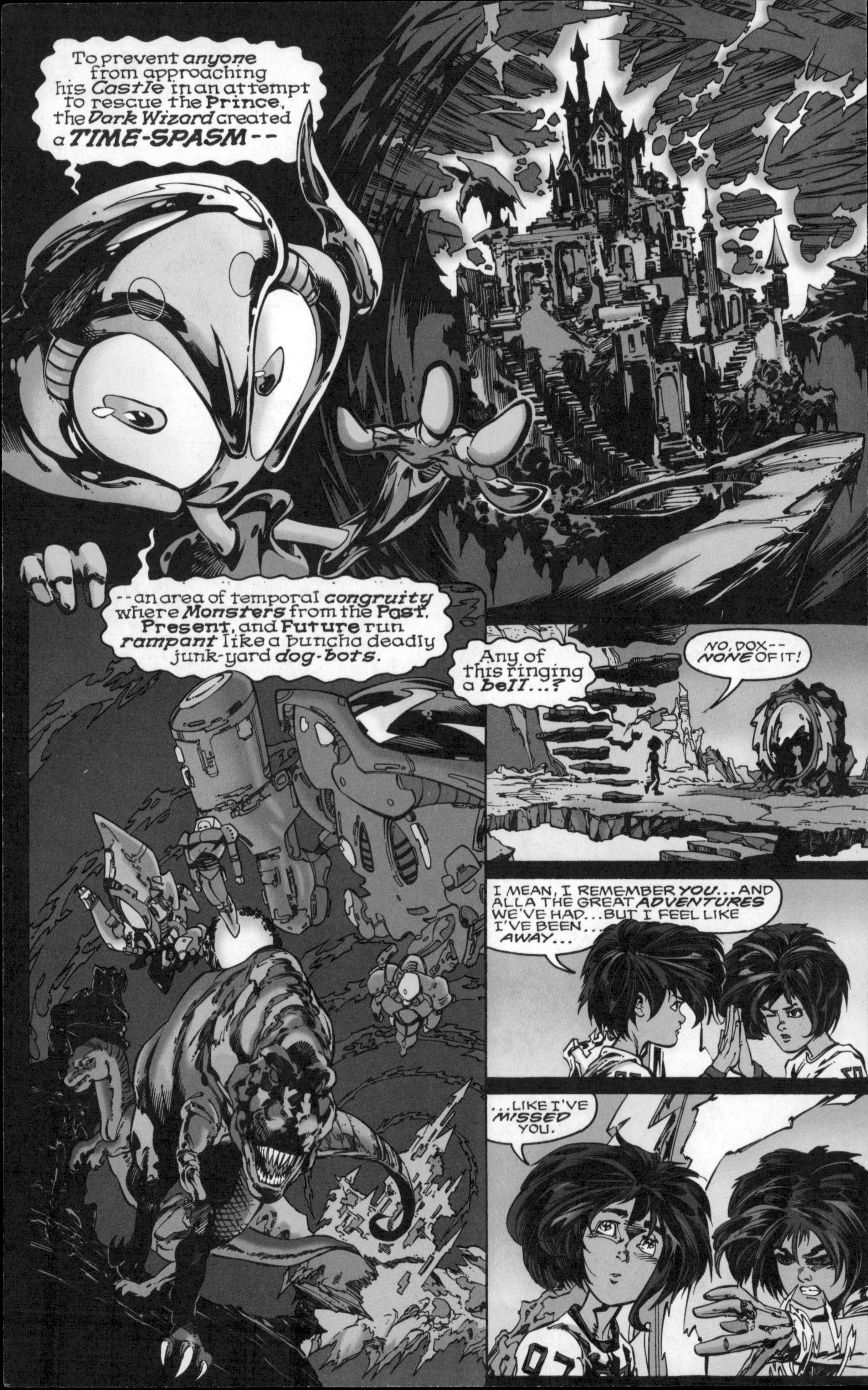
To prevent anyone from approaching his Castle in an attempt to rescue the Prince, the Dark Wizard created a TIME-SPASM--
--an area of temporal congruity where Monsters from the Past, Present, and Future run rampant like a buncha deadly junk-yard dog-bots.
Any of this ringing a bell...?
NO, DOX--NONE OF IT!
I MEAN, I REMEMBER YOU...AND ALLA THE GREAT ADVENTURES WE'VE HAD...BUT I FEEL LIKE I'VE BEEN... AWAY...
...LIKE I'VE MISSED YOU.

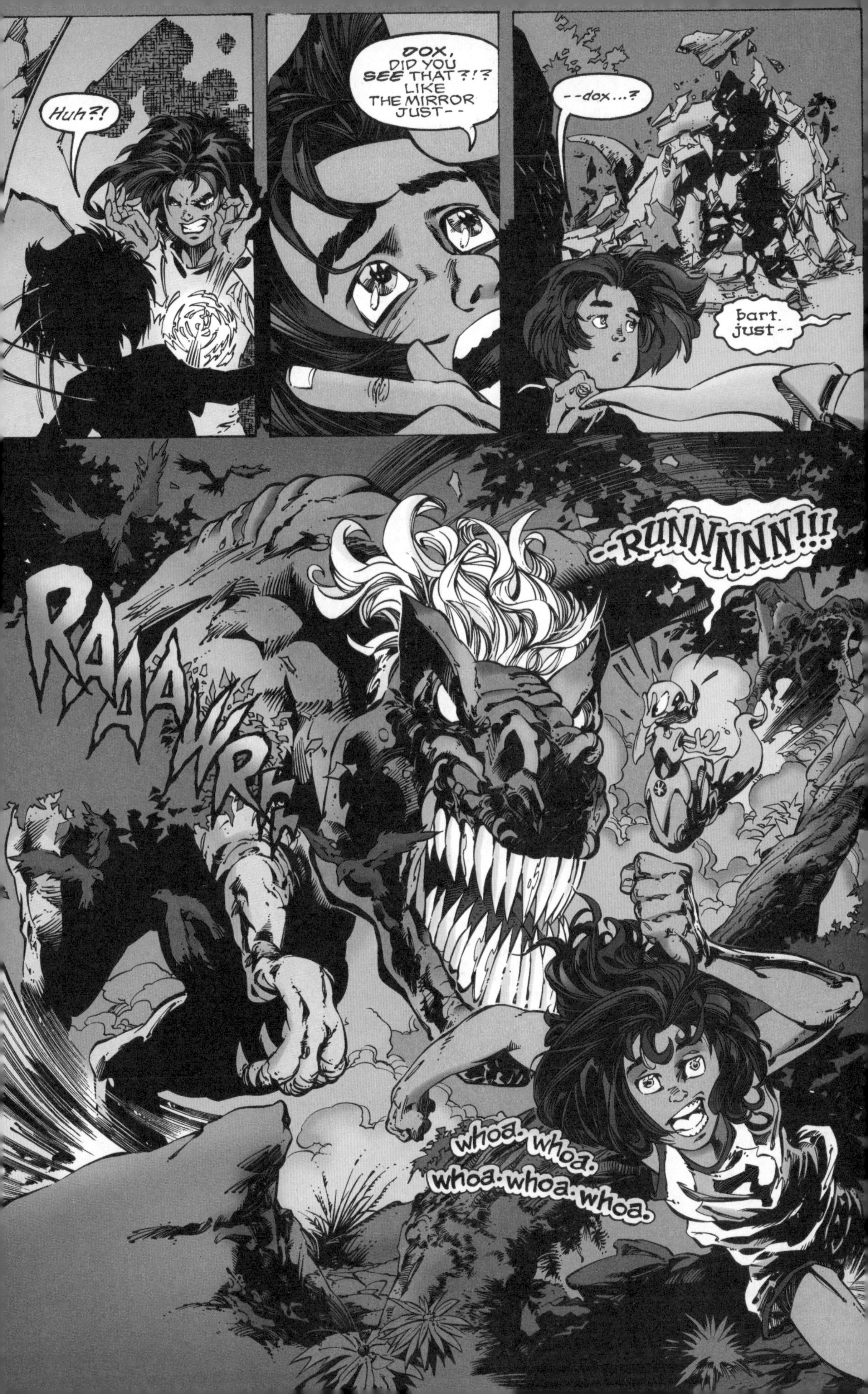
Huh?!
DOX, DID YOU SEE THAT?!? LIKE THE MIRROR JUST--
--dox...?
bart. just--
RAAAWR
--RUNNNNN!!!
whoa. whoa. whoa.whoa.whoa.

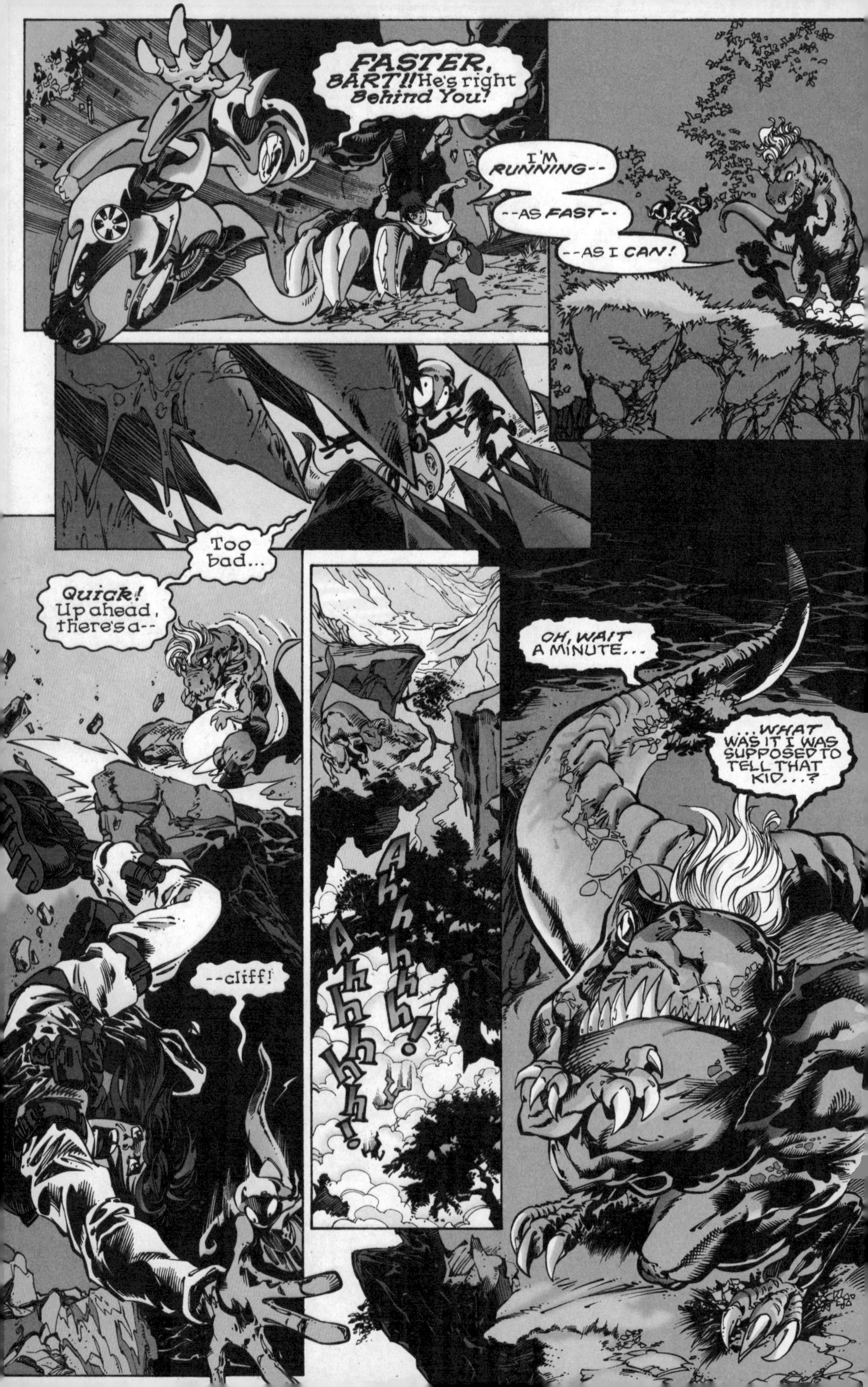
FASTER, BART!! He's right Behind You!
I'M RUNNING--
--AS FAST--
--AS I CAN!
Too bad...
Quick! Up ahead, there's a--
--cliff!
Ahhhhh!
Ahhhhhh!
OH, WAIT A MINUTE...
...WHAT WAS IT I WAS SUPPOSED TO TELL THAT KID...?

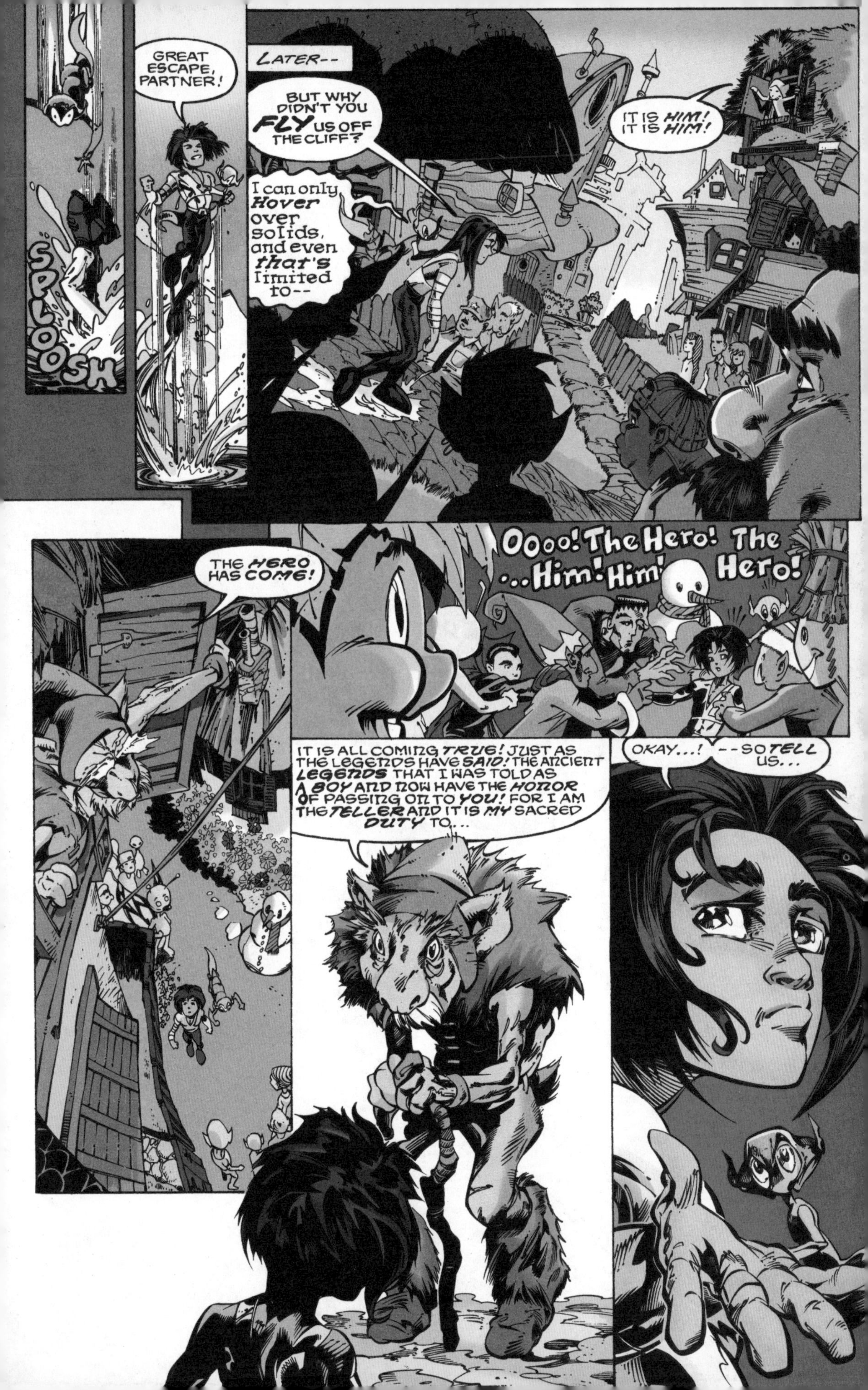
SPLOOSH
GREAT ESCAPE, PARTNER!
LATER--
BUT WHY DIDN'T YOU FLY US OFF THE CLIFF?
I can only Hover over solids, and even that's limited to--
IT IS HIM! IT IS HIM!
THE HERO HAS COME!
Oooo! The Hero! The ...Him! Him! Hero!
IT IS ALL COMING TRUE! JUST AS THE LEGENDS HAVE SAID! THE ANCIENT LEGENDS THAT I WAS TOLD AS A BOY AND NOW HAVE THE HONOR OF PASSING ON TO YOU! FOR I AM THE TELLER AND IT IS MY SACRED DUTY TO...
OKAY...! --SO TELL US...

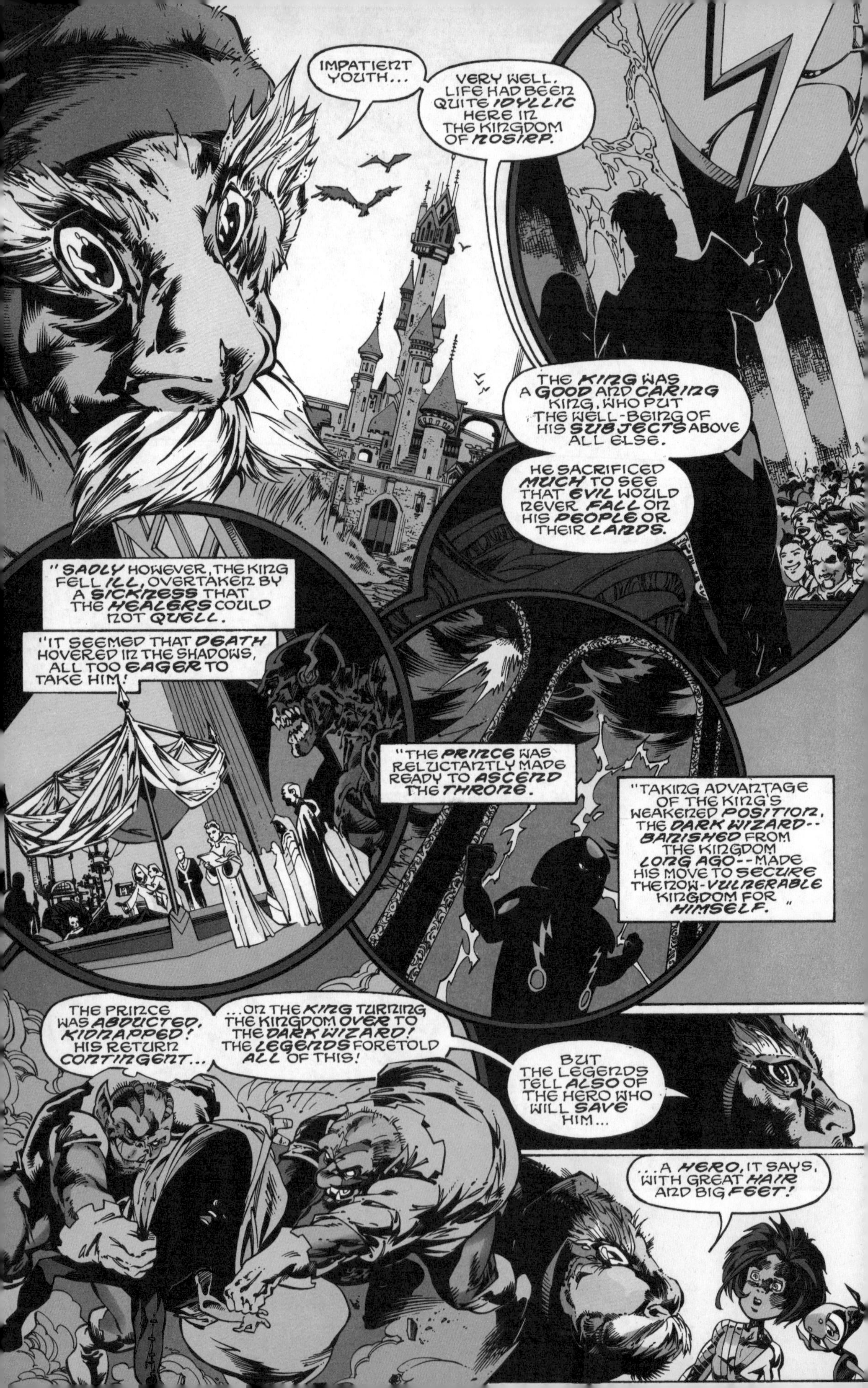
IMPATIENT YOUTH...
VERY WELL. LIFE HAD BEEN QUITE IDYLLIC HERE IN THE KINGDOM OF NOSIRP.
THE KING WAS A GOOD AND CARING KING, WHO PUT THE WELL-BEING OF HIS SUBJECTS ABOVE ALL ELSE.
HE SACRIFICED MUCH TO SEE THAT EVIL WOULD NEVER FALL ON HIS PEOPLE OR THEIR LANDS.
"SADLY HOWEVER, THE KING FELL ILL, OVERTAKEN BY A SICKNESS THAT THE HEALERS COULD NOT QUELL.
"IT SEEMED THAT DEATH HOVERED IN THE SHADOWS, ALL TOO EAGER TO TAKE HIM!
"THE PRINCE WAS RELUCTANTLY MADE READY TO ASCEND THE THRONE.
"TAKING ADVANTAGE OF THE KING'S WEAKENED POSITION, THE DARK WIZARD--BANISHED FROM THE KINGDOM LONG AGO--MADE HIS MOVE TO SECURE THE NOW-VULNERABLE KINGDOM FOR HIMSELF."
THE PRINCE WAS ABDUCTED, KIDNAPPED! HIS RETURN CONTINGENT...
...ON THE KING TURNING THE KINGDOM OVER TO THE DARK WIZARD! THE LEGENDS FORETOLD ALL OF THIS!
BUT THE LEGENDS TELL ALSO OF THE HERO WHO WILL SAVE HIM...
...A HERO, IT SAYS, WITH GREAT HAIR AND BIG FEET!

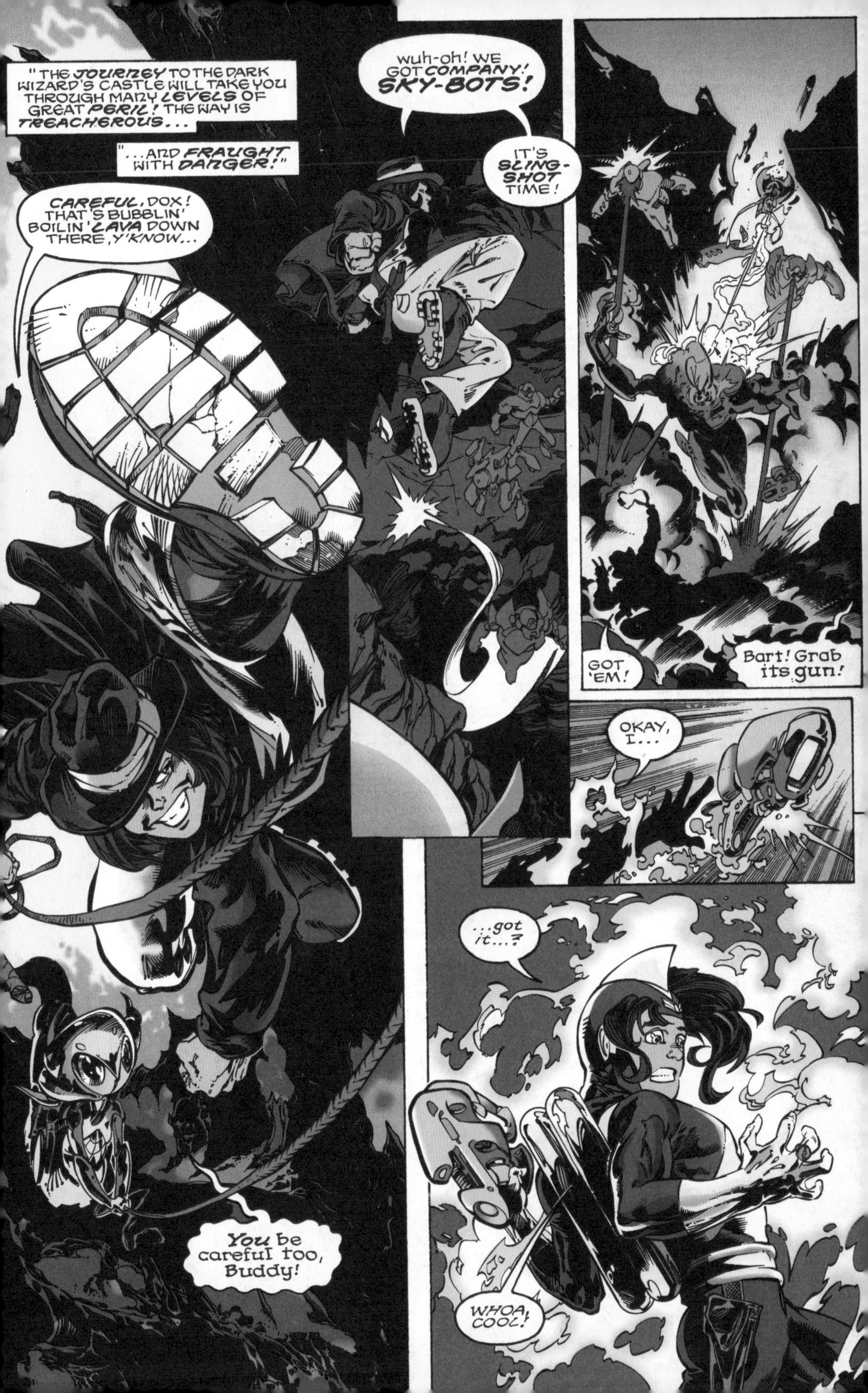
"THE JOURNEY TO THE DARK WIZARD'S CASTLE WILL TAKE YOU THROUGH MANY LEVELS OF GREAT PERIL! THE WAY IS TREACHEROUS...
"...AND FRAUGHT WITH DANGER!"
CAREFUL, DOX! THAT'S BUBBLIN' BOILIN' LAVA DOWN THERE, Y'KNOW...
You be careful too, Buddy!
WUH-OH! WE GOT COMPANY! SKY-BOTS!
IT'S SLING-SHOT TIME!
GOT 'EM!
Bart! Grab its gun!
OKAY, I...
...got it...?
WHOA, COOL!

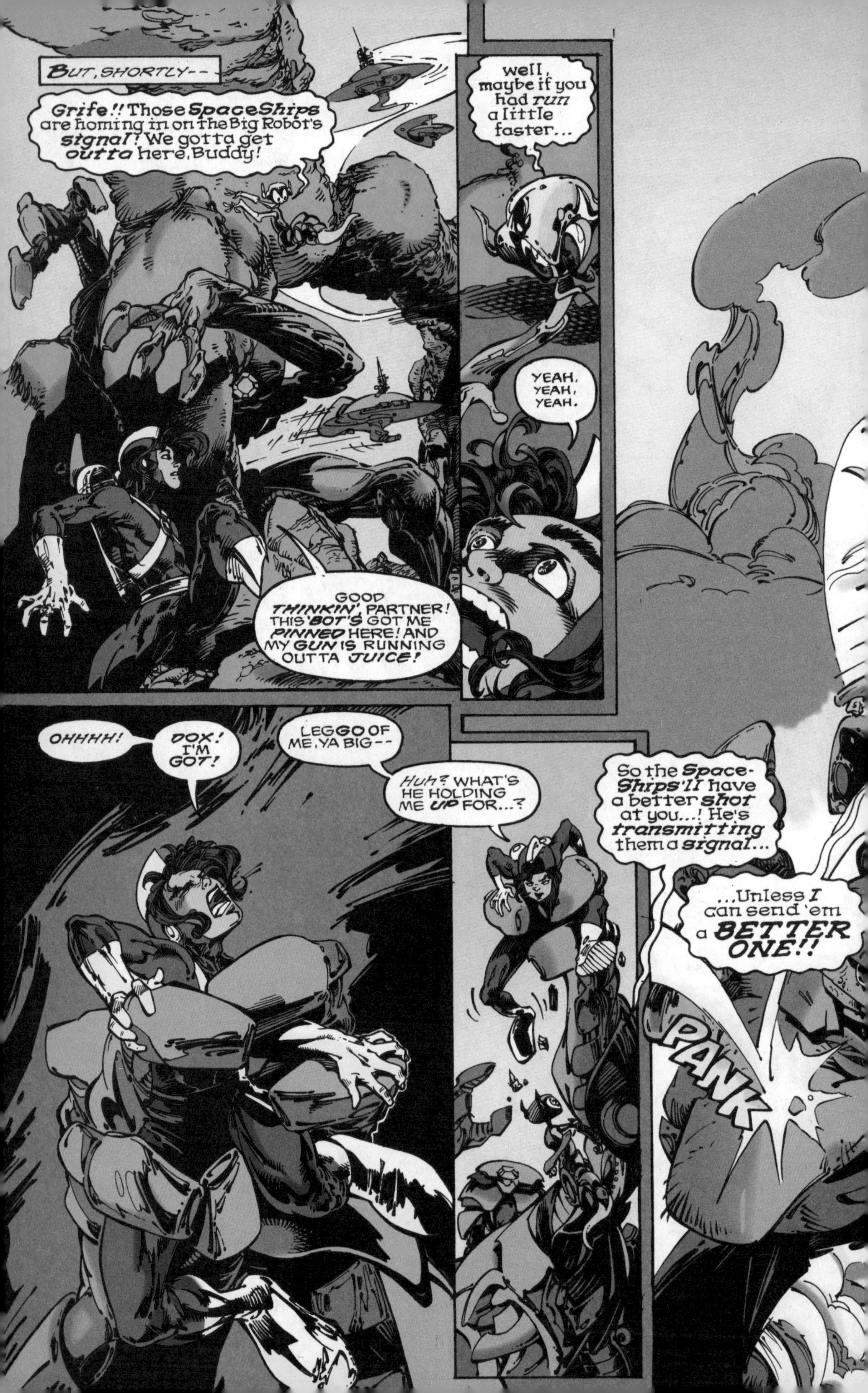

BUT, SHORTLY--
Grife!! Those SpaceShips are homing in on the Big Robot's signal! We gotta get outta here, Buddy!
GOOD THINKIN', PARTNER! THIS 'BOT'S GOT ME PINNED HERE! AND MY GUN IS RUNNING OUTTA JUICE!
well, maybe if you had run a little faster...
YEAH, YEAH, YEAH.
OHHHH!
DOX! I'M GOT!
LEGGO OF ME, YA BIG--
Huh? WHAT'S HE HOLDING ME UP FOR...?
So the Space-Ships'll have a better shot at you...! He's transmitting them a signal...
...Unless I can send 'em a BETTER ONE!!
PANK

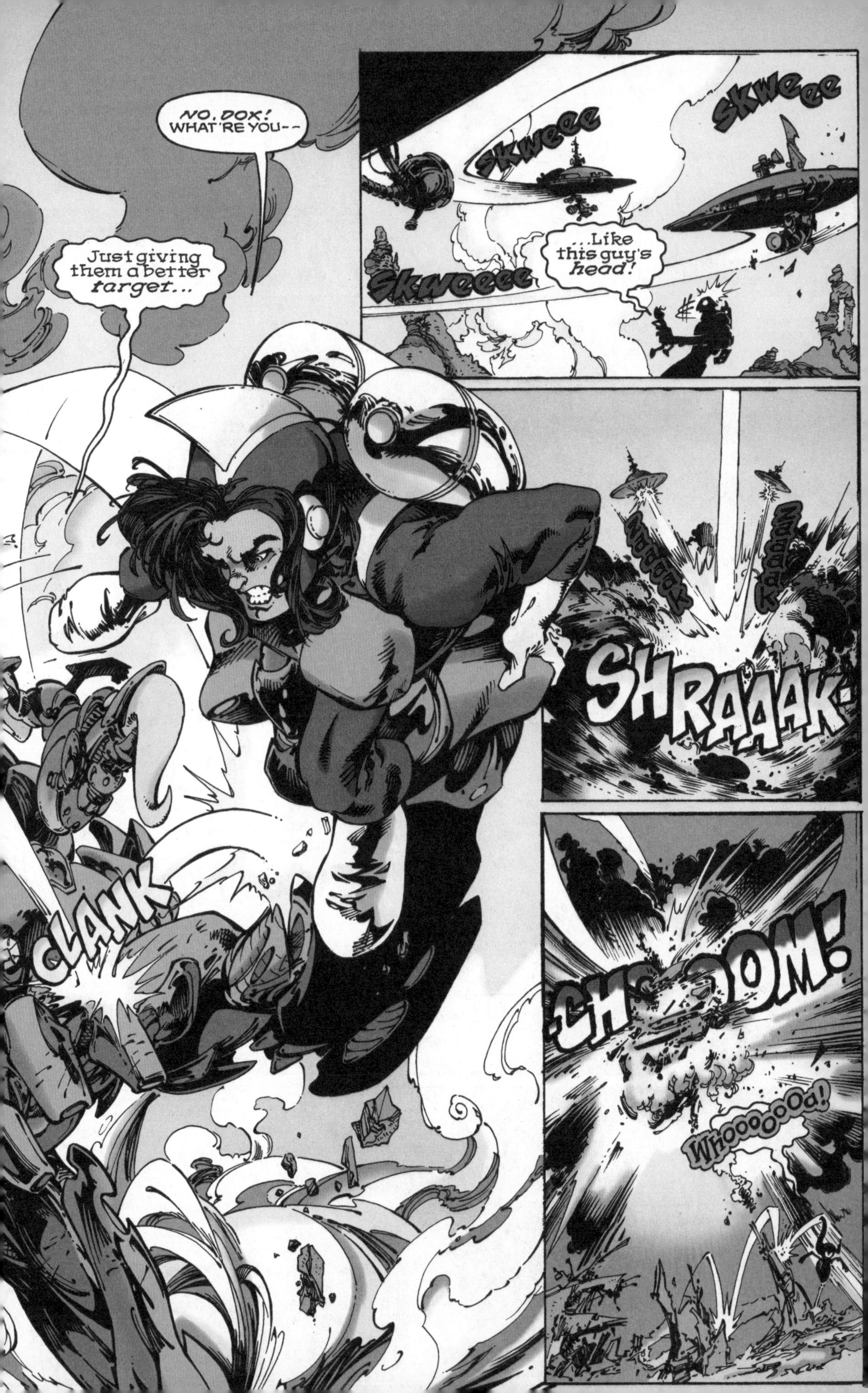
NO. DOX! WHAT'RE YOU--
Just giving them a better target...
SKWEEE
SKWEEE
SKWEEEE
...Like this guy's head!
SHRAAAK
CLANK
CHOOOM!
WHOOOOOOA!

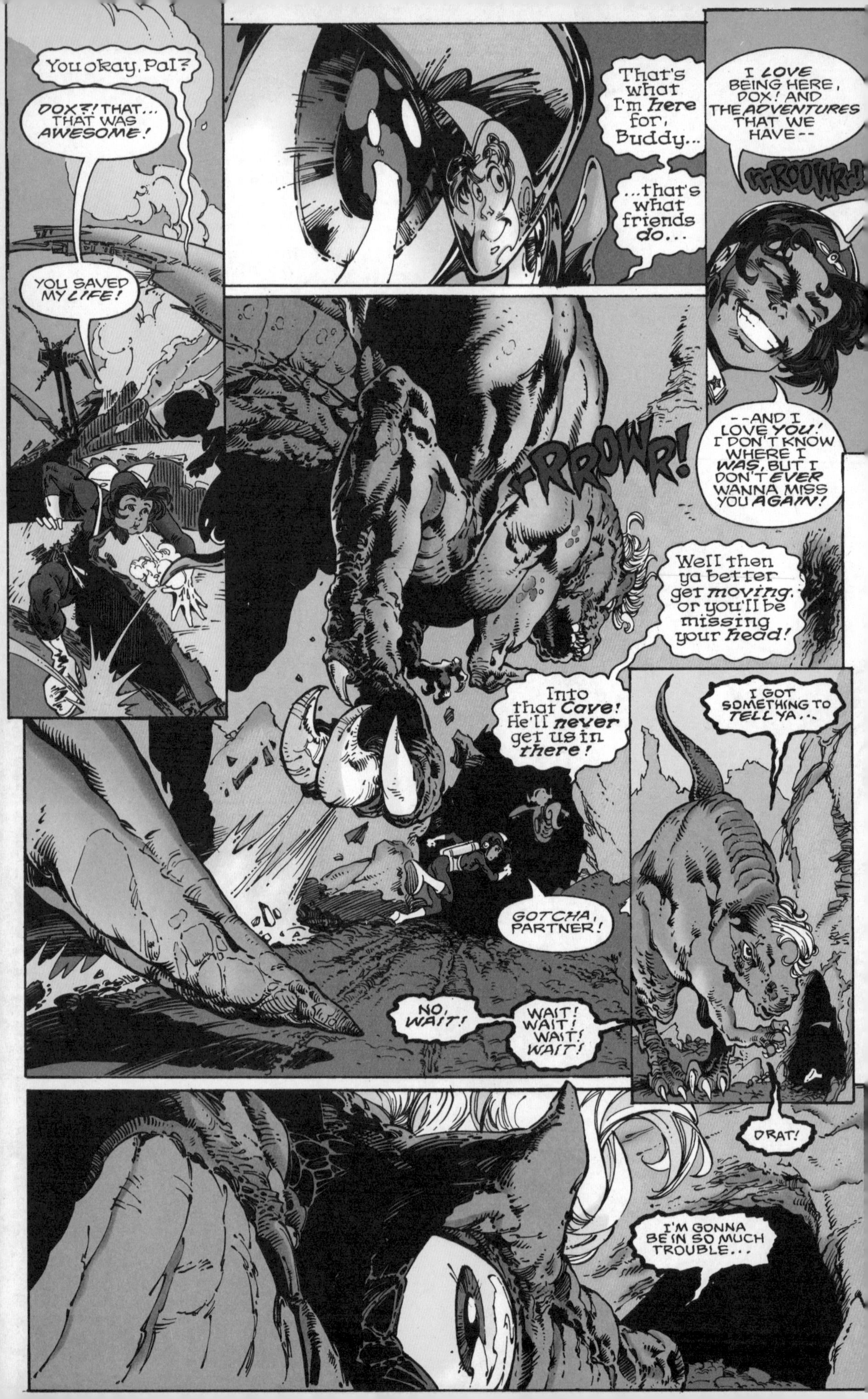
You okay, Pal?
DOX?! THAT... THAT WAS AWESOME!
YOU SAVED MY LIFE!
That's what I'm here for, Buddy...
...that's what friends do...
I LOVE BEING HERE, DOX! AND THE ADVENTURES THAT WE HAVE--
rr-ROOWRr!
--AND I LOVE YOU! I DON'T KNOW WHERE I WAS, BUT I DON'T EVER WANNA MISS YOU AGAIN!
rrRROWR!
Well then ya better get moving, or you'll be missing your head!
Into that Cave! He'll never get us in there!
GOTCHA, PARTNER!
I GOT SOMETHING TO TELL YA...
NO, WAIT!
WAIT! WAIT! WAIT! WAIT!
DRAT!
I'M GONNA BE IN SO MUCH TROUBLE...

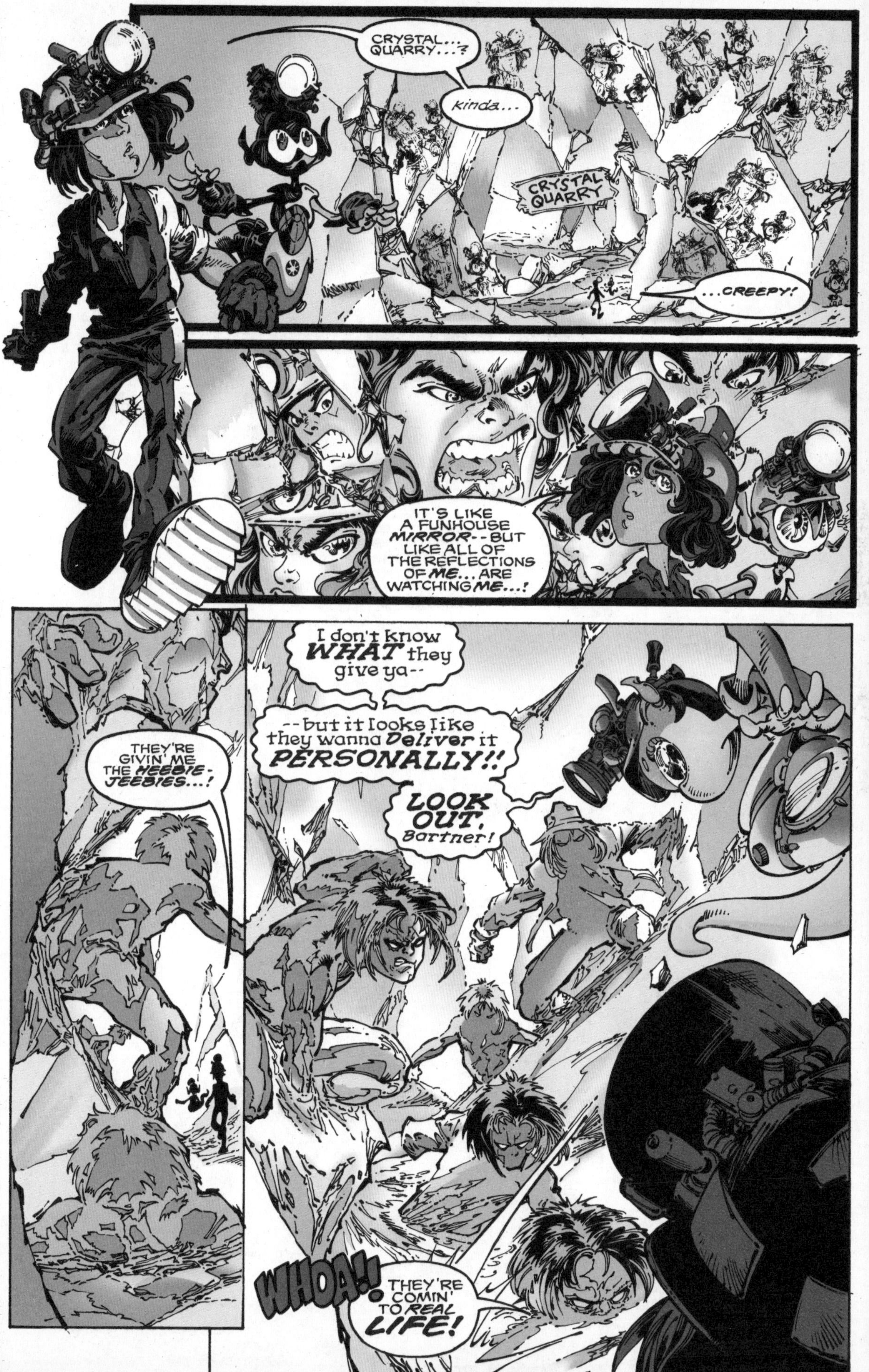
CRYSTAL... QUARRY...?
kinda...
CRYSTAL QUARRY
...CREEPY!
IT'S LIKE A FUNHOUSE MIRROR--BUT LIKE ALL OF THE REFLECTIONS OF ME... ARE WATCHING ME...!
THEY'RE GIVIN' ME THE HEEBIE-JEEBIES...!
I don't know WHAT they give ya--
--but it looks like they wanna Deliver it PERSONALLY!!
LOOK OUT, Bartner!
WHOA!!
THEY'RE COMIN' TO REAL LIFE!

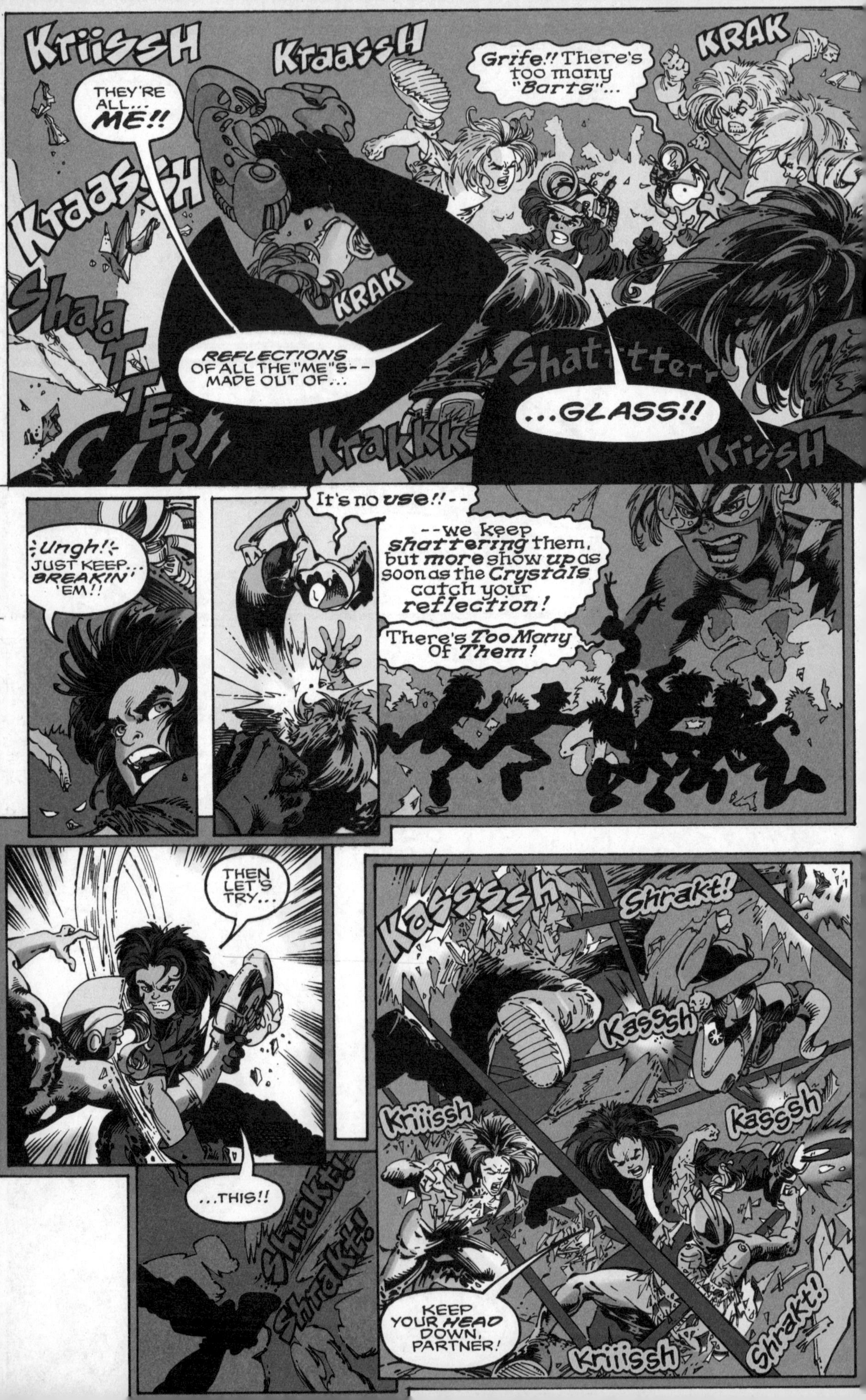

Kriissh
Kraassh
They're all... me!!
Grife!! There's too many "Barts"...
KRAK
Kraassh
Shaatter!
KRAK
Reflections of all the "me"s-- made out of...
Shattterr
...glass!!
Krakkk
Krissh
Ungh!- Just keep... breakin' 'em!!
It's no use!!--
--we keep shattering them, but more show up as soon as the Crystals catch your reflection!
There's Too Many Of Them!
Then let's try...
...this!!
Shrakt!
Shrakt!
Kassssh
Shrakt!
Kasssh
Kriiissh
Kasssh
Keep your head down, partner!
Kriiissh
Shrakt!

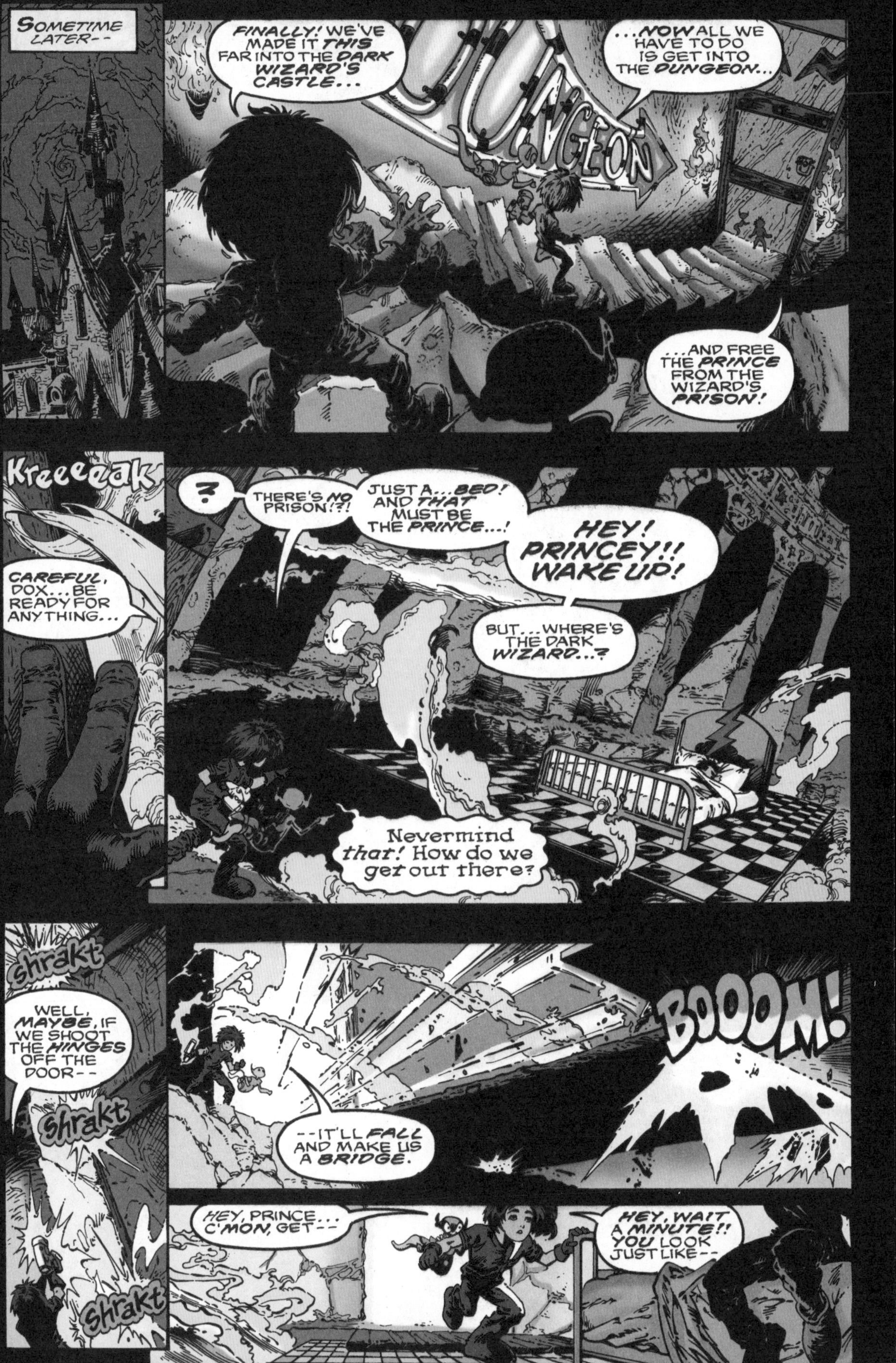
SOMETIME LATER--
FINALLY! WE'VE MADE IT THIS FAR INTO THE DARK WIZARD'S CASTLE...
...NOW ALL WE HAVE TO DO IS GET INTO THE DUNGEON...
DUNGEON
...AND FREE THE PRINCE FROM THE WIZARD'S PRISON!
Kreeeeak
CAREFUL, DOX... BE READY FOR ANYTHING...
?
THERE'S NO PRISON!?!
JUST A... BED! AND THAT MUST BE THE PRINCE...!
HEY! PRINCEY!! WAKE UP!
BUT... WHERE'S THE DARK WIZARD...?
Nevermind that! How do we get out there?
shrakt
WELL, MAYBE, IF WE SHOOT THE HINGES OFF THE DOOR--
shrakt
--IT'LL FALL AND MAKE US A BRIDGE.
BOOOM!
shrakt
HEY, PRINCE... C'MON, GET--
HEY, WAIT A MINUTE!! YOU LOOK JUST LIKE--

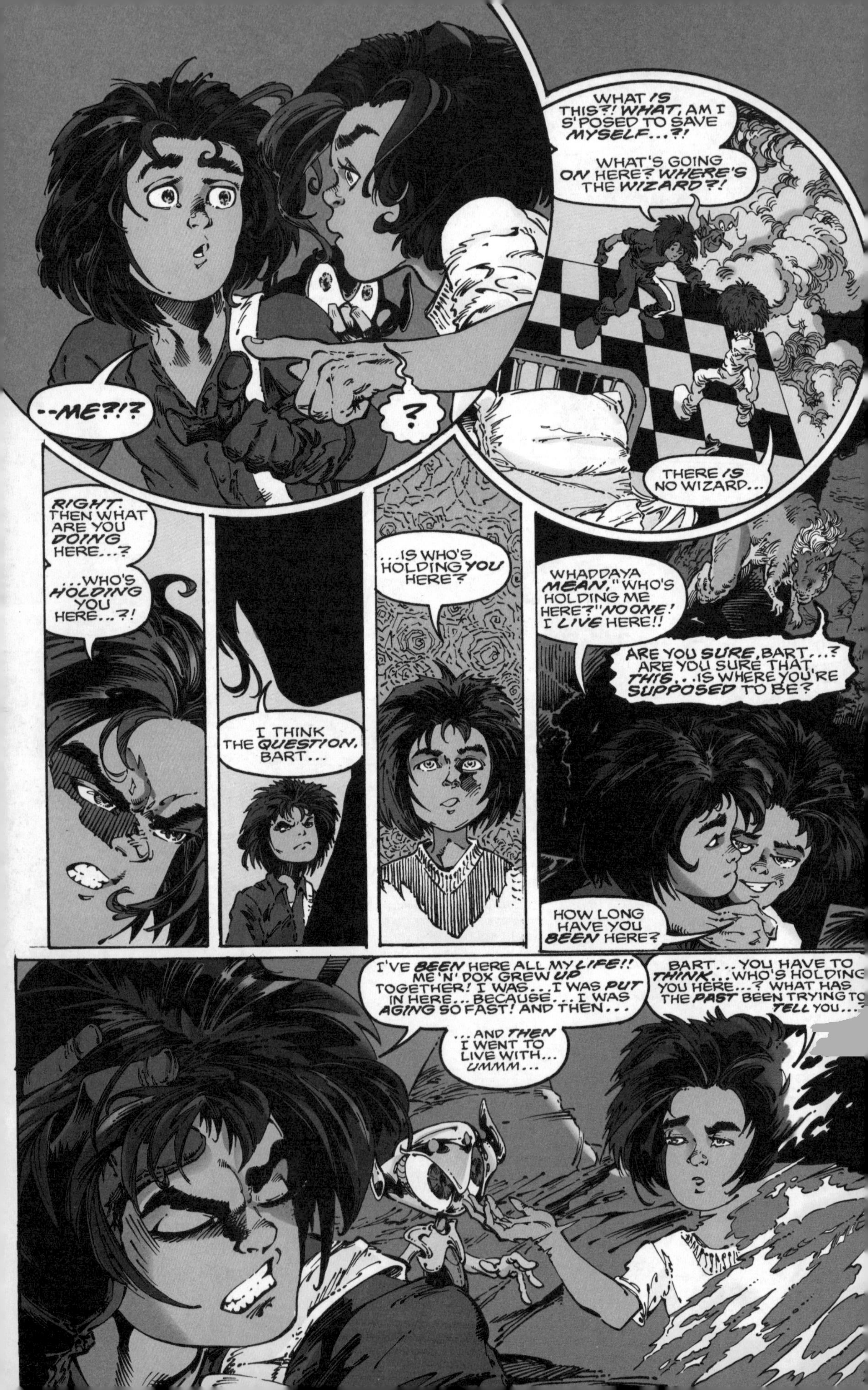

--ME?!?
?
WHAT IS THIS?! WHAT, AM I S'POSED TO SAVE MYSELF...?!
WHAT'S GOING ON HERE? WHERE'S THE WIZARD?!
THERE IS NO WIZARD...
RIGHT. THEN WHAT ARE YOU DOING HERE...?
...WHO'S HOLDING YOU HERE...?!
I THINK THE QUESTION, BART...
...IS WHO'S HOLDING YOU HERE?
WHADDAYA MEAN, "WHO'S HOLDING ME HERE?" NO ONE! I LIVE HERE!!
ARE YOU SURE, BART...? ARE YOU SURE THAT THIS... IS WHERE YOU'RE SUPPOSED TO BE?
HOW LONG HAVE YOU BEEN HERE?
I'VE BEEN HERE ALL MY LIFE!! ME 'N' DOX GREW UP TOGETHER! I WAS... I WAS PUT IN HERE... BECAUSE... I WAS AGING SO FAST! AND THEN...
...AND THEN I WENT TO LIVE WITH... UMMM...
BART... YOU HAVE TO THINK... WHO'S HOLDING YOU HERE...? WHAT HAS THE PAST BEEN TRYING TO TELL YOU...?

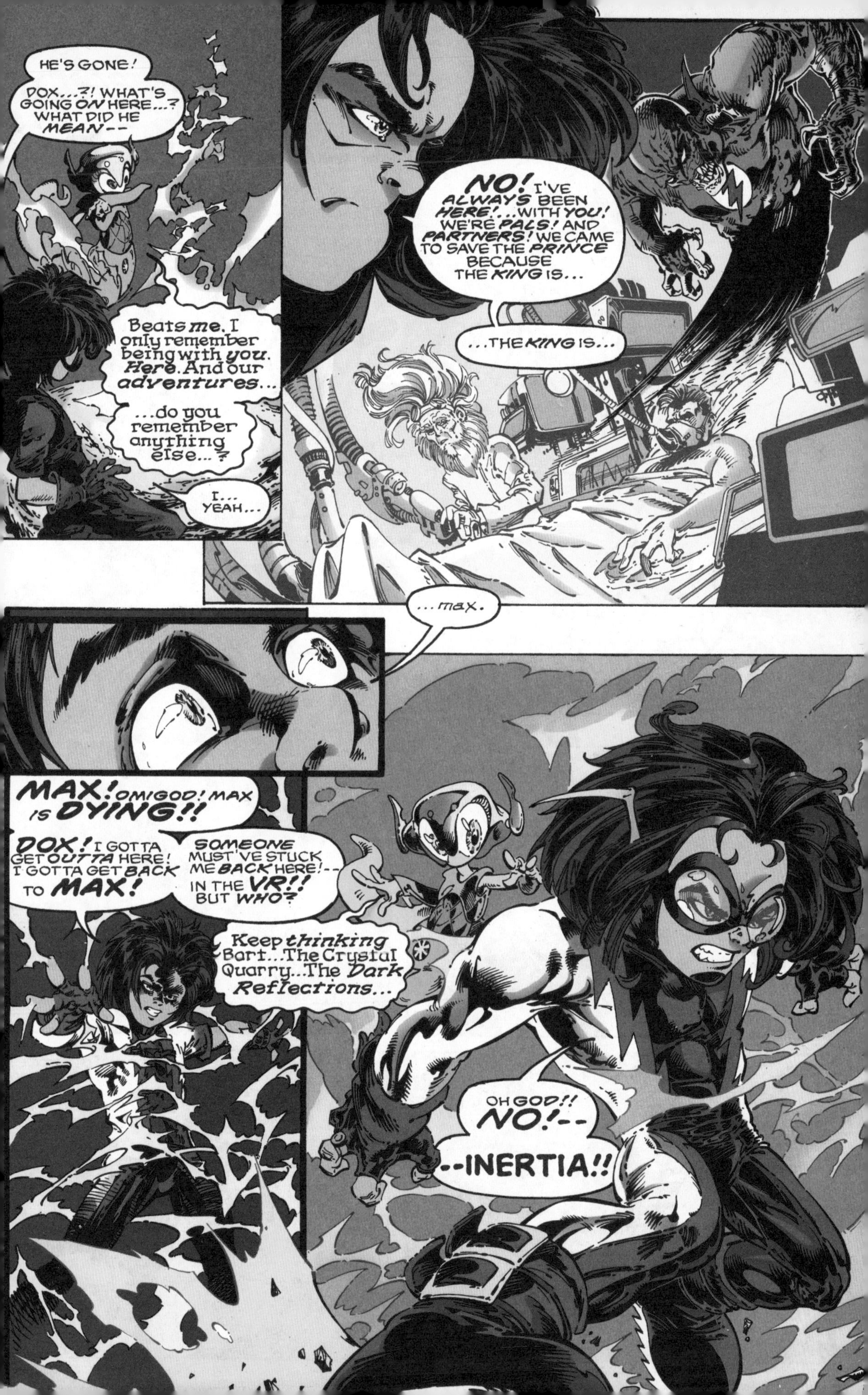
HE'S GONE!
DOX...?! WHAT'S GOING ON HERE...? WHAT DID HE MEAN--
Beats me. I only remember being with you. Here. And our adventures...
...do you remember anything else...?
I... YEAH...
NO! I'VE ALWAYS BEEN HERE!...WITH YOU! WE'RE PALS! AND PARTNERS! WE CAME TO SAVE THE PRINCE BECAUSE THE KING IS...
...THE KING IS...
...max.
MAX! OMIGOD! MAX IS DYING!!
DOX! I GOTTA GET OUTTA HERE! I GOTTA GET BACK TO MAX!
SOMEONE MUST'VE STUCK ME BACK HERE!-- IN THE VR!! BUT WHO?
Keep thinking Bart...The Crystal Quarry...The Dark Reflections...
OH GOD!! NO!--
--INERTIA!!

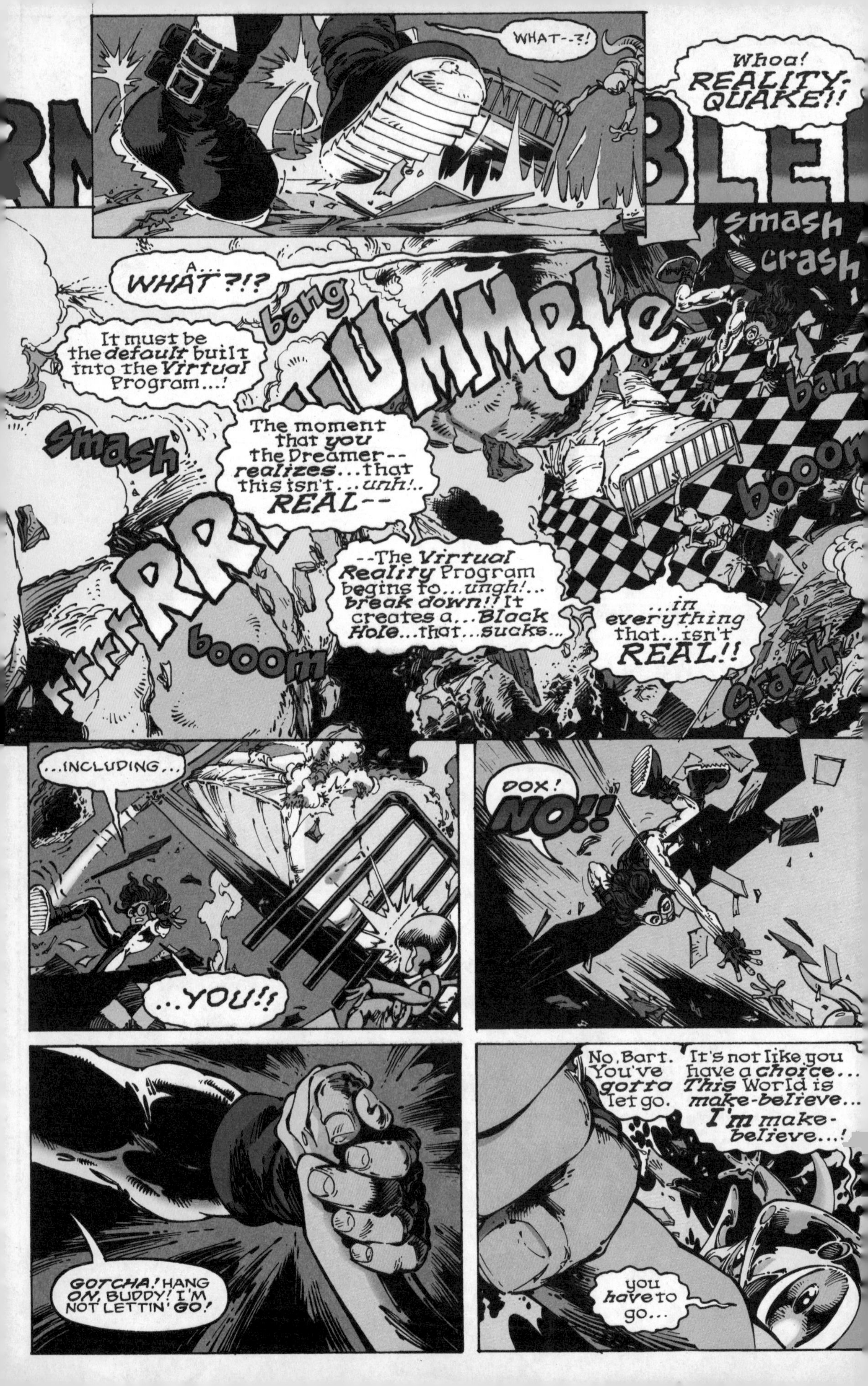

WHAT--?!
Whoa! REALITY-QUAKE!!
A... WHAT?!?
It must be the default built into the Virtual Program...!
The moment that you the Dreamer--realizes...that this isn't...unh!..REAL--
--The Virtual Reality Program begins to...ungh!...break down!! It creates a...Black Hole...that...sucks...
...in everything that...isn't REAL!!
...INCLUDING...
...YOU!!
DOX! NO!!
GOTCHA! HANG ON, BUDDY! I'M NOT LETTIN' GO!
No, Bart. You've gotta let go.
It's not like you have a choice... This World is make-believe... I'm make-believe...!
you have to go...

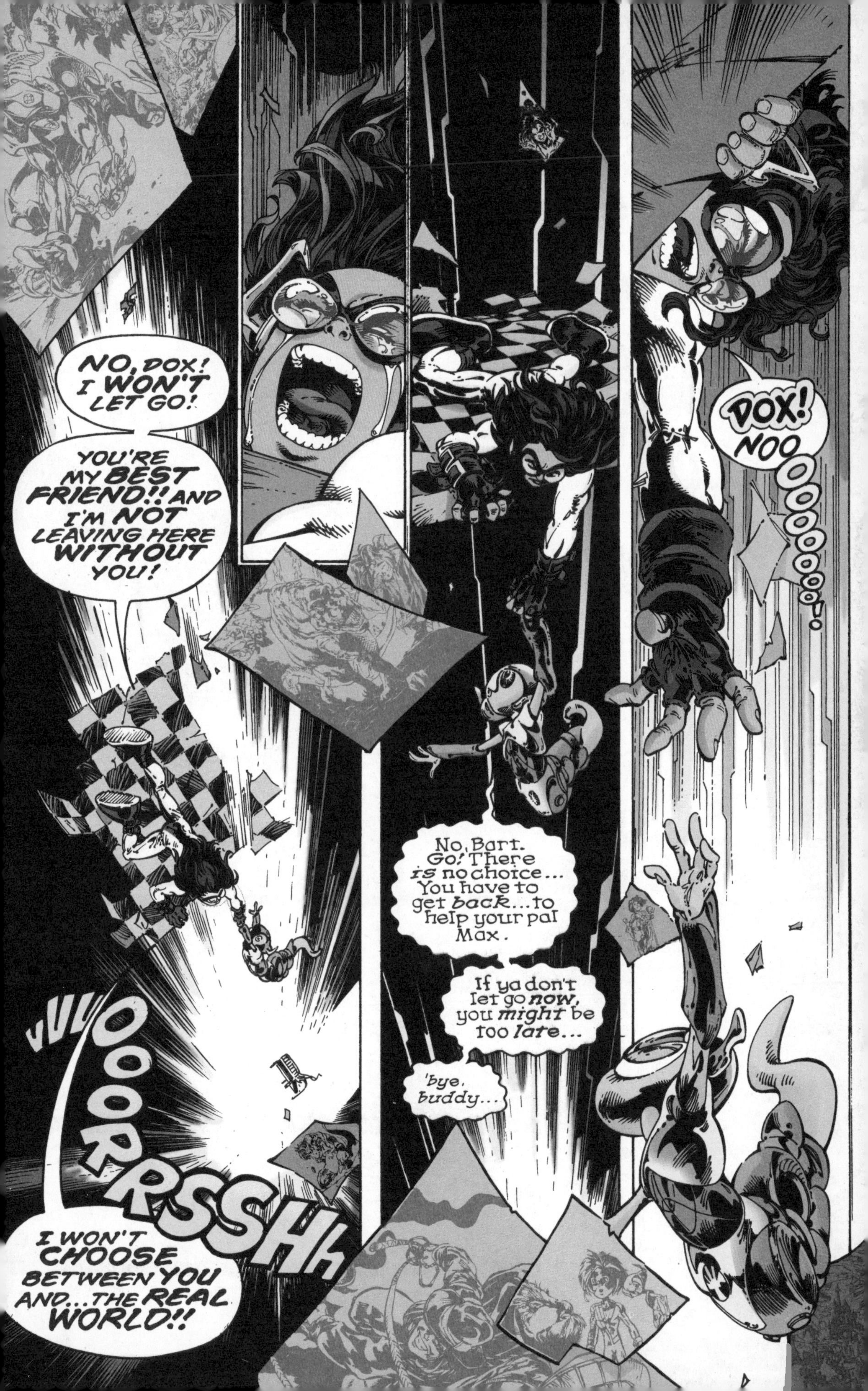

NO, DOX! I WON'T LET GO!
YOU'RE MY BEST FRIEND!! AND I'M NOT LEAVING HERE WITHOUT YOU!
VVVOOOORRSSHH
I WON'T CHOOSE BETWEEN YOU AND... THE REAL WORLD!!
No, Bart. Go! There is no choice... You have to get back... to help your pal Max.
If ya don't let go now, you might be too late...
'bye, buddy...
DOX! NOOOOOOOOOO!

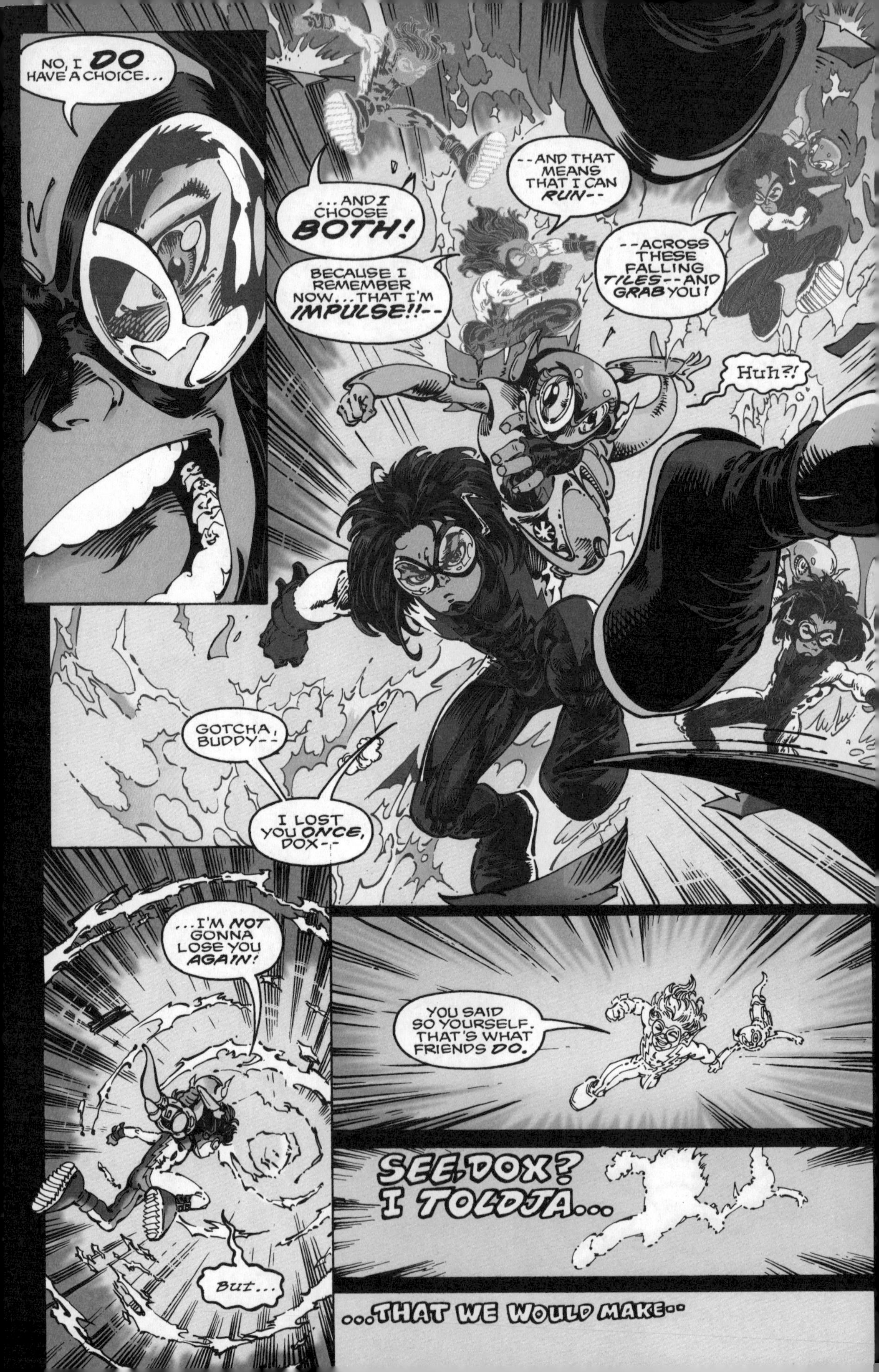
NO, I DO HAVE A CHOICE...
...AND I CHOOSE BOTH!
BECAUSE I REMEMBER NOW... THAT I'M IMPULSE!!--
--AND THAT MEANS THAT I CAN RUN--
--ACROSS THESE FALLING TILES--AND GRAB YOU!
Huh?!
GOTCHA, BUDDY--
I LOST YOU ONCE, DOX--
...I'M NOT GONNA LOSE YOU AGAIN!
But...
YOU SAID SO YOURSELF. THAT'S WHAT FRIENDS DO.
SEE, DOX? I TOLDJA...
...THAT WE WOULD MAKE--

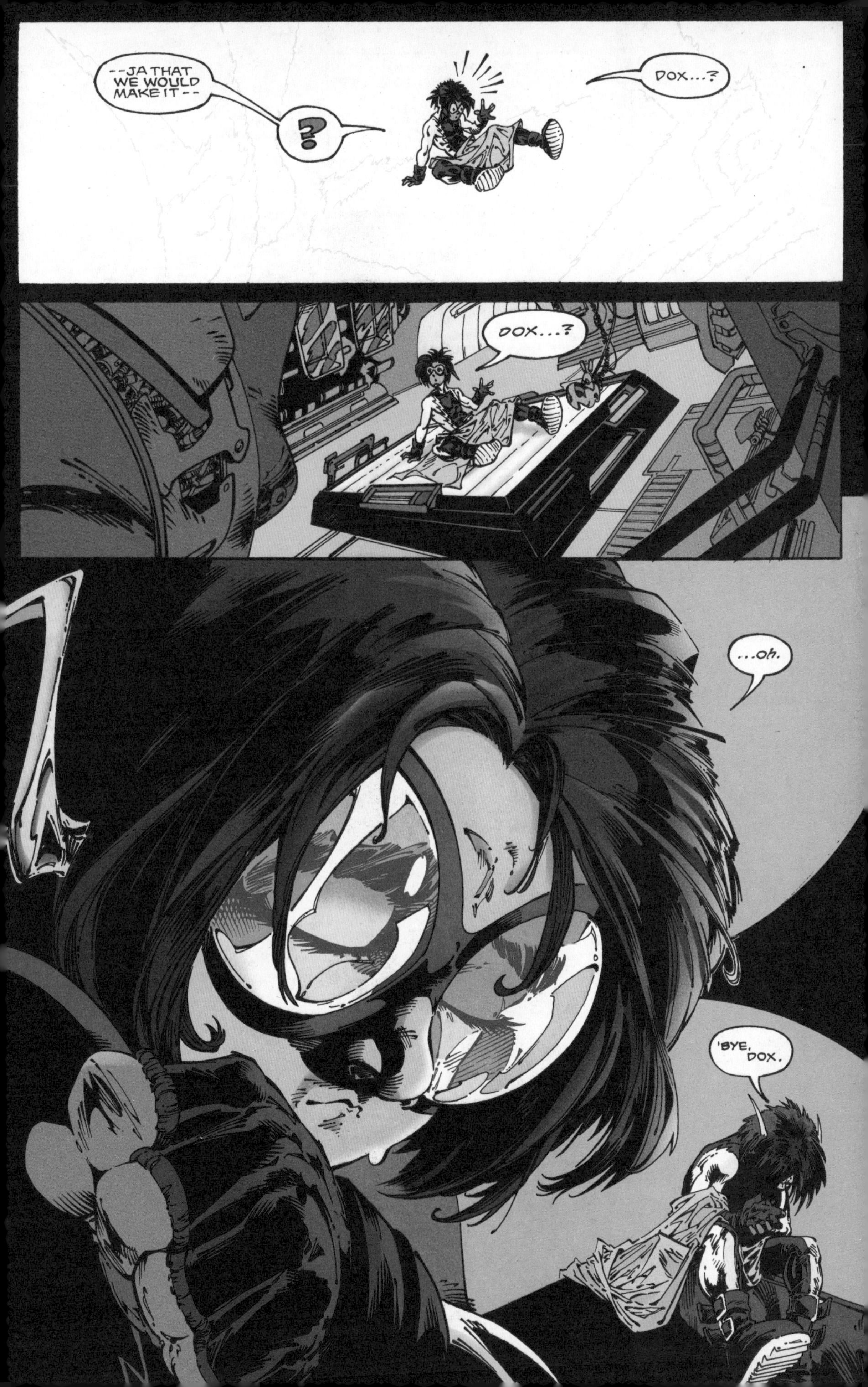
--JA THAT WE WOULD MAKE IT--
?
DOX...?
DOX...?
...oh.
'BYE, DOX.

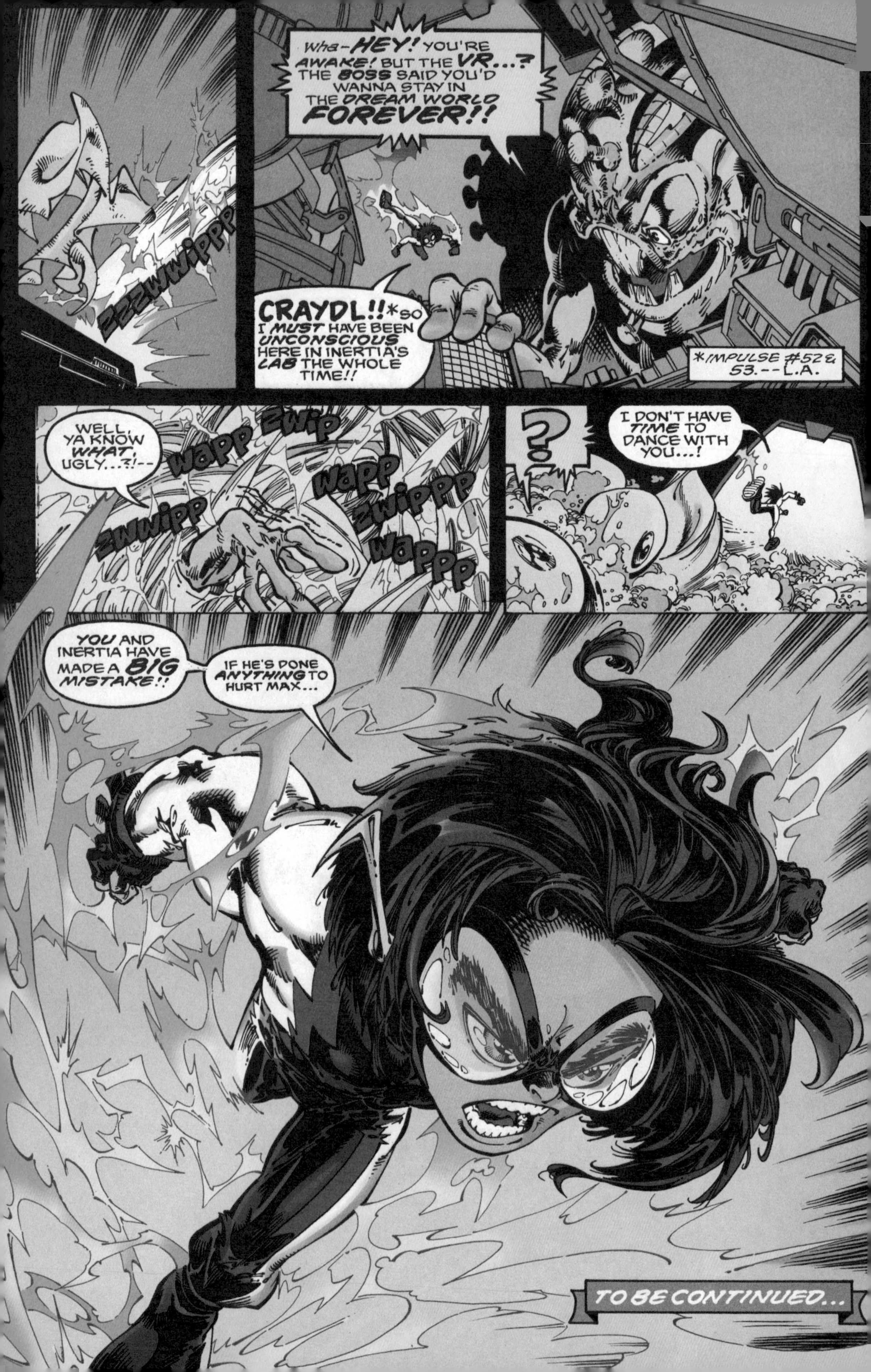

ZZZWWWIPPP
Wha-HEY! YOU'RE AWAKE! BUT THE VR...? THE BOSS SAID YOU'D WANNA STAY IN THE DREAM WORLD FOREVER!!
CRAYDL!!* SO I MUST HAVE BEEN UNCONSCIOUS HERE IN INERTIA'S LAB THE WHOLE TIME!!
*IMPULSE #52 & 53.--L.A.
WELL, YA KNOW WHAT, UGLY...?!--
ZWIP WAPP ZWWIPP WAPP ZWIPPP WAPPP
?
I DON'T HAVE TIME TO DANCE WITH YOU...!
YOU AND INERTIA HAVE MADE A BIG MISTAKE!!
IF HE'S DONE ANYTHING TO HURT MAX...
TO BE CONTINUED...

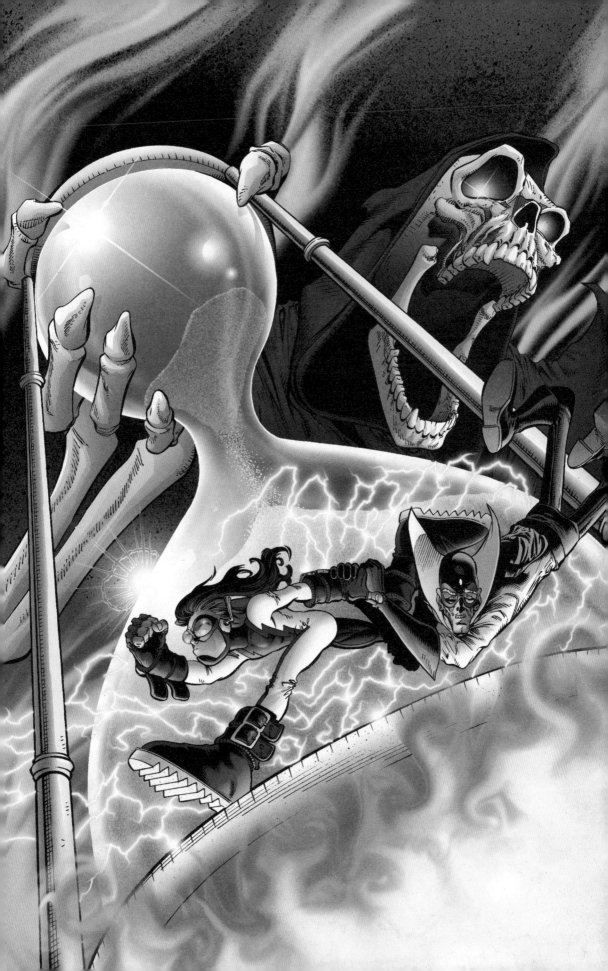

BART ALLEN'S EVIL TWIN
MERCURY FALLING Part 4
a dezago - van sciver - kaalberg & rollins - chiang - jones - jamison - l.a. collabo
OH, I COULD TELL YOU MY NAME, BUT THEN I'D HAVE TO KILL YOU...!
oh, wait a minute...
...right...
THE NAME IS GLORY SHREDDER, SMOKEY--
--AND IT'S THE LAST NAME YOU'RE GONNA SEE BEFORE I SNUFF YOUR GREEN CIGARETTE BUTT OUT FOR GOOD!
cof... cof...
COULD THIS GUY BE ANY MORE INSANE...?
IMPULSE created by WAID & WIERINGO

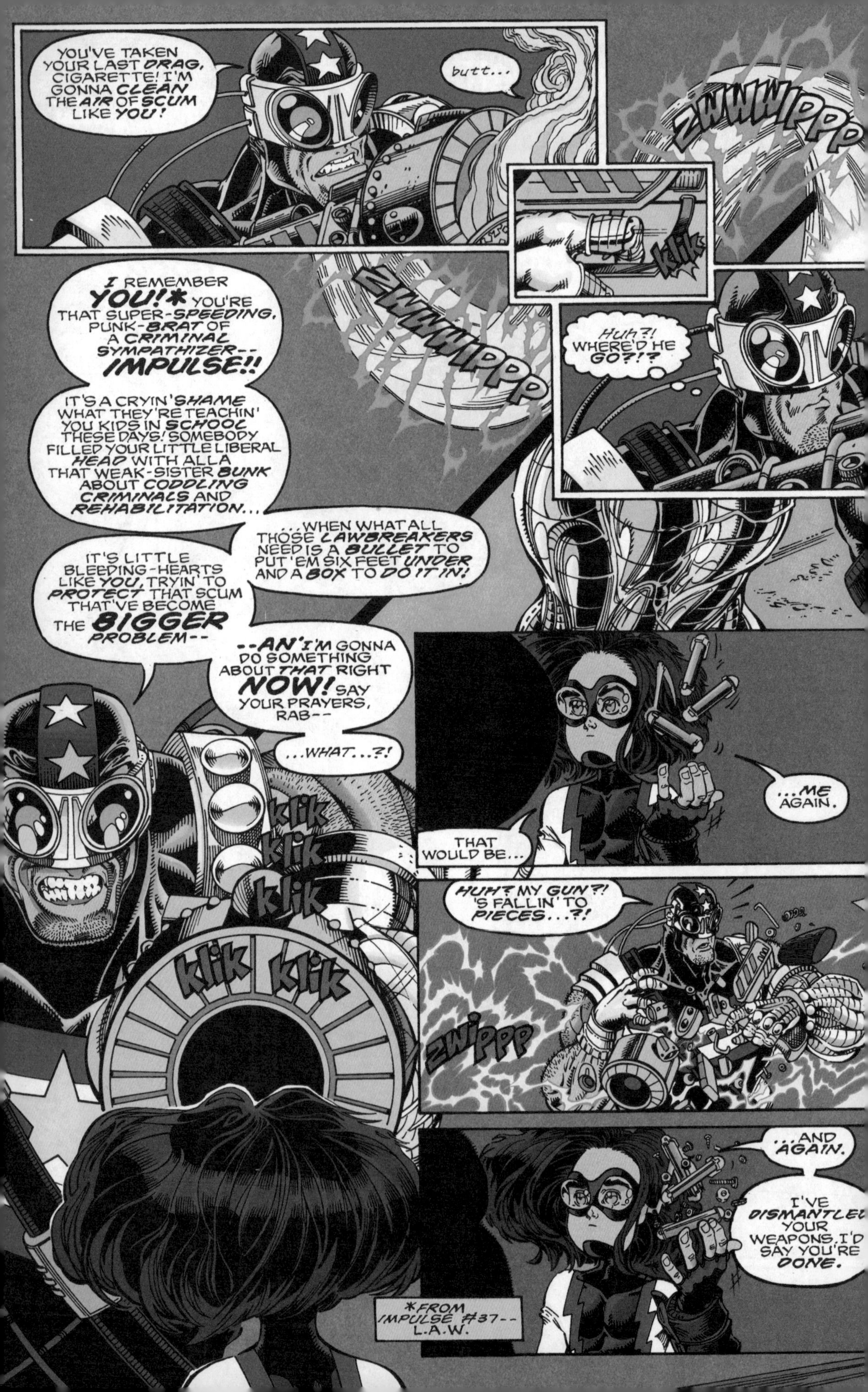
YOU'VE TAKEN YOUR LAST DRAG, CIGARETTE! I'M GONNA CLEAN THE AIR OF SCUM LIKE YOU!
butt...
ZWWWIPPP
klik
ZWWWIPPP
I REMEMBER YOU!* YOU'RE THAT SUPER-SPEEDING, PUNK-BRAT OF A CRIMINAL SYMPATHIZER-- IMPULSE!!
IT'S A CRYIN' SHAME WHAT THEY'RE TEACHIN' YOU KIDS IN SCHOOL THESE DAYS! SOMEBODY FILLED YOUR LITTLE LIBERAL HEAD WITH ALLA THAT WEAK-SISTER BUNK ABOUT CODDLING CRIMINALS AND REHABILITATION...
...WHEN WHAT ALL THOSE LAWBREAKERS NEED IS A BULLET TO PUT 'EM SIX FEET UNDER AND A BOX TO DO IT IN!
IT'S LITTLE BLEEDING-HEARTS LIKE YOU, TRYIN' TO PROTECT THAT SCUM THAT'VE BECOME THE BIGGER PROBLEM--
HUH?! WHERE'D HE GO?!?
--AN' I'M GONNA DO SOMETHING ABOUT THAT RIGHT NOW! SAY YOUR PRAYERS, RAB--
...WHAT...?!
klik klik klik
klik klik
THAT WOULD BE...
...ME AGAIN.
HUH? MY GUN?! 'S FALLIN' TO PIECES...?!
ZWIPPP
...AND AGAIN.
I'VE DISMANTLED YOUR WEAPONS, I'D SAY YOU'RE DONE.
*FROM IMPULSE #37-- L.A.W.

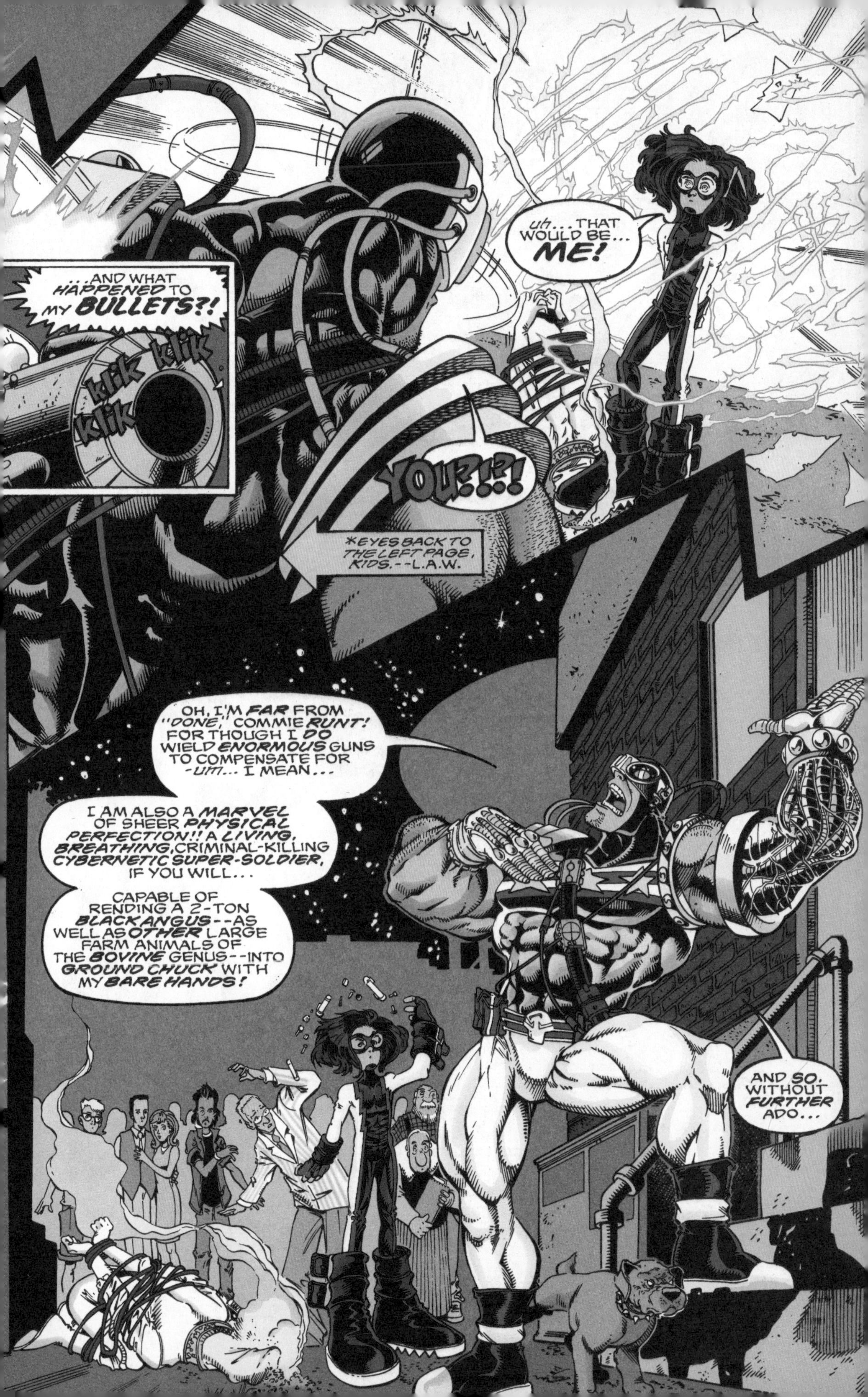
uh... THAT WOULD BE... ME!
...AND WHAT HAPPENED TO MY BULLETS?!
klik klik klik
YOU?!?!...
*EYES BACK TO THE LEFT PAGE, KIDS.--L.A.W.
OH, I'M FAR FROM "DONE," COMMIE RUNT! FOR THOUGH I DO WIELD ENORMOUS GUNS TO COMPENSATE FOR -UM... I MEAN...
I AM ALSO A MARVEL OF SHEER PHYSICAL PERFECTION!! A LIVING, BREATHING, CRIMINAL-KILLING CYBERNETIC SUPER-SOLDIER, IF YOU WILL...
CAPABLE OF RENDING A 2-TON BLACK ANGUS--AS WELL AS OTHER LARGE FARM ANIMALS OF THE BOVINE GENUS--INTO GROUND CHUCK WITH MY BARE HANDS!
AND SO, WITHOUT FURTHER ADO...

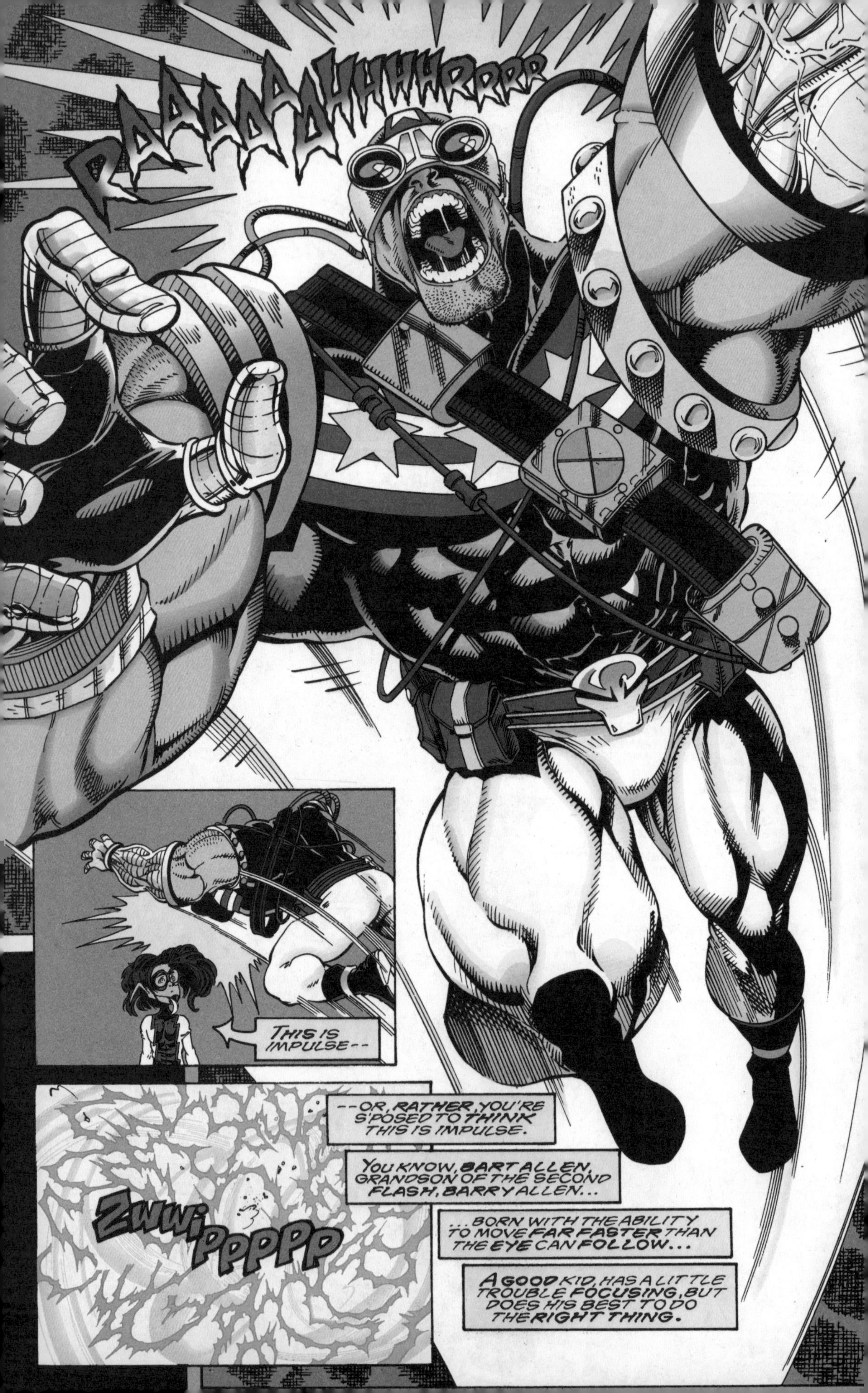
RAAAAAAHHHHRRRRR
THIS IS IMPULSE--
--OR, RATHER, YOU'RE S'POSED TO THINK THIS IS IMPULSE.
YOU KNOW, BART ALLEN, GRANDSON OF THE SECOND FLASH, BARRY ALLEN...
...BORN WITH THE ABILITY TO MOVE FAR FASTER THAN THE EYE CAN FOLLOW...
A GOOD KID, HAS A LITTLE TROUBLE FOCUSING, BUT DOES HIS BEST TO DO THE RIGHT THING.
ZWWIPPPPP

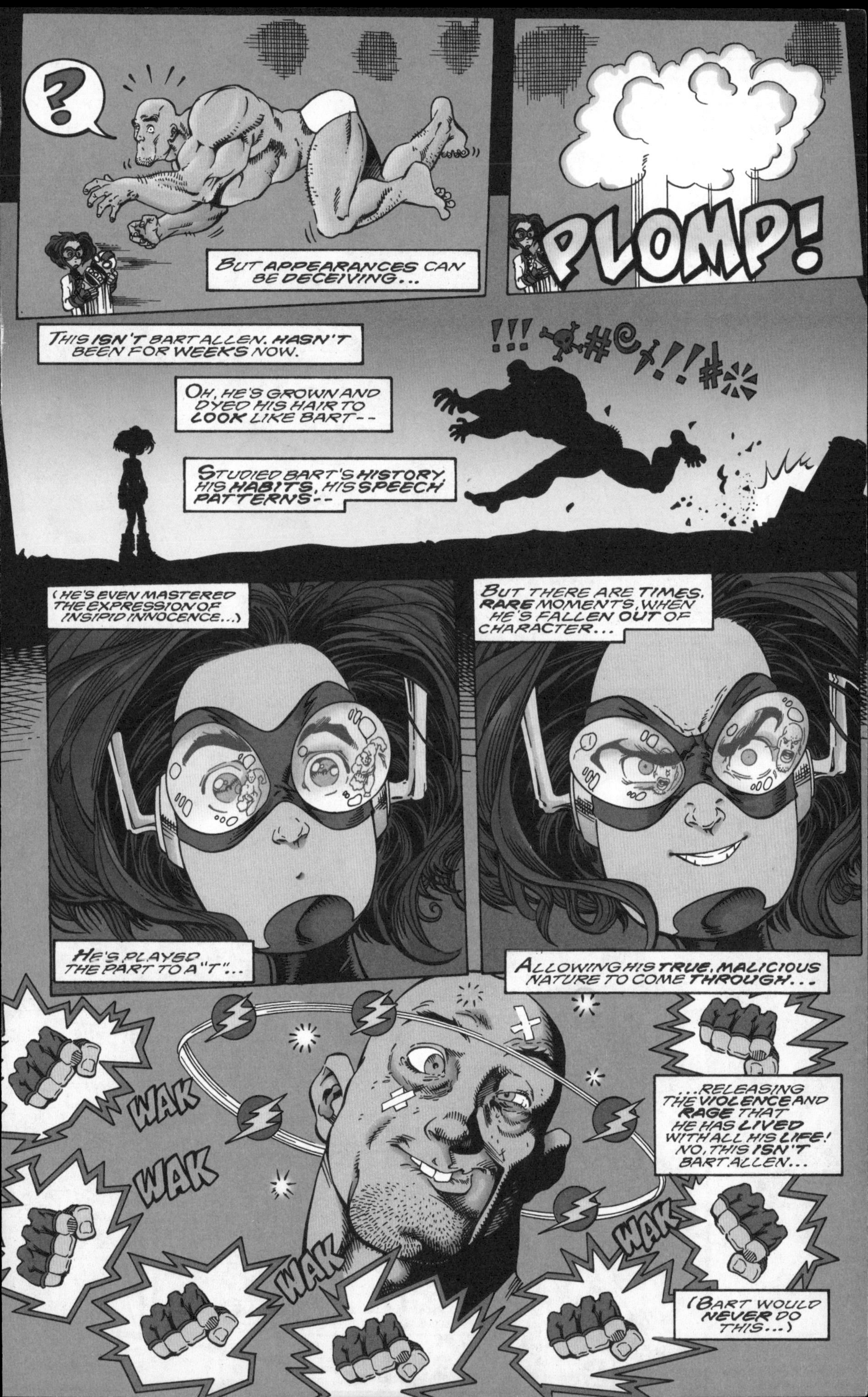
?
BUT APPEARANCES CAN BE DECEIVING...
PLOMP!
THIS ISN'T BART ALLEN. HASN'T BEEN FOR WEEKS NOW.
!!! #@!!#
OH, HE'S GROWN AND DYED HIS HAIR TO LOOK LIKE BART--
STUDIED BART'S HISTORY, HIS HABITS, HIS SPEECH PATTERNS--
(HE'S EVEN MASTERED THE EXPRESSION OF INSIPID INNOCENCE...)
HE'S PLAYED THE PART TO A "T"...
BUT THERE ARE TIMES, RARE MOMENTS, WHEN HE'S FALLEN OUT OF CHARACTER...
ALLOWING HIS TRUE, MALICIOUS NATURE TO COME THROUGH...
WAK
WAK
...RELEASING THE VIOLENCE AND RAGE THAT HE HAS LIVED WITH ALL HIS LIFE! NO, THIS ISN'T BART ALLEN...
WAK
WAK
(BART WOULD NEVER DO THIS...)

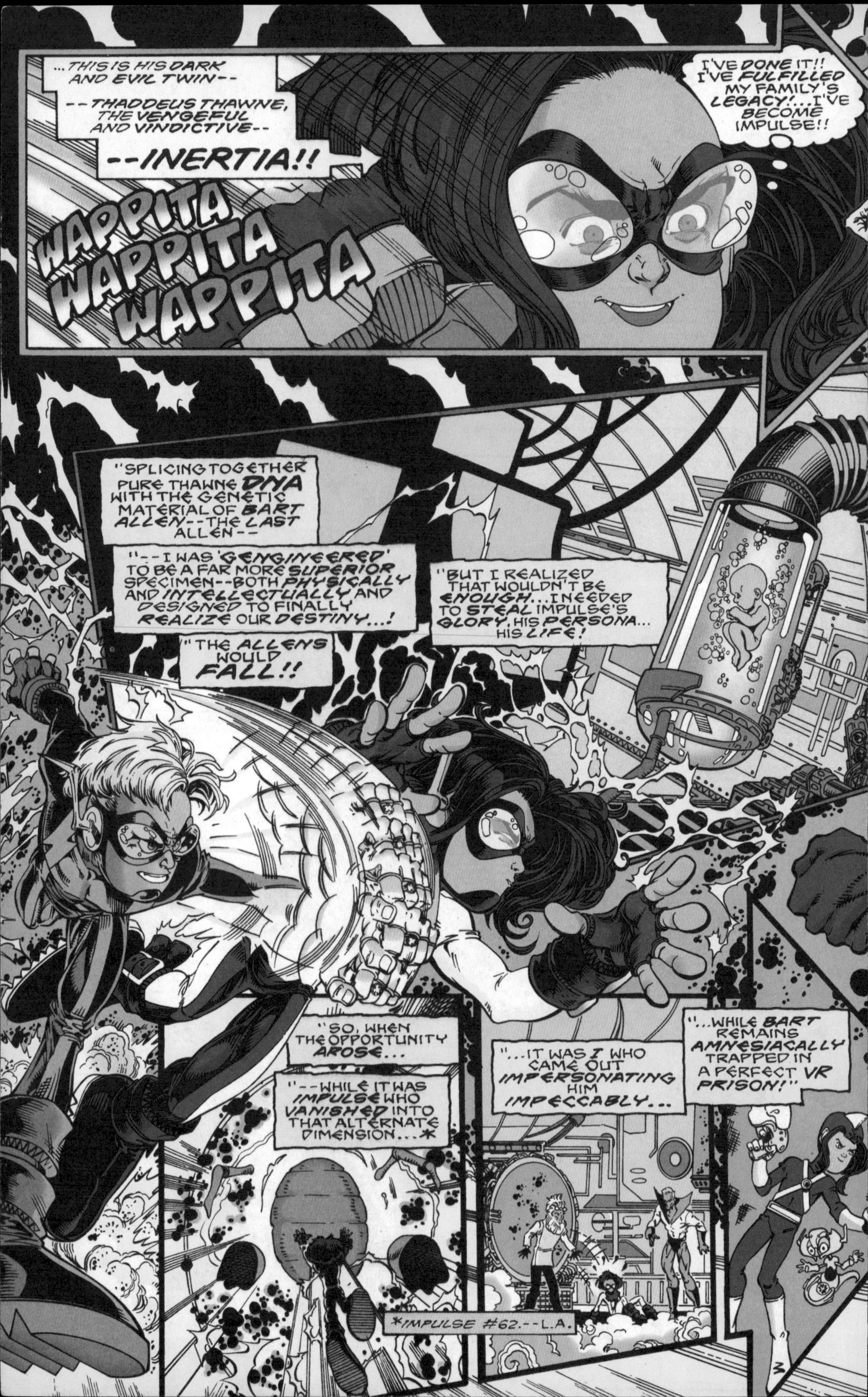
...THIS IS HIS DARK AND EVIL TWIN--
--THADDEUS THAWNE, THE VENGEFUL AND VINDICTIVE--
--INERTIA!!
I'VE DONE IT!! I'VE FULFILLED MY FAMILY'S LEGACY!...I'VE BECOME IMPULSE!!
WAPPITA WAPPITA WAPPITA
"SPLICING TOGETHER PURE THAWNE DNA WITH THE GENETIC MATERIAL OF BART ALLEN--THE LAST ALLEN--
"--I WAS 'GENGINEERED' TO BE A FAR MORE SUPERIOR SPECIMEN--BOTH PHYSICALLY AND INTELLECTUALLY AND DESIGNED TO FINALLY REALIZE OUR DESTINY...!
"THE ALLENS WOULD FALL!!
"BUT I REALIZED THAT WOULDN'T BE ENOUGH...I NEEDED TO STEAL IMPULSE'S GLORY, HIS PERSONA... HIS LIFE!
"SO, WHEN THE OPPORTUNITY AROSE...
"--WHILE IT WAS IMPULSE WHO VANISHED INTO THAT ALTERNATE DIMENSION...*
*IMPULSE #62.--L.A.
"...IT WAS I WHO CAME OUT IMPERSONATING HIM IMPECCABLY...
"...WHILE BART REMAINS AMNESIACALLY TRAPPED IN A PERFECT VR PRISON!"

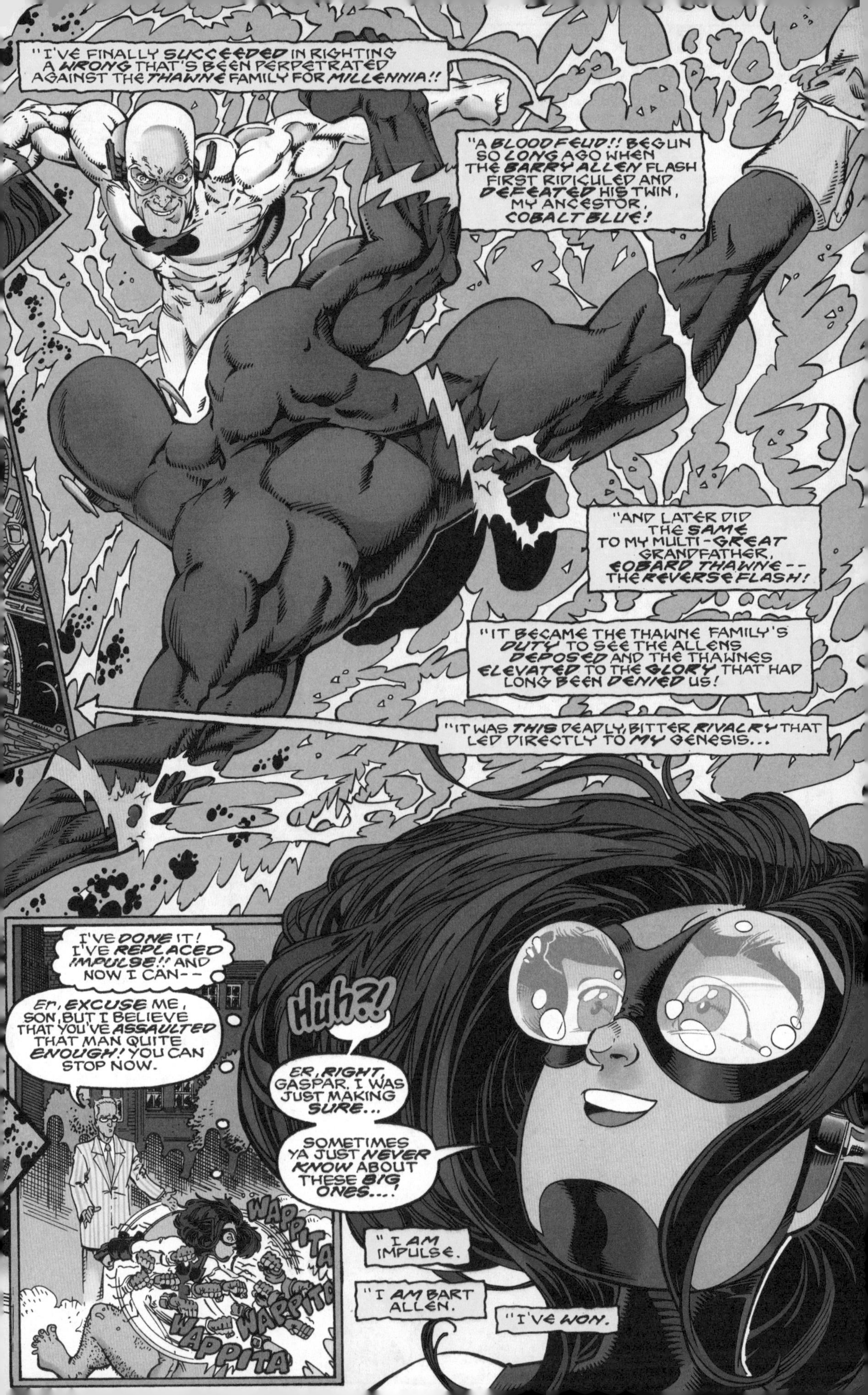
"I'VE FINALLY SUCCEEDED IN RIGHTING A WRONG THAT'S BEEN PERPETRATED AGAINST THE THAWNE FAMILY FOR MILLENNIA!!
"A BLOOD FEUD!! BEGUN SO LONG AGO WHEN THE BARRY ALLEN FLASH FIRST RIDICULED AND DEFEATED HIS TWIN, MY ANCESTOR, COBALT BLUE!
"AND LATER DID THE SAME TO MY MULTI-GREAT GRANDFATHER, EOBARD THAWNE-- THE REVERSE FLASH!
"IT BECAME THE THAWNE FAMILY'S DUTY TO SEE THE ALLENS DEPOSED AND THE THAWNES ELEVATED TO THE GLORY THAT HAD LONG BEEN DENIED US!
"IT WAS THIS DEADLY, BITTER RIVALRY THAT LED DIRECTLY TO MY GENESIS...
I'VE DONE IT! I'VE REPLACED IMPULSE!! AND NOW I CAN--
Er, EXCUSE ME, SON, BUT I BELIEVE THAT YOU'VE ASSAULTED THAT MAN QUITE ENOUGH! YOU CAN STOP NOW.
WAPPITA
WAPPITA
WAPPITA
WAPPITA
HUH?!
ER, RIGHT, GASPAR. I WAS JUST MAKING SURE...
SOMETIMES YA JUST NEVER KNOW ABOUT THESE BIG ONES...
"I AM IMPULSE.
"I AM BART ALLEN.
"I'VE WON.

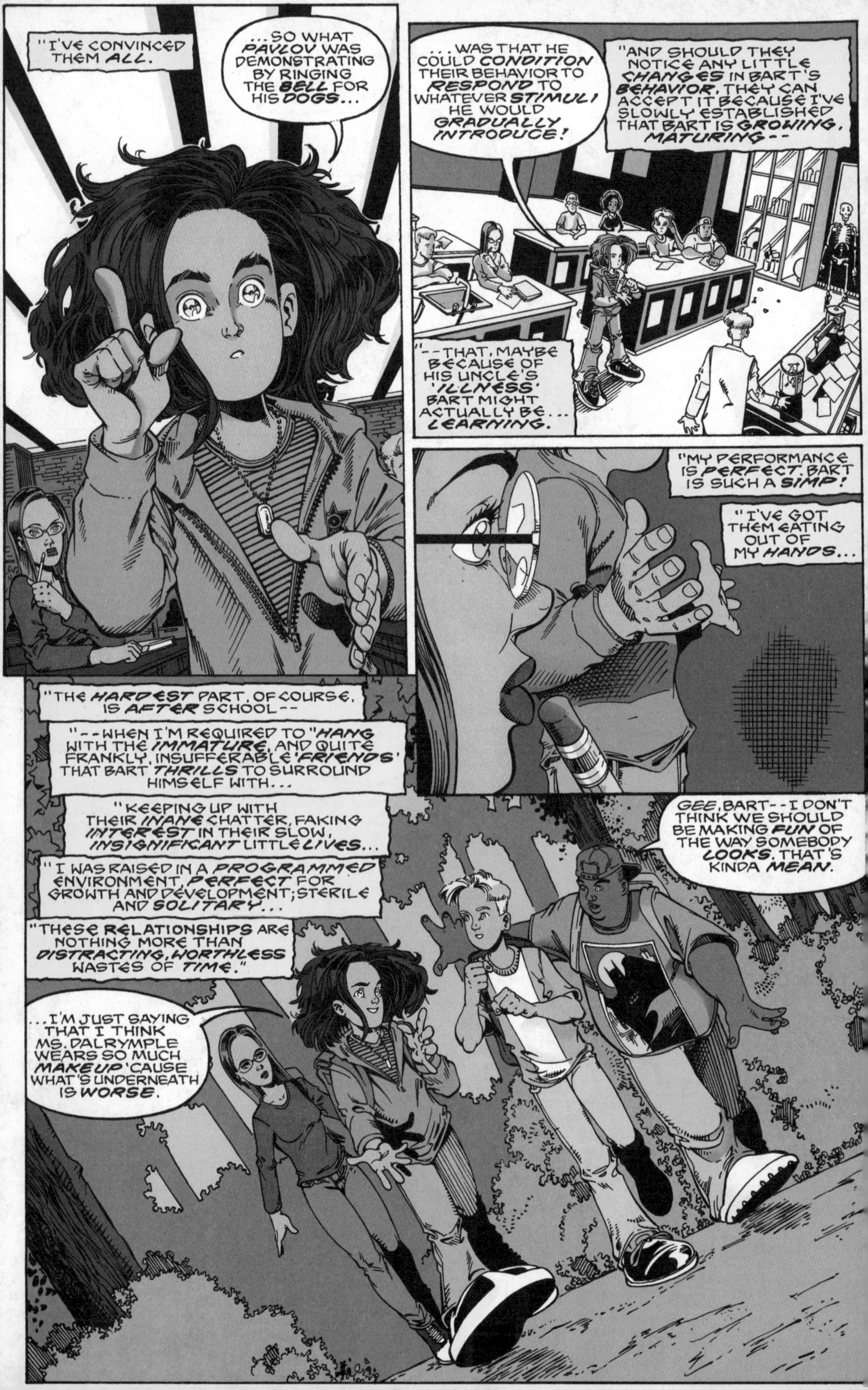
"I'VE CONVINCED THEM ALL.
...SO WHAT PAVLOV WAS DEMONSTRATING BY RINGING THE BELL FOR HIS DOGS...
...WAS THAT HE COULD CONDITION THEIR BEHAVIOR TO RESPOND TO WHATEVER STIMULI HE WOULD GRADUALLY INTRODUCE!
"AND SHOULD THEY NOTICE ANY LITTLE CHANGES IN BART'S BEHAVIOR, THEY CAN ACCEPT IT BECAUSE I'VE SLOWLY ESTABLISHED THAT BART IS GROWING, MATURING--
"--THAT, MAYBE BECAUSE OF HIS UNCLE'S 'ILLNESS' BART MIGHT ACTUALLY BE... LEARNING.
"MY PERFORMANCE IS PERFECT. BART IS SUCH A SIMP!
"I'VE GOT THEM EATING OUT OF MY HANDS...
"THE HARDEST PART, OF COURSE, IS AFTER SCHOOL--
"--WHEN I'M REQUIRED TO "HANG" WITH THE IMMATURE, AND QUITE FRANKLY, INSUFFERABLE 'FRIENDS' THAT BART THRILLS TO SURROUND HIMSELF WITH...
"KEEPING UP WITH THEIR INANE CHATTER, FAKING INTEREST IN THEIR SLOW, INSIGNIFICANT LITTLE LIVES...
"I WAS RAISED IN A PROGRAMMED ENVIRONMENT, PERFECT FOR GROWTH AND DEVELOPMENT; STERILE AND SOLITARY...
"THESE RELATIONSHIPS ARE NOTHING MORE THAN DISTRACTING, WORTHLESS WASTES OF TIME."
GEE, BART--I DON'T THINK WE SHOULD BE MAKING FUN OF THE WAY SOMEBODY LOOKS. THAT'S KINDA MEAN.
...I'M JUST SAYING THAT I THINK MS. DALRYMPLE WEARS SO MUCH MAKEUP 'CAUSE WHAT'S UNDERNEATH IS WORSE.

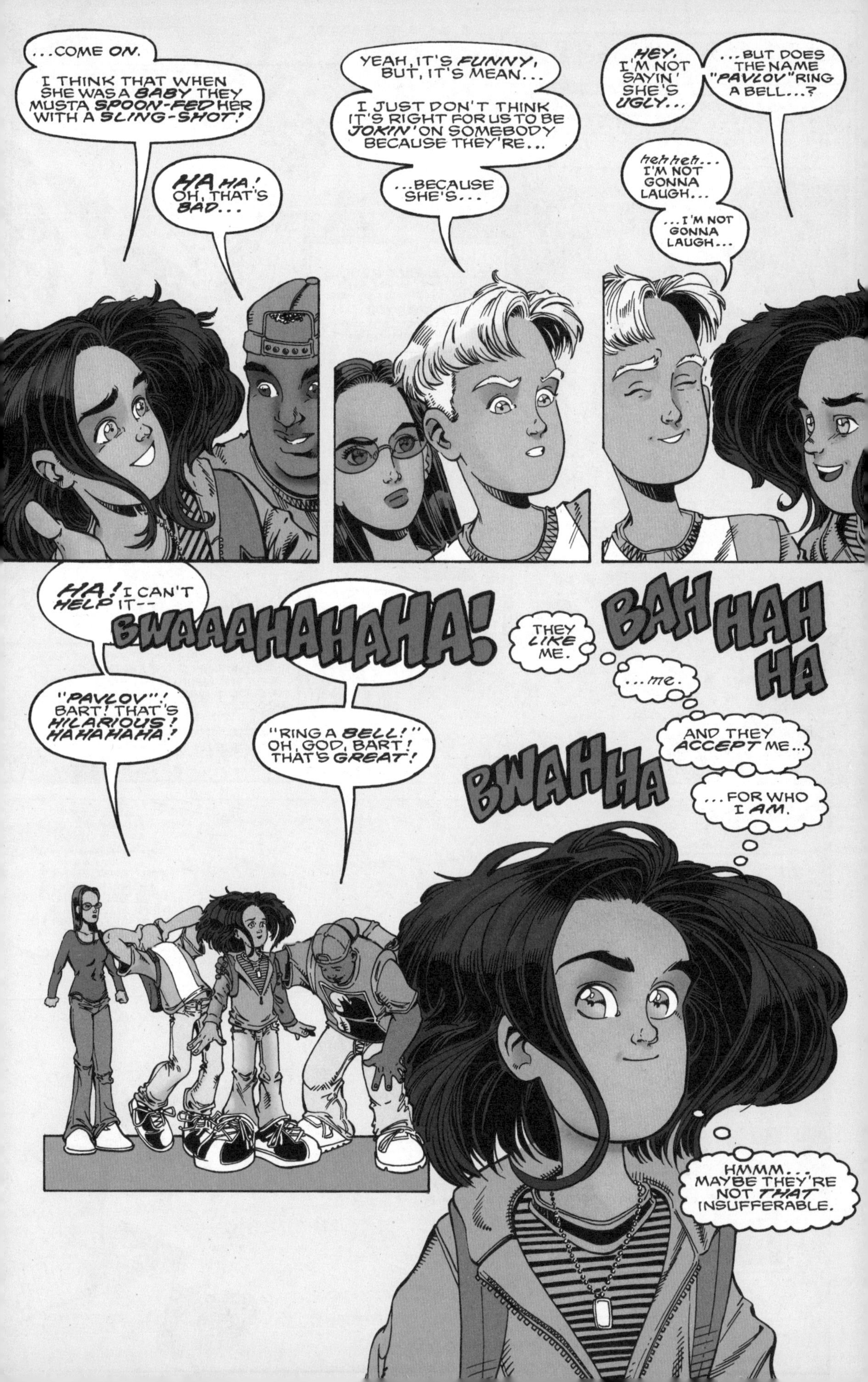
...COME ON.
I THINK THAT WHEN SHE WAS A BABY THEY MUSTA SPOON-FED HER WITH A SLING-SHOT!
HA HA! OH, THAT'S BAD...
YEAH, IT'S FUNNY, BUT, IT'S MEAN...
I JUST DON'T THINK IT'S RIGHT FOR US TO BE JOKIN' ON SOMEBODY BECAUSE THEY'RE...
...BECAUSE SHE'S...
HEY, I'M NOT SAYIN' SHE'S UGLY...
...BUT DOES THE NAME "PAVLOV" RING A BELL...?
hehheh... I'M NOT GONNA LAUGH...
...I'M NOT GONNA LAUGH...
HA! I CAN'T HELP IT--
BWAAAHAHAHAHA!
"PAVLOV"! BART! THAT'S HILARIOUS! HAHAHAHA!
"RING A BELL!" OH, GOD, BART! THAT'S GREAT!
THEY LIKE ME.
BAH HAH HA
...me.
AND THEY ACCEPT ME...
BWAHHA
...FOR WHO I AM.
HMMM... MAYBE THEY'RE NOT THAT INSUFFERABLE.

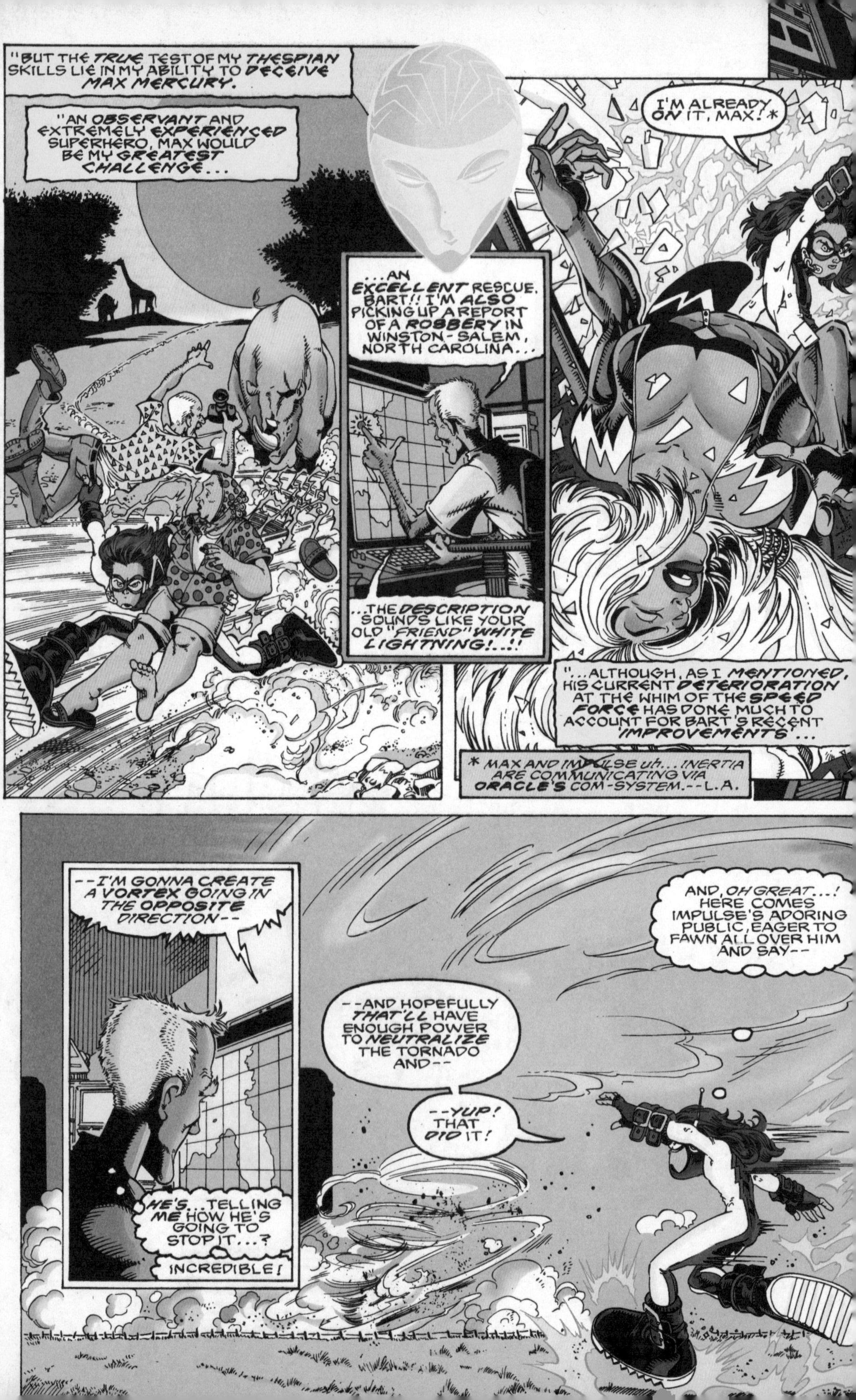
"BUT THE TRUE TEST OF MY THESPIAN SKILLS LIE IN MY ABILITY TO DECEIVE MAX MERCURY.
"AN OBSERVANT AND EXTREMELY EXPERIENCED SUPERHERO, MAX WOULD BE MY GREATEST CHALLENGE...
...AN EXCELLENT RESCUE, BART!! I'M ALSO PICKING UP A REPORT OF A ROBBERY IN WINSTON-SALEM, NORTH CAROLINA...
...THE DESCRIPTION SOUNDS LIKE YOUR OLD "FRIEND" WHITE LIGHTNING!..!!
I'M ALREADY ON IT, MAX! *
"...ALTHOUGH, AS I MENTIONED, HIS CURRENT DETERIORATION AT THE WHIM OF THE SPEED FORCE HAS DONE MUCH TO ACCOUNT FOR BART'S RECENT 'IMPROVEMENTS'...
* MAX AND IMPULSE uh... INERTIA ARE COMMUNICATING VIA ORACLE'S COM-SYSTEM.--L.A.
--I'M GONNA CREATE A VORTEX GOING IN THE OPPOSITE DIRECTION--
--AND HOPEFULLY THAT'LL HAVE ENOUGH POWER TO NEUTRALIZE THE TORNADO AND--
--YUP! THAT DID IT!
HE'S...TELLING ME HOW HE'S GOING TO STOP IT...?
INCREDIBLE!
AND, OH GREAT...! HERE COMES IMPULSE'S ADORING PUBLIC, EAGER TO FAWN ALL OVER HIM AND SAY--

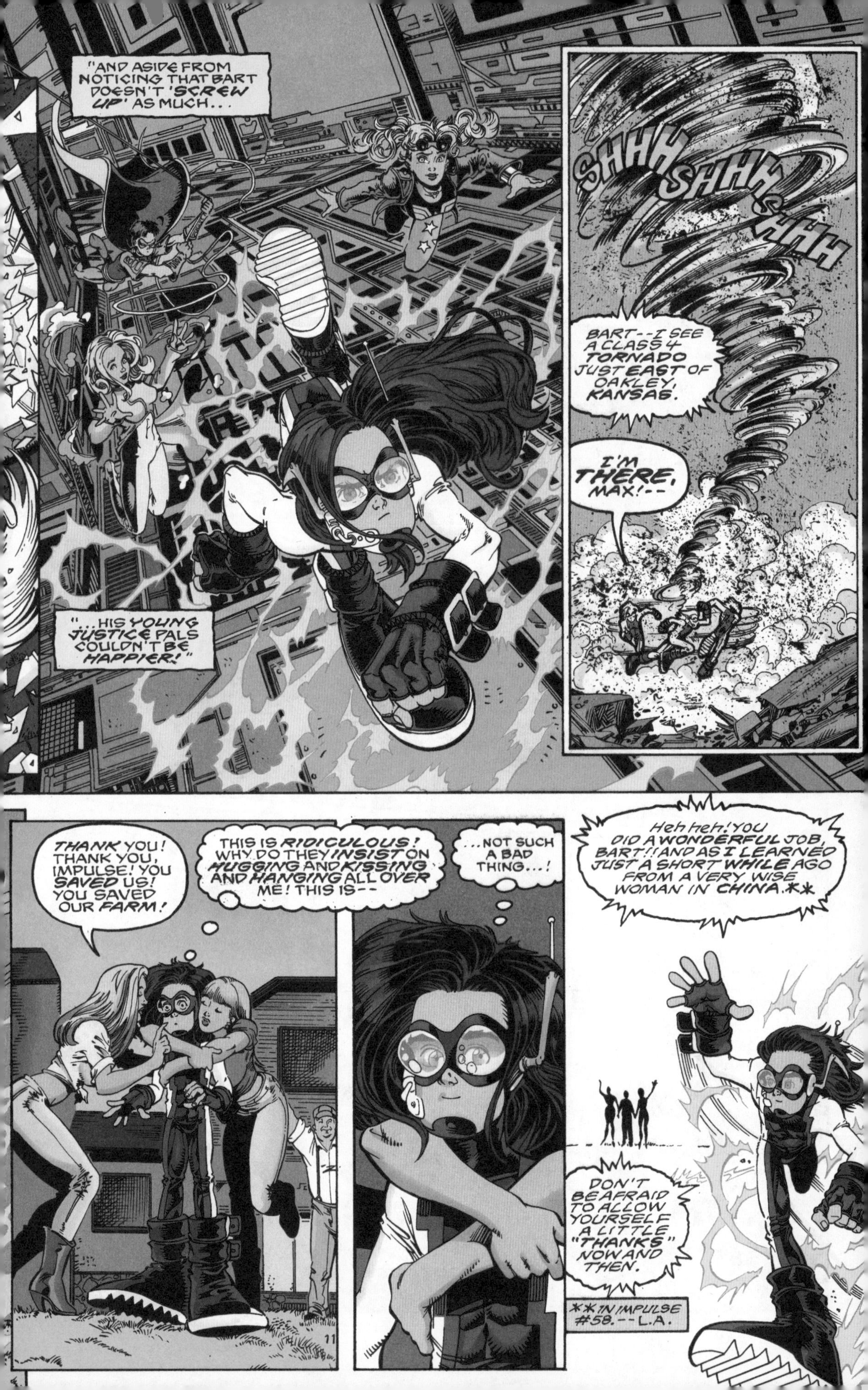
"AND ASIDE FROM NOTICING THAT BART DOESN'T 'SCREW UP' AS MUCH...
"...HIS YOUNG JUSTICE PALS COULDN'T BE HAPPIER!"
SHHH SHHH SHHH
BART--I SEE A CLASS 4 TORNADO JUST EAST OF OAKLEY, KANSAS.
I'M THERE, MAX!--
THANK YOU! THANK YOU, IMPULSE! YOU SAVED US! YOU SAVED OUR FARM!
THIS IS RIDICULOUS! WHY DO THEY INSIST ON HUGGING AND KISSING AND HANGING ALL OVER ME! THIS IS--
...NOT SUCH A BAD THING...!
Heh heh! YOU DID A WONDERFUL JOB, BART!! AND AS I LEARNED JUST A SHORT WHILE AGO FROM A VERY WISE WOMAN IN CHINA.**
DON'T BE AFRAID TO ALLOW YOURSELF A LITTLE "THANKS" NOW AND THEN.
**IN IMPULSE #58.--L.A.

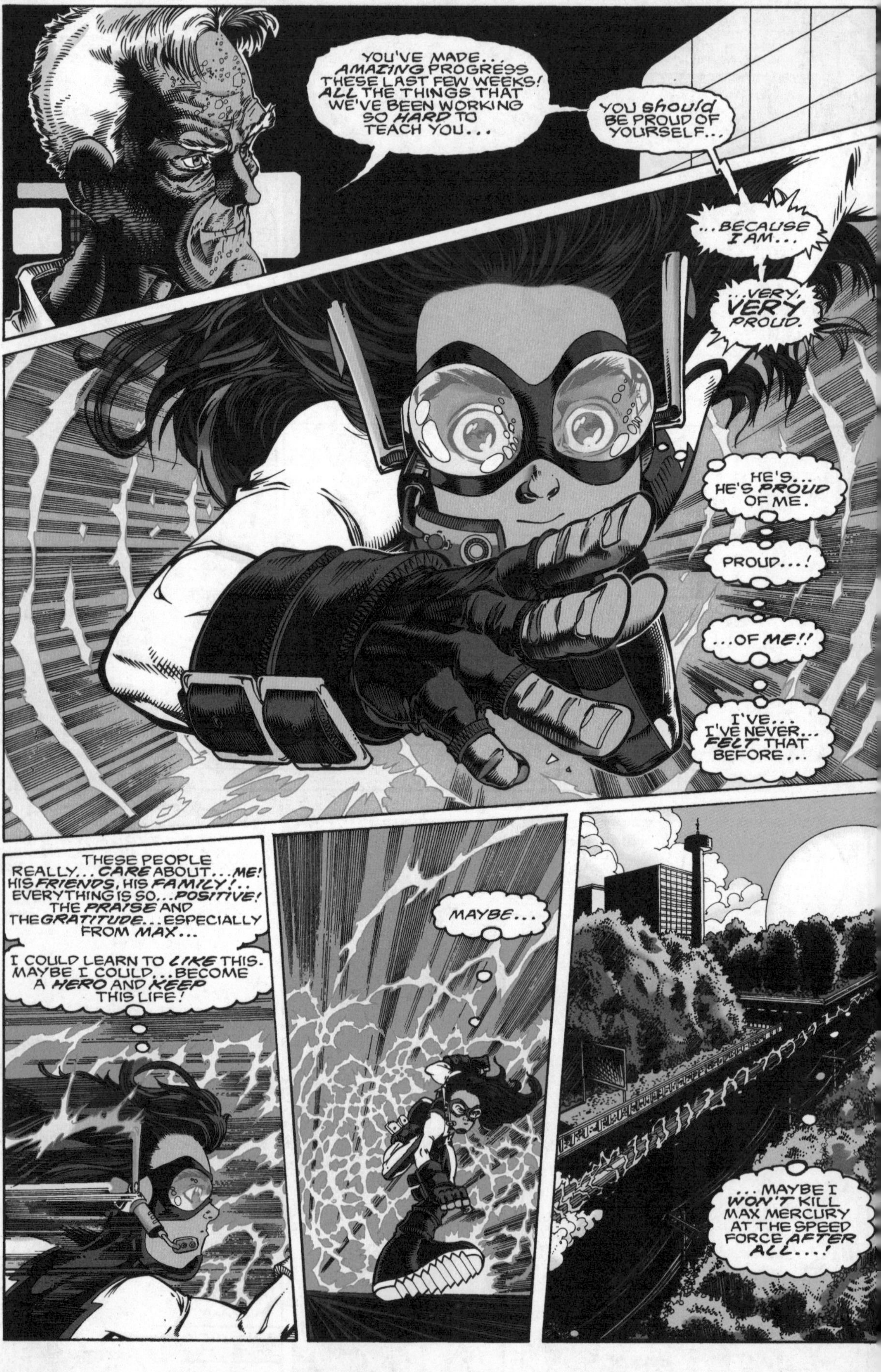

YOU'VE MADE... AMAZING PROGRESS THESE LAST FEW WEEKS! ALL THE THINGS THAT WE'VE BEEN WORKING SO HARD TO TEACH YOU...
YOU SHOULD BE PROUD OF YOURSELF...
...BECAUSE I AM...
...VERY, VERY PROUD.
HE'S... HE'S PROUD OF ME.
PROUD...!
...OF ME!!
I'VE... I'VE NEVER... FELT THAT BEFORE...
THESE PEOPLE REALLY... CARE ABOUT... ME! HIS FRIENDS, HIS FAMILY!.. EVERYTHING IS SO... POSITIVE! THE PRAISE AND THE GRATITUDE... ESPECIALLY FROM MAX...
I COULD LEARN TO LIKE THIS. MAYBE I COULD... BECOME A HERO AND KEEP THIS LIFE!
MAYBE...
...MAYBE I WON'T KILL MAX MERCURY AT THE SPEED FORCE AFTER ALL...!

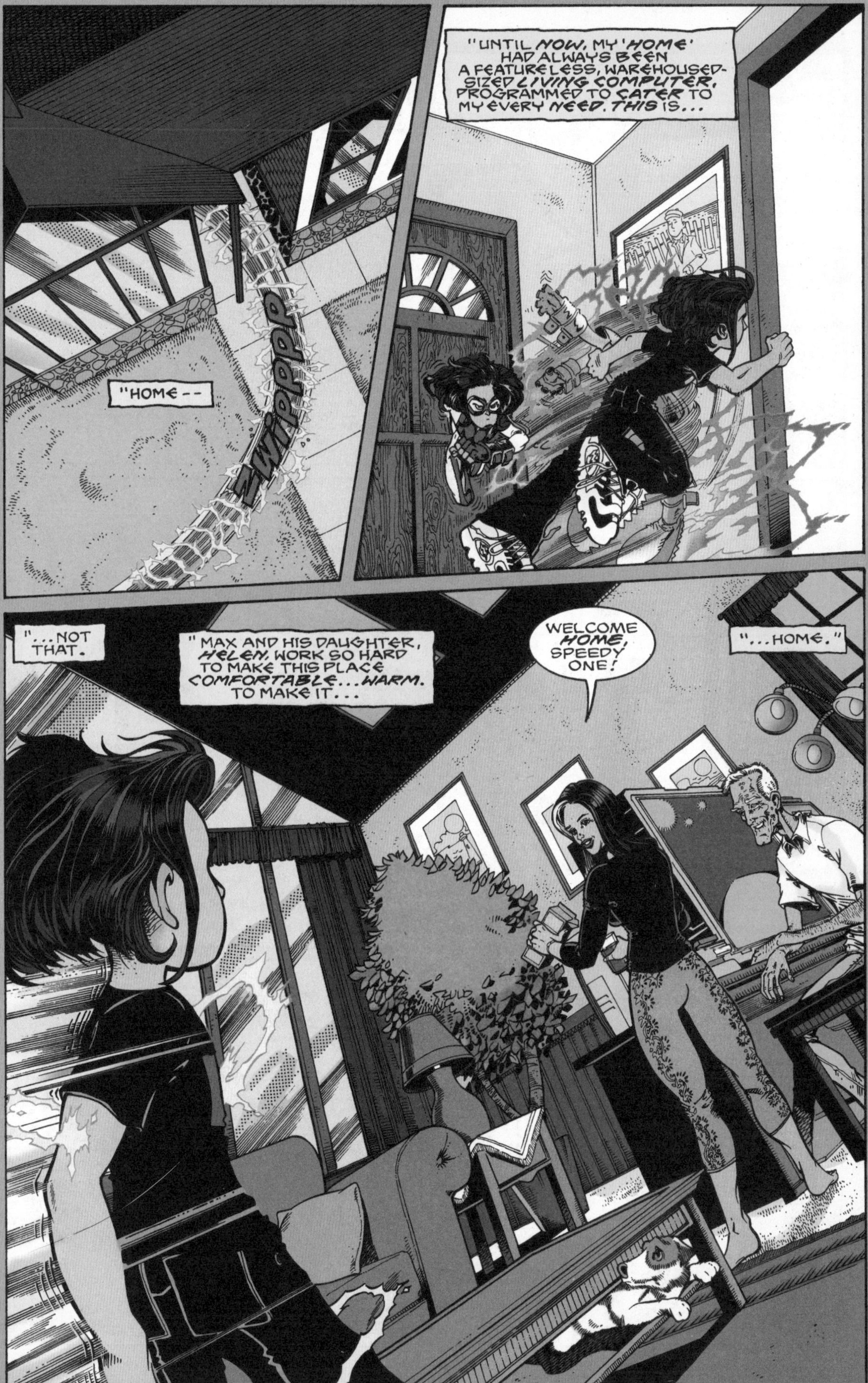
"HOME --
ZWIPPP
"UNTIL NOW, MY 'HOME' HAD ALWAYS BEEN A FEATURELESS, WAREHOUSED-SIZED LIVING COMPUTER, PROGRAMMED TO CATER TO MY EVERY NEED. THIS IS...
"...NOT THAT.
"MAX AND HIS DAUGHTER, HELEN, WORK SO HARD TO MAKE THIS PLACE COMFORTABLE...WARM. TO MAKE IT...
WELCOME HOME, SPEEDY ONE!
"...HOME."

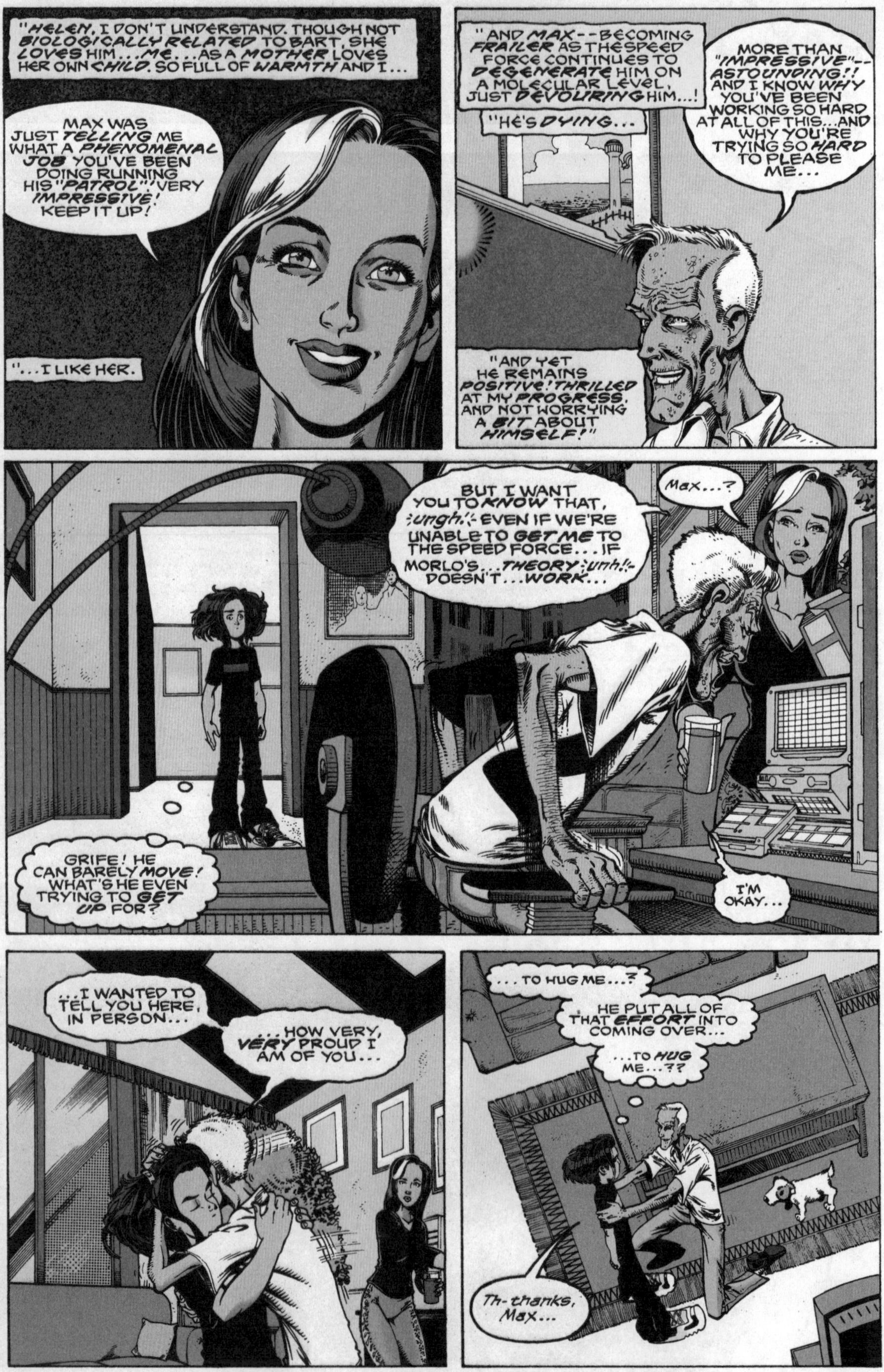
"HELEN, I DON'T UNDERSTAND. THOUGH NOT BIOLOGICALLY RELATED TO BART, SHE LOVES HIM... ME... AS A MOTHER LOVES HER OWN CHILD. SO FULL OF WARMTH AND I...
MAX WAS JUST TELLING ME WHAT A PHENOMENAL JOB YOU'VE BEEN DOING RUNNING HIS "PATROL"! VERY IMPRESSIVE! KEEP IT UP!
"...I LIKE HER.
"AND MAX--BECOMING FRAILER AS THE SPEED FORCE CONTINUES TO DEGENERATE HIM ON A MOLECULAR LEVEL, JUST DEVOURING HIM...!
"HE'S DYING...
MORE THAN "IMPRESSIVE"-- ASTOUNDING!! AND I KNOW WHY YOU'VE BEEN WORKING SO HARD AT ALL OF THIS...AND WHY YOU'RE TRYING SO HARD TO PLEASE ME...
"AND YET HE REMAINS POSITIVE! THRILLED AT MY PROGRESS, AND NOT WORRYING A BIT ABOUT HIMSELF!"
BUT I WANT YOU TO KNOW THAT, ;ungh!;- EVEN IF WE'RE UNABLE TO GET ME TO THE SPEED FORCE... IF MORLO'S... THEORY ;unh!;- DOESN'T... WORK...
Max...?
GRIFE! HE CAN BARELY MOVE! WHAT'S HE EVEN TRYING TO GET UP FOR?
I'M OKAY...
...I WANTED TO TELL YOU HERE, IN PERSON...
...HOW VERY, VERY PROUD I AM OF YOU...
...TO HUG ME...?
HE PUT ALL OF THAT EFFORT INTO COMING OVER...
...TO HUG ME...??
Th-thanks, Max...

"THE **DOG**, OF COURSE, KNEW FROM THE **START**...

"THE **JLA** AND **YOUNG JUSTICE** COMPUTERS MIGHT BE **FOOLED** BY A GENETIC MATCH --

"--BUT THERE'S **NO WAY** TO TRICK AN ANIMAL INTO **BELIEVING** YOU'RE ITS **MASTER**...!

"BUT I FOUND A WAY **AROUND** THAT...

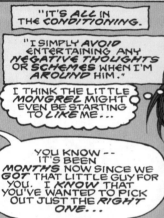

"IT'S **ALL** IN THE **CONDITIONING**.

"I SIMPLY **AVOID** ENTERTAINING ANY **NEGATIVE** THOUGHTS OR **SCHEMES** WHEN I'M **AROUND** HIM."

I THINK THE LITTLE **MONGREL** MIGHT EVEN BE STARTING TO **LIKE** ME...

YOU KNOW -- IT'S BEEN **MONTHS** NOW SINCE WE **GOT** THAT LITTLE GUY FOR YOU. I **KNOW** THAT YOU'VE WANTED TO PICK OUT JUST THE **RIGHT** ONE...

...BUT DON'T YOU THINK IT'S TIME HE HAD A **NAME**...?

WELL, ACTUALLY, HELEN -- I'VE BEEN THINKING ABOUT THAT A **LOT** LATELY... AND I THINK IT'D BE GOOD IF WE CALLED HIM...

...IVAN!

OH! HEH HEH... I **GET** IT! LIKE "IVAN THE TERRIBLE"! --

--HE'S "IVAN THE **TERRIER**"! VERY GOOD! CUTE!

NO. AS IN **IVAN PAVLOV**... THE **BEHAVIORIST**. YOU KNOW... PAVLOV'S DOGS.

CLEVER, NO?

OH, uh... YEAH...

?

...OKAY...

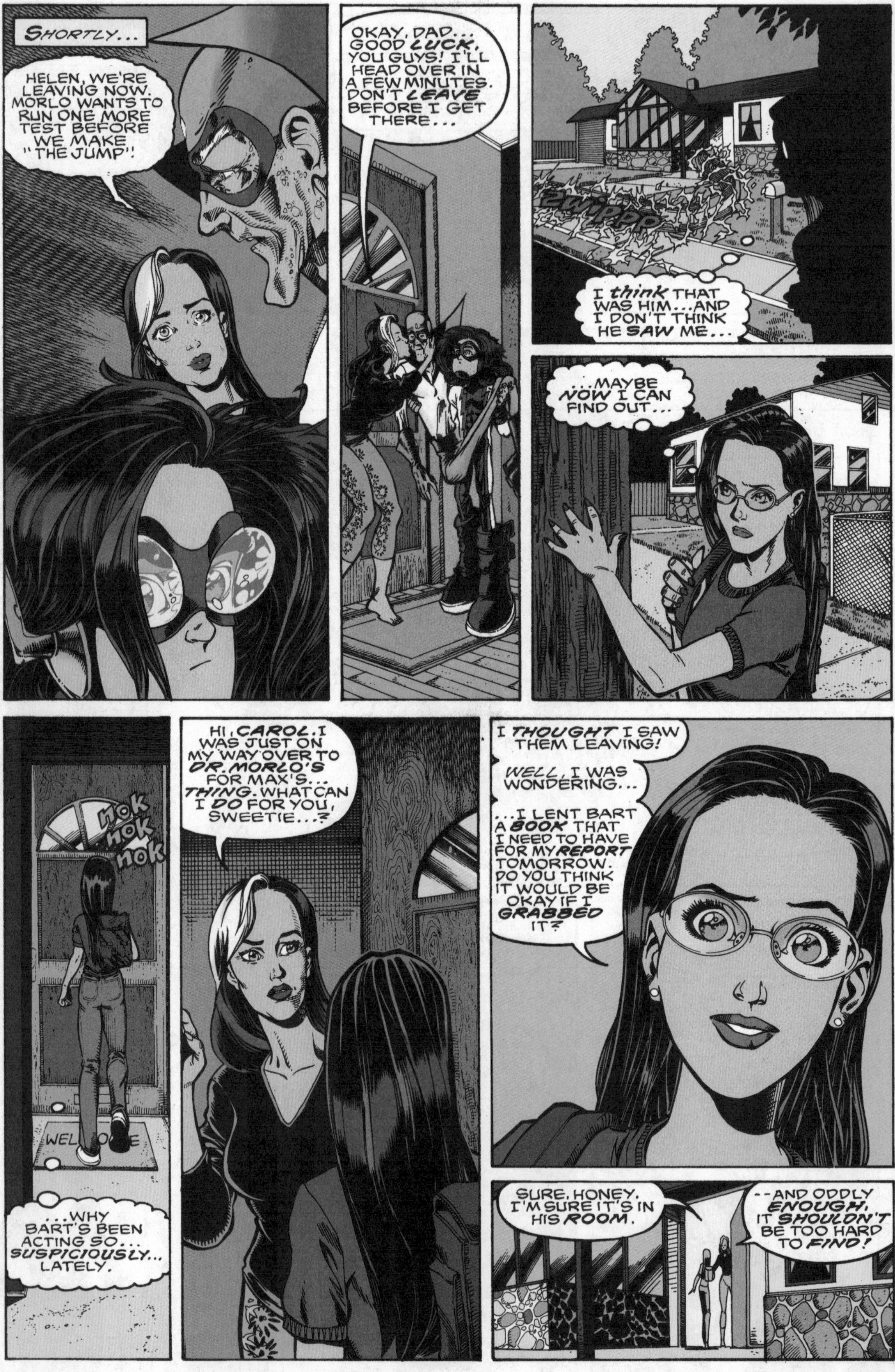
SHORTLY...
HELEN, WE'RE LEAVING NOW. MORLO WANTS TO RUN ONE MORE TEST BEFORE WE MAKE "THE JUMP"!
OKAY, DAD... GOOD LUCK, YOU GUYS! I'LL HEAD OVER IN A FEW MINUTES. DON'T LEAVE BEFORE I GET THERE...
ZWIPPP
I think THAT WAS HIM...AND I DON'T THINK HE SAW ME...
...MAYBE NOW I CAN FIND OUT...
NOK NOK NOK
WELCOME
...WHY BART'S BEEN ACTING SO... SUSPICIOUSLY... LATELY.
HI, CAROL. I WAS JUST ON MY WAY OVER TO DR. MORLO'S FOR MAX'S... THING. WHAT CAN I DO FOR YOU, SWEETIE...?
I THOUGHT I SAW THEM LEAVING!
WELL, I WAS WONDERING...
...I LENT BART A BOOK THAT I NEED TO HAVE FOR MY REPORT TOMORROW. DO YOU THINK IT WOULD BE OKAY IF I GRABBED IT?
SURE, HONEY. I'M SURE IT'S IN HIS ROOM.
--AND ODDLY ENOUGH, IT SHOULDN'T BE TOO HARD TO FIND!

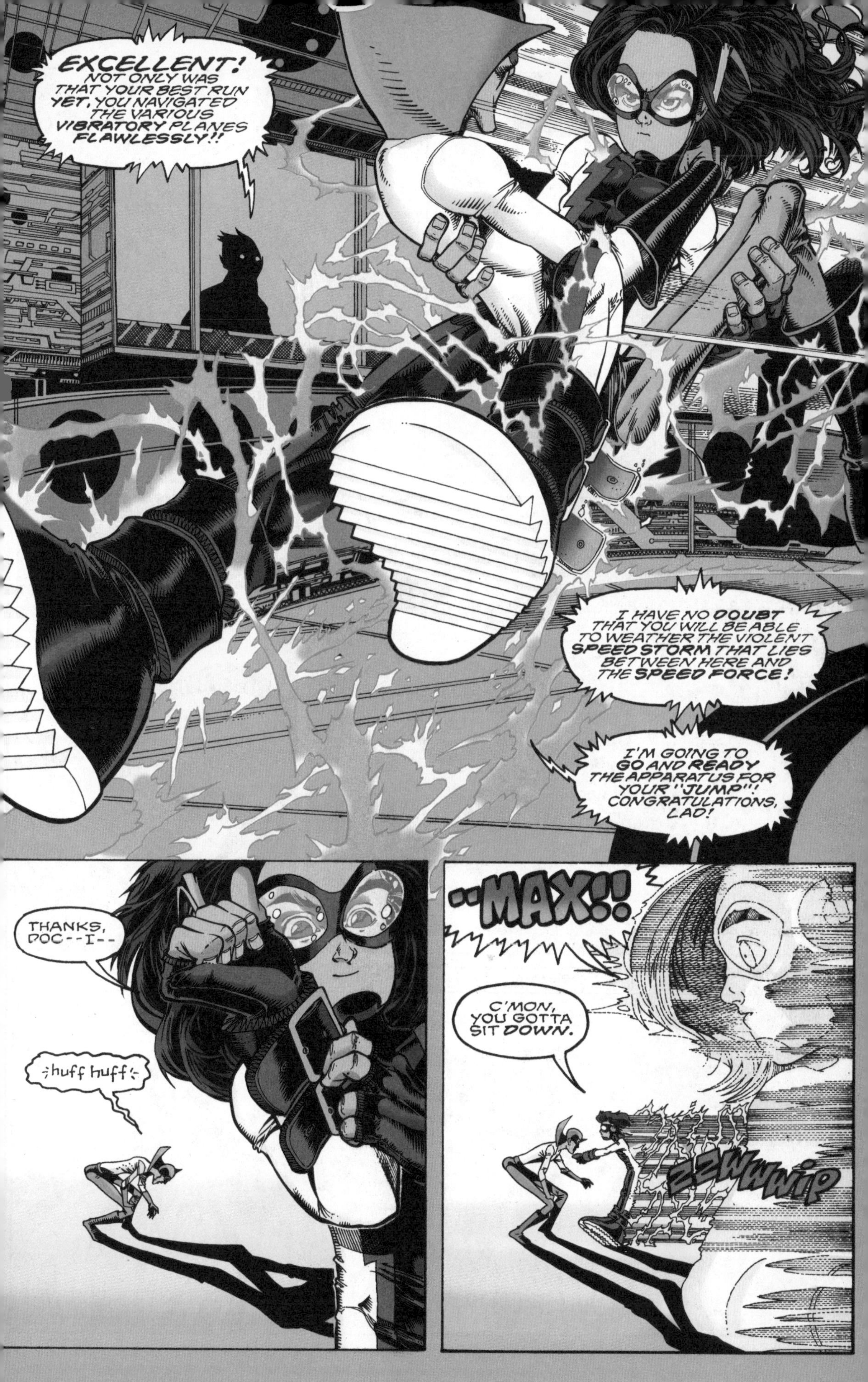
EXCELLENT! NOT ONLY WAS THAT YOUR BEST RUN YET, YOU NAVIGATED THE VARIOUS VIBRATORY PLANES FLAWLESSLY!!
I HAVE NO DOUBT THAT YOU WILL BE ABLE TO WEATHER THE VIOLENT SPEED STORM THAT LIES BETWEEN HERE AND THE SPEED FORCE!
I'M GOING TO GO AND READY THE APPARATUS FOR YOUR "JUMP"! CONGRATULATIONS, LAD!
THANKS, DOC--I--
huff huff
"MAX!!
C'MON, YOU GOTTA SIT DOWN.
ZZWWWIP

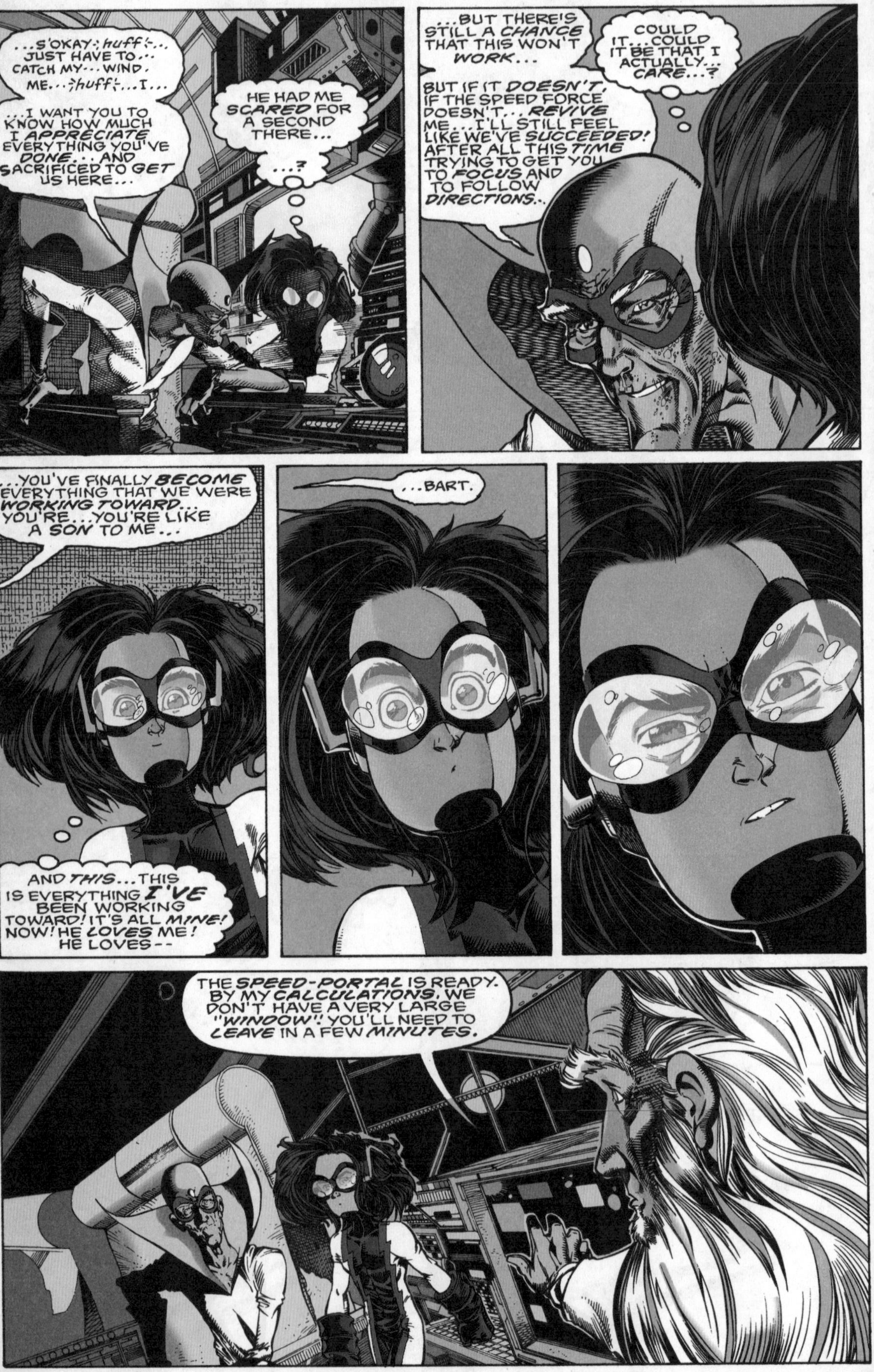
...S'OKAY-;huff;-... JUST HAVE TO... CATCH MY... WIND. ME...;huff;-...I...
...I WANT YOU TO KNOW HOW MUCH I APPRECIATE EVERYTHING YOU'VE DONE... AND SACRIFICED TO GET US HERE...
HE HAD ME SCARED FOR A SECOND THERE...
...?
...BUT THERE'S STILL A CHANCE THAT THIS WON'T WORK...
BUT IF IT DOESN'T, IF THE SPEED FORCE DOESN'T... REVIVE ME... I'LL STILL FEEL LIKE WE'VE SUCCEEDED! AFTER ALL THIS TIME TRYING TO GET YOU TO FOCUS AND TO FOLLOW DIRECTIONS...
COULD IT... COULD IT BE THAT I ACTUALLY... CARE...?
...YOU'VE FINALLY BECOME EVERYTHING THAT WE WERE WORKING TOWARD... YOU'RE... YOU'RE LIKE A SON TO ME...
AND THIS... THIS IS EVERYTHING I'VE BEEN WORKING TOWARD! IT'S ALL MINE! NOW! HE LOVES ME! HE LOVES--
...BART.
THE SPEED-PORTAL IS READY. BY MY CALCULATIONS, WE DON'T HAVE A VERY LARGE "WINDOW". YOU'LL NEED TO LEAVE IN A FEW MINUTES.

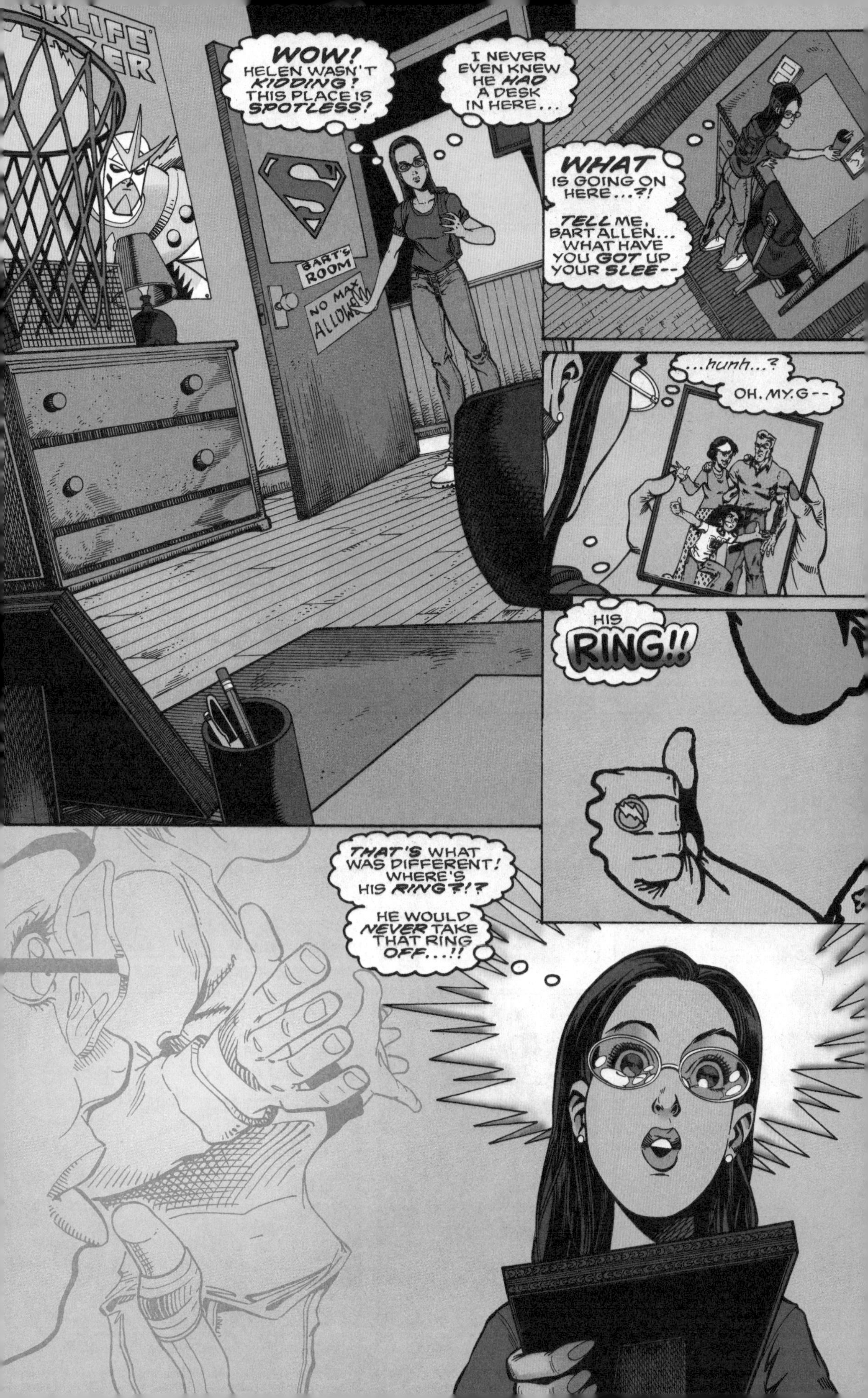
WOW! HELEN WASN'T KIDDING? THIS PLACE IS SPOTLESS!
I NEVER EVEN KNEW HE HAD A DESK IN HERE...
BART'S ROOM
NO MAX ALLOWED
WHAT IS GOING ON HERE...?!
TELL ME, BART ALLEN... WHAT HAVE YOU GOT UP YOUR SLEE--
...hunh...?
OH. MY. G--
HIS RING!!
THAT'S WHAT WAS DIFFERENT! WHERE'S HIS RING?!?
HE WOULD NEVER TAKE THAT RING OFF...!!

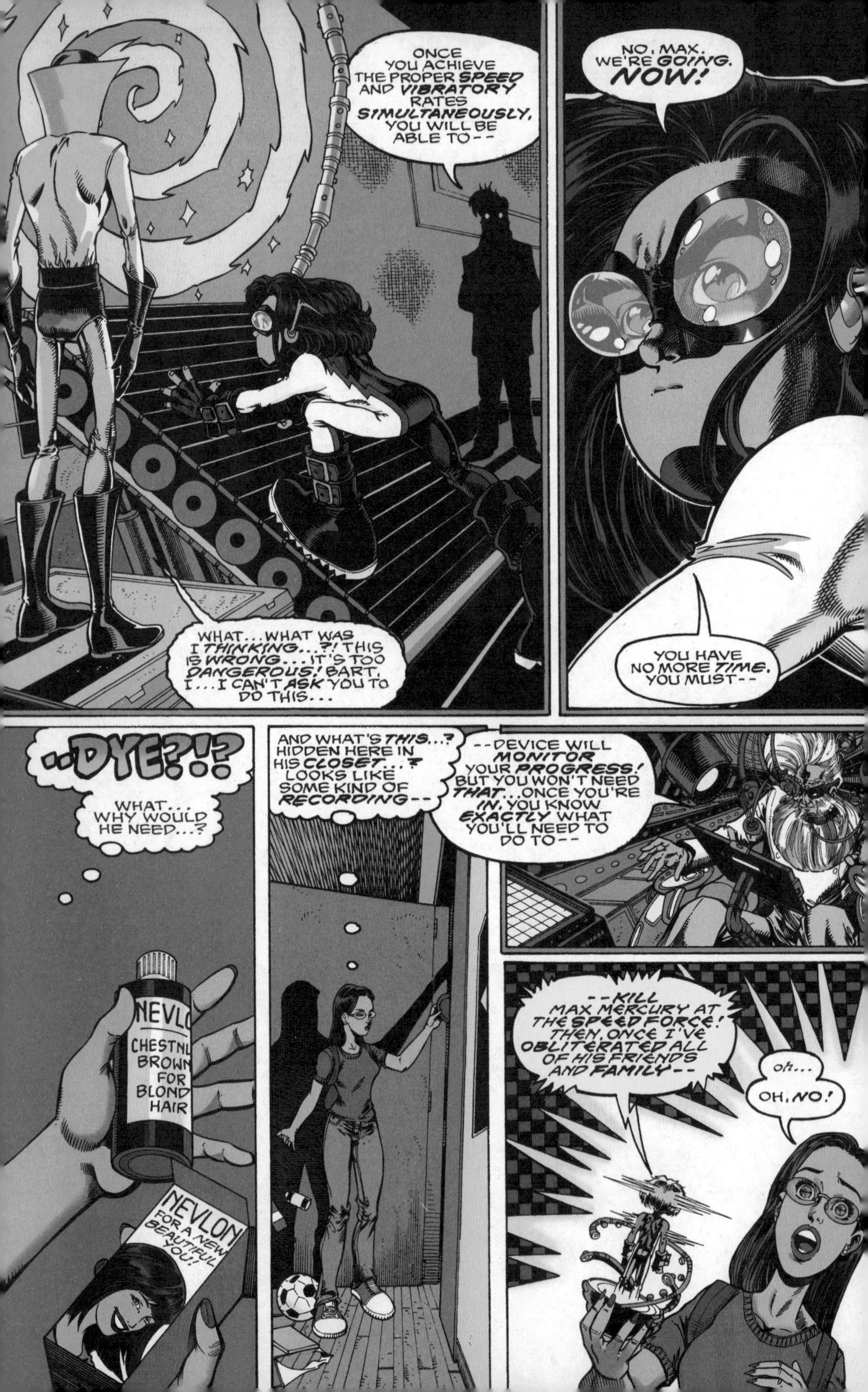
ONCE YOU ACHIEVE THE PROPER SPEED AND VIBRATORY RATES SIMULTANEOUSLY, YOU WILL BE ABLE TO--
WHAT...WHAT WAS I THINKING...?! THIS IS WRONG...IT'S TOO DANGEROUS! BART, I...I CAN'T ASK YOU TO DO THIS...
NO, MAX. WE'RE GOING. NOW!
YOU HAVE NO MORE TIME. YOU MUST--
..DYE?!?
WHAT... WHY WOULD HE NEED...?
NEVLO
CHESTNU BROWN FOR BLOND HAIR
NEVLON FOR A NEW BEAUTIFUL YOU!
AND WHAT'S THIS...? HIDDEN HERE IN HIS CLOSET...? LOOKS LIKE SOME KIND OF RECORDING--
--DEVICE WILL MONITOR YOUR PROGRESS! BUT YOU WON'T NEED THAT...ONCE YOU'RE IN, YOU KNOW EXACTLY WHAT YOU'LL NEED TO DO TO--
--KILL MAX MERCURY AT THE SPEED FORCE! THEN, ONCE I'VE OBLITERATED ALL OF HIS FRIENDS AND FAMILY--
oh...
OH, NO!

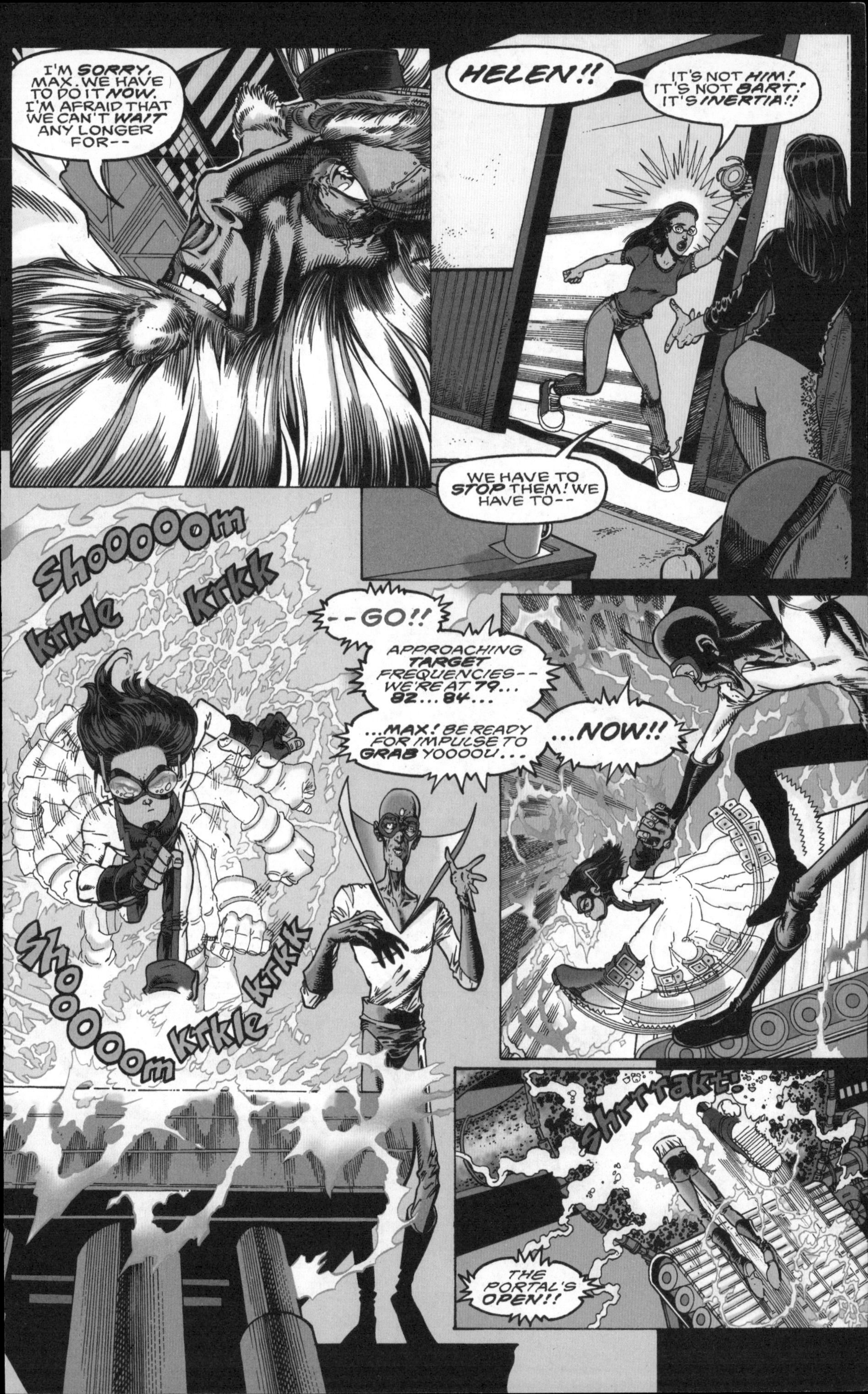
I'M SORRY, MAX. WE HAVE TO DO IT NOW. I'M AFRAID THAT WE CAN'T WAIT ANY LONGER FOR--
HELEN!!
IT'S NOT HIM! IT'S NOT BART! IT'S INERTIA!!
WE HAVE TO STOP THEM! WE HAVE TO--
ShoOOOOm
krkle
krkk
--GO!!
APPROACHING TARGET FREQUENCIES-- WE'RE AT 79... 82... 84...
...MAX! BE READY FOR IMPULSE TO GRAB YOOOOU...
...NOW!!
ShoOOOOm
krkle
krkk
shrrrakt!
THE PORTAL'S OPEN!!

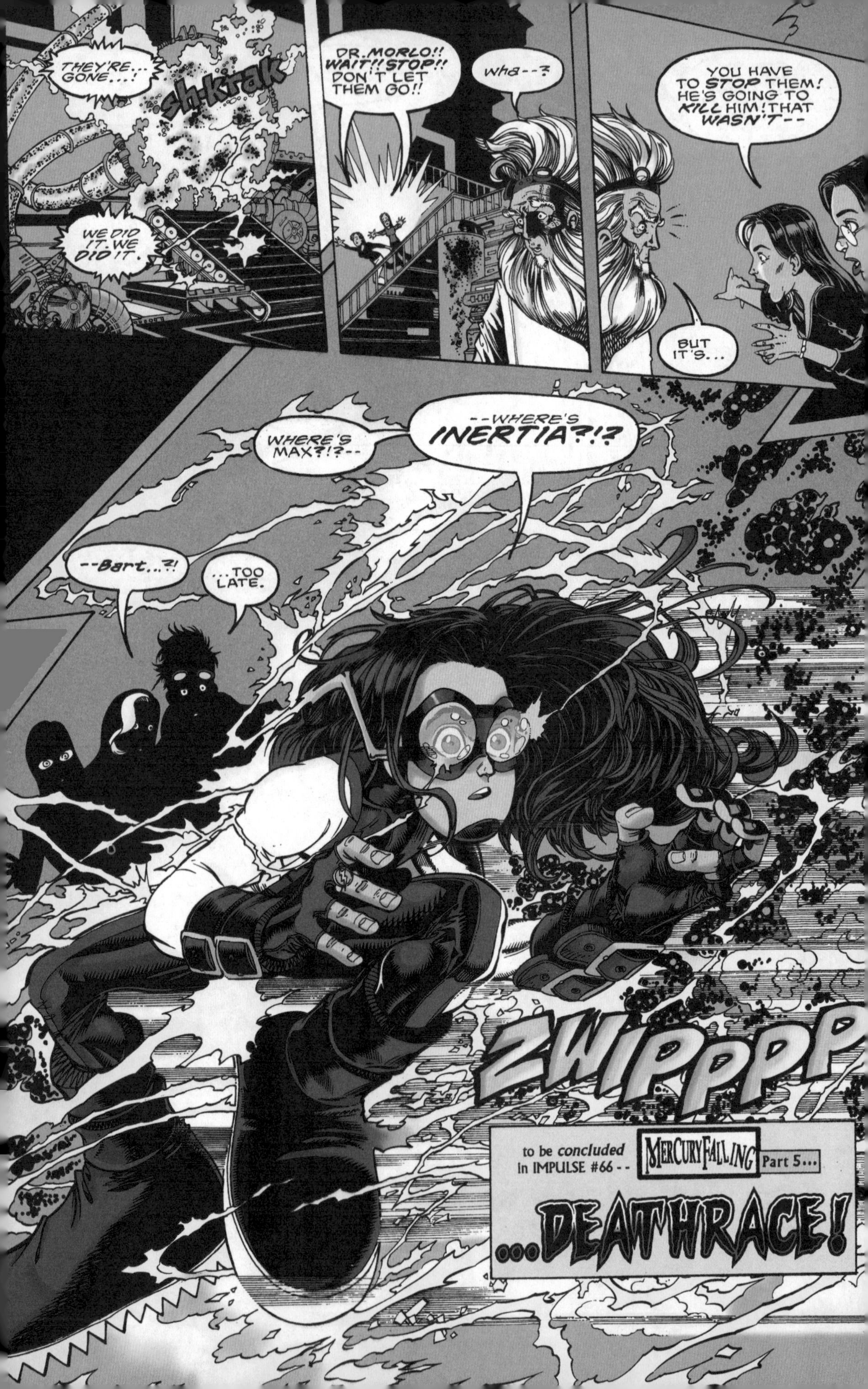
THEY'RE... GONE...!
sh-krak
WE DID IT. WE DID IT.
DR. MORLO!! WAIT!! STOP!! DON'T LET THEM GO!!
Wha--?
YOU HAVE TO STOP THEM! HE'S GOING TO KILL HIM! THAT WASN'T--
BUT IT'S...
WHERE'S MAX?!?--
--WHERE'S INERTIA?!?
--Bart...?!
...TOO LATE.
ZWIPPPP
to be concluded in IMPULSE #66 -- MERCURY FALLING Part 5...
...DEATHRACE!

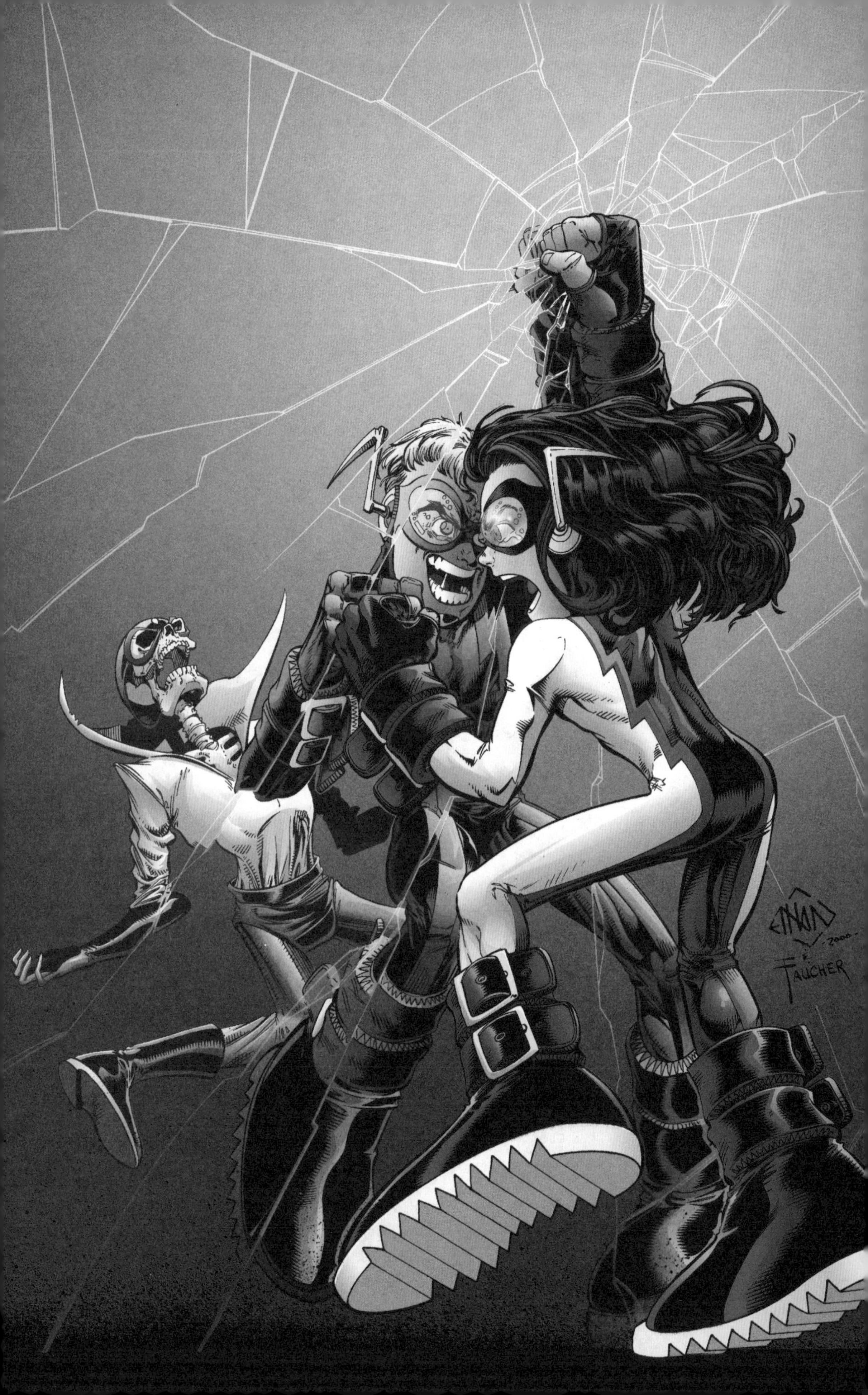

-2000-
FAUCHER

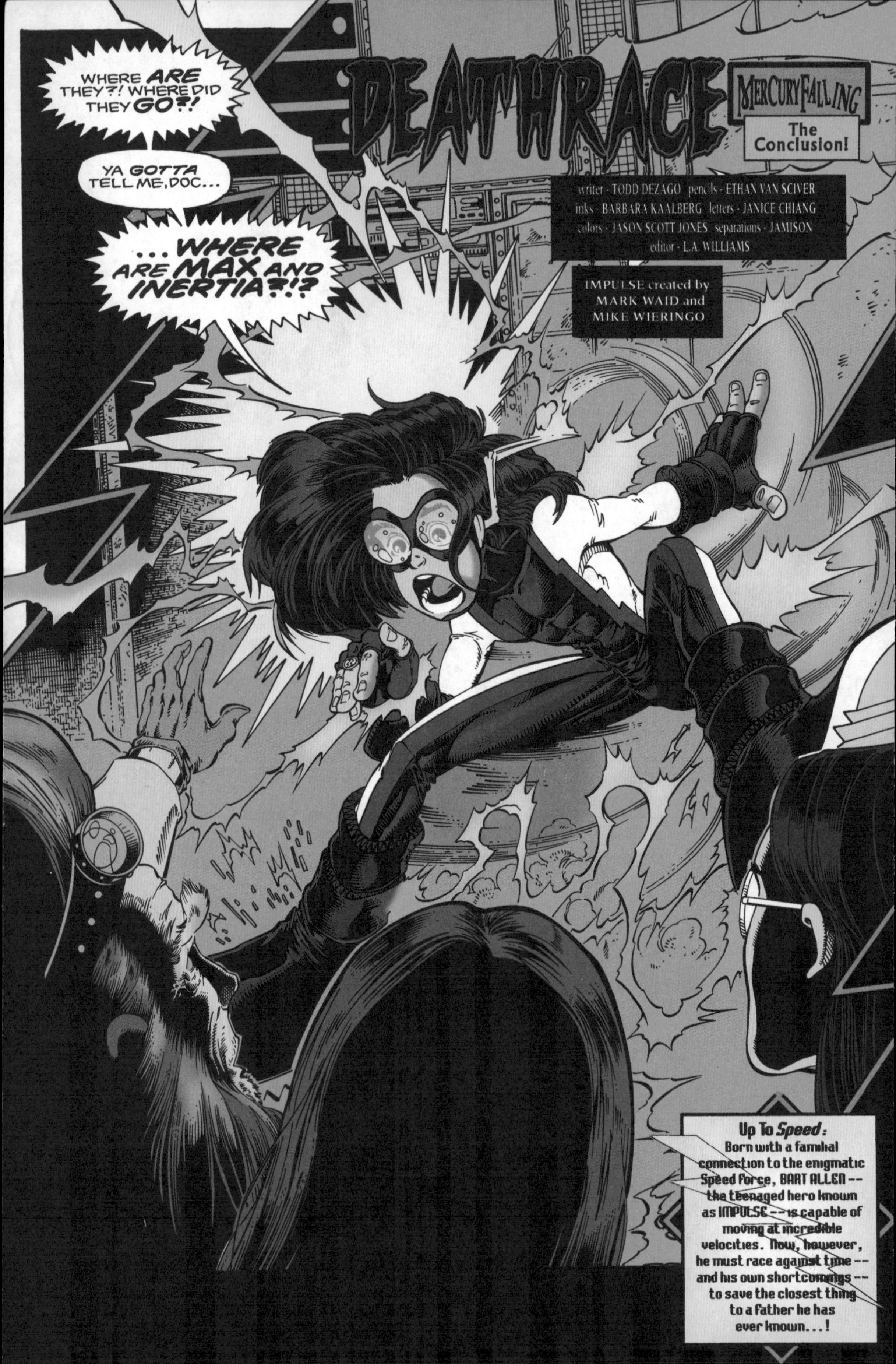
WHERE ARE THEY?! WHERE DID THEY GO?!
YA GOTTA TELL ME, DOC...
...WHERE ARE MAX AND INERTIA?!?
DEATHRACE
MERCURY FALLING
The Conclusion!
writer - TODD DEZAGO pencils - ETHAN VAN SCIVER inks - BARBARA KAALBERG letters - JANICE CHIANG colors - JASON SCOTT JONES separations - JAMISON editor - L.A. WILLIAMS
IMPULSE created by MARK WAID and MIKE WIERINGO
Up To Speed: Born with a familial connection to the enigmatic Speed Force, BART ALLEN -- the teenaged hero known as IMPULSE -- is capable of moving at incredible velocities. Now, however, he must race against time -- and his own shortcomings -- to save the closest thing to a father he has ever known...!

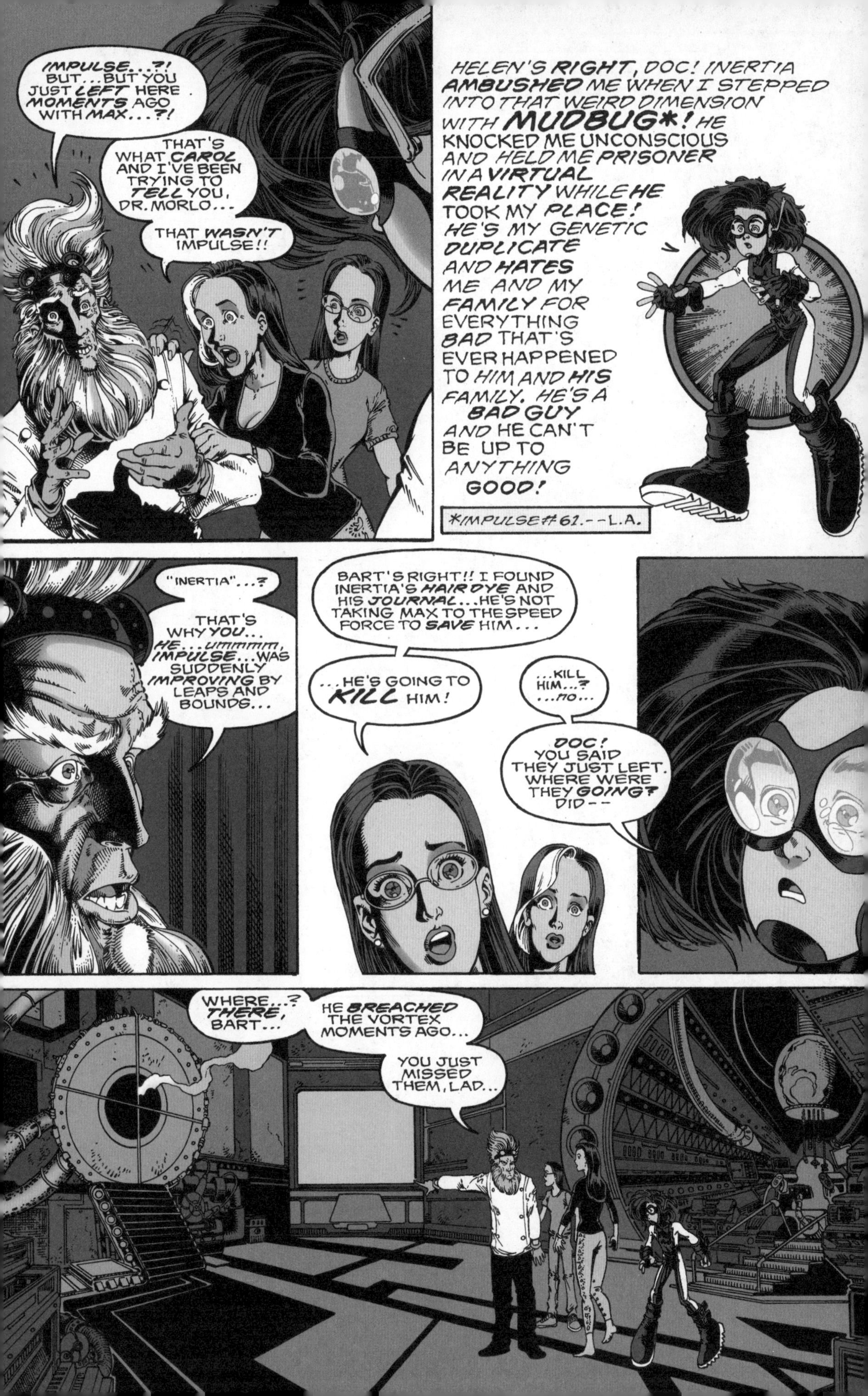
IMPULSE...?! BUT...BUT YOU JUST LEFT HERE MOMENTS AGO WITH MAX...?!
THAT'S WHAT CAROL AND I'VE BEEN TRYING TO TELL YOU, DR. MORLO...
THAT WASN'T IMPULSE!!
HELEN'S RIGHT, DOC! INERTIA AMBUSHED ME WHEN I STEPPED INTO THAT WEIRD DIMENSION WITH MUDBUG*! HE KNOCKED ME UNCONSCIOUS AND HELD ME PRISONER IN A VIRTUAL REALITY WHILE HE TOOK MY PLACE! HE'S MY GENETIC DUPLICATE AND HATES ME AND MY FAMILY FOR EVERYTHING BAD THAT'S EVER HAPPENED TO HIM AND HIS FAMILY. HE'S A BAD GUY AND HE CAN'T BE UP TO ANYTHING GOOD!
*IMPULSE #61.--L.A.
"INERTIA"...?
THAT'S WHY YOU... HE...ummmm, IMPULSE...WAS SUDDENLY IMPROVING BY LEAPS AND BOUNDS...
BART'S RIGHT!! I FOUND INERTIA'S HAIR DYE AND HIS JOURNAL...HE'S NOT TAKING MAX TO THE SPEED FORCE TO SAVE HIM...
...HE'S GOING TO KILL HIM!
...KILL HIM...? ...no...
DOC! YOU SAID THEY JUST LEFT. WHERE WERE THEY GOING? DID--
WHERE...? THERE, BART...
HE BREACHED THE VORTEX MOMENTS AGO...
YOU JUST MISSED THEM, LAD...

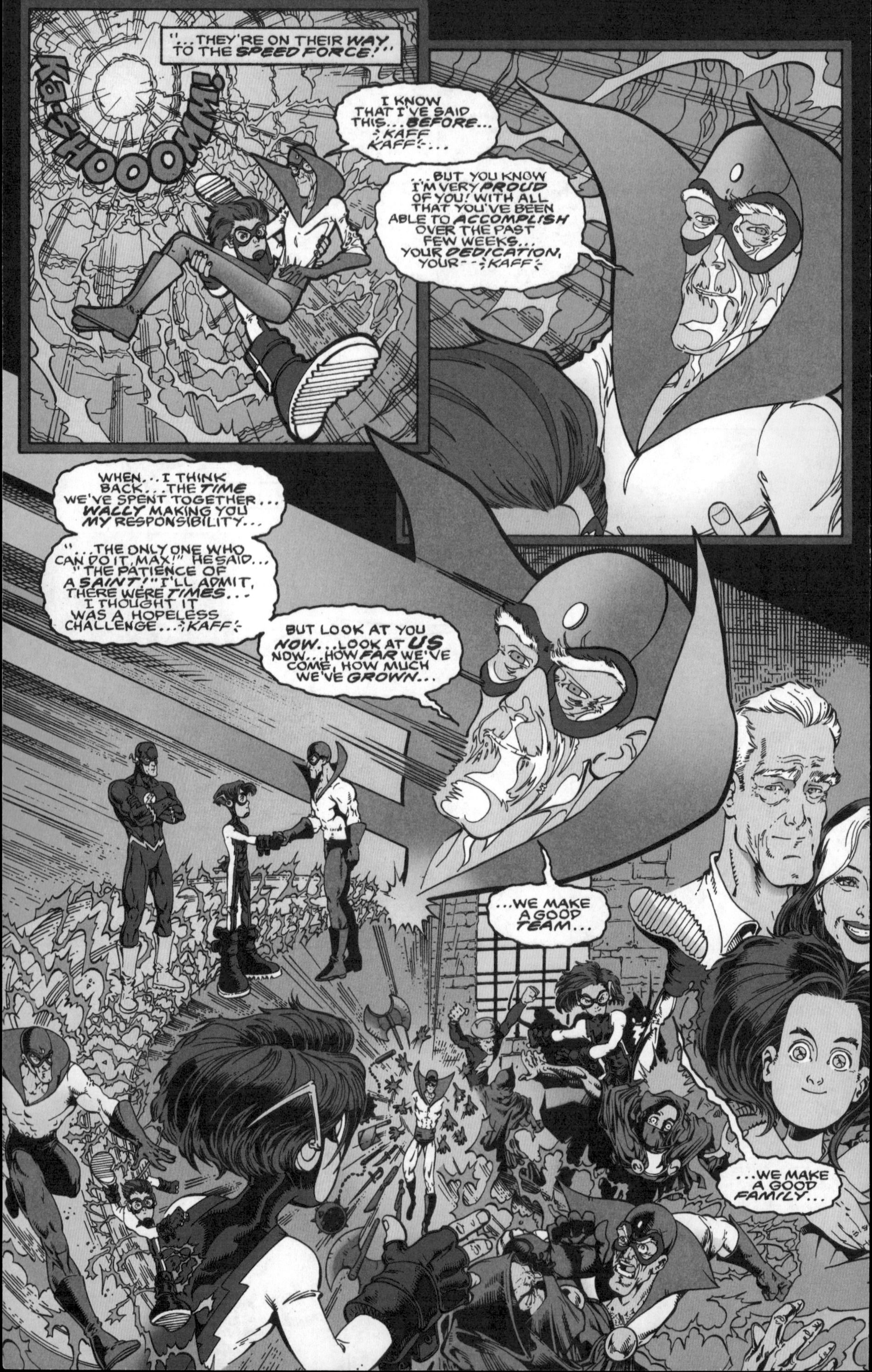
"...THEY'RE ON THEIR WAY TO THE SPEED FORCE!"
KA-SHOOOMM!
I KNOW THAT I'VE SAID THIS...BEFORE... KAFF KAFF...
...BUT YOU KNOW I'M VERY PROUD OF YOU! WITH ALL THAT YOU'VE BEEN ABLE TO ACCOMPLISH OVER THE PAST FEW WEEKS... YOUR DEDICATION, YOUR-- KAFF
WHEN...I THINK BACK...THE TIME WE'VE SPENT TOGETHER... WALLY MAKING YOU MY RESPONSIBILITY...
"...THE ONLY ONE WHO CAN DO IT, MAX!" HE SAID... "THE PATIENCE OF A SAINT!" I'LL ADMIT, THERE WERE TIMES... I THOUGHT IT WAS A HOPELESS CHALLENGE... KAFF
BUT LOOK AT YOU NOW...LOOK AT US NOW...HOW FAR WE'VE COME, HOW MUCH WE'VE GROWN...
...WE MAKE A GOOD TEAM...
...WE MAKE A GOOD FAMILY...

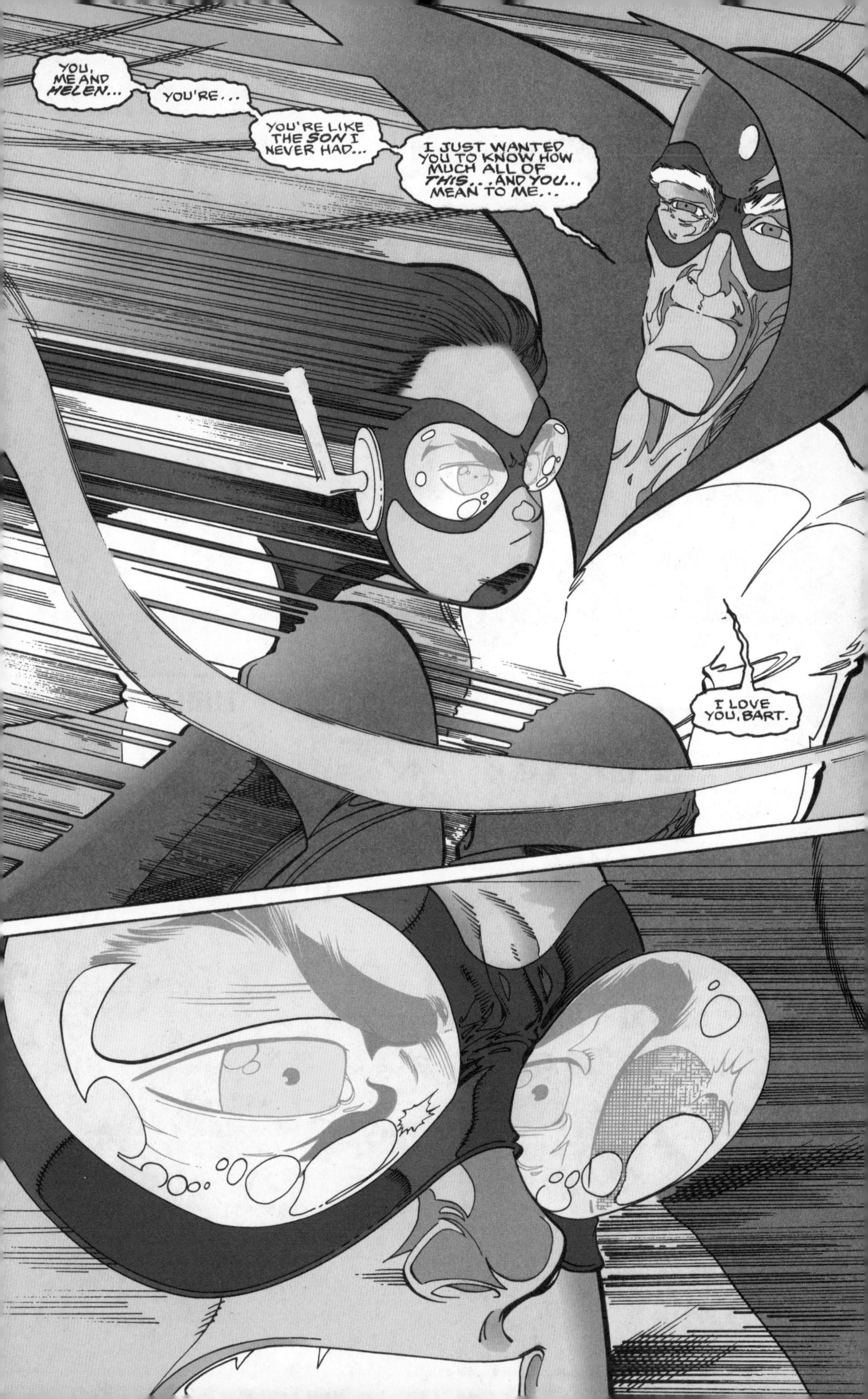
YOU, ME AND HELEN...
YOU'RE...
YOU'RE LIKE THE SON I NEVER HAD...
I JUST WANTED YOU TO KNOW HOW MUCH ALL OF THIS... AND YOU... MEAN TO ME...
I LOVE YOU, BART.

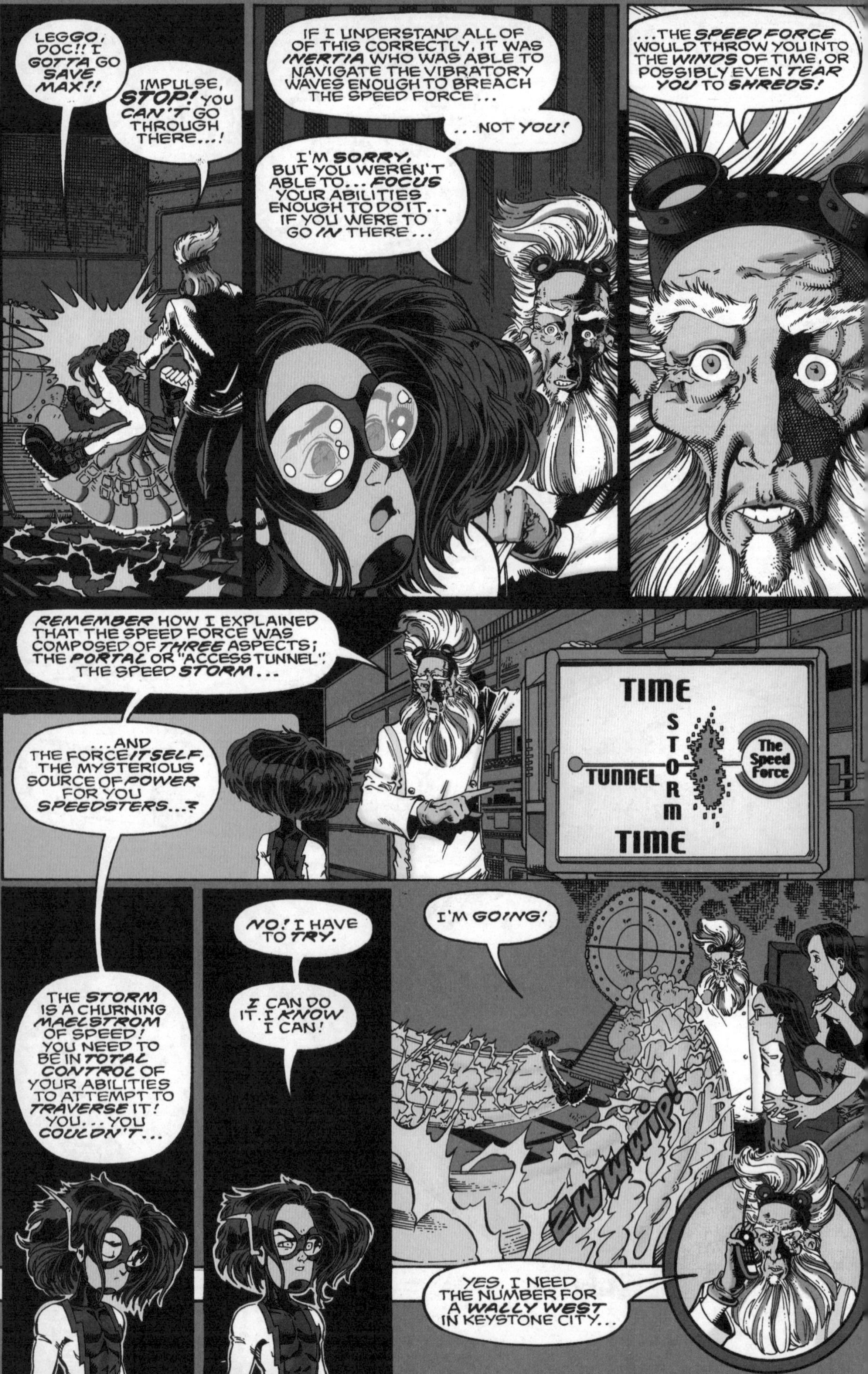

LEGGO, DOC!! I GOTTA GO SAVE MAX!!
IMPULSE, STOP! YOU CAN'T GO THROUGH THERE...!
IF I UNDERSTAND ALL OF THIS CORRECTLY, IT WAS INERTIA WHO WAS ABLE TO NAVIGATE THE VIBRATORY WAVES ENOUGH TO BREACH THE SPEED FORCE...
...NOT YOU!
I'M SORRY, BUT YOU WEREN'T ABLE TO... FOCUS YOUR ABILITIES ENOUGH TO DO IT... IF YOU WERE TO GO IN THERE...
...THE SPEED FORCE WOULD THROW YOU INTO THE WINDS OF TIME, OR POSSIBLY EVEN TEAR YOU TO SHREDS!
REMEMBER HOW I EXPLAINED THAT THE SPEED FORCE WAS COMPOSED OF THREE ASPECTS; THE PORTAL OR "ACCESS TUNNEL", THE SPEED STORM...
...AND THE FORCE ITSELF, THE MYSTERIOUS SOURCE OF POWER FOR YOU SPEEDSTERS...?
TIME
STORM
TUNNEL
The Speed Force
TIME
THE STORM IS A CHURNING MAELSTROM OF SPEED! YOU NEED TO BE IN TOTAL CONTROL OF YOUR ABILITIES TO ATTEMPT TO TRAVERSE IT! YOU... YOU COULDN'T...
NO! I HAVE TO TRY.
I CAN DO IT. I KNOW I CAN!
I'M GOING!
EWWWUP!
YES, I NEED THE NUMBER FOR A WALLY WEST IN KEYSTONE CITY...

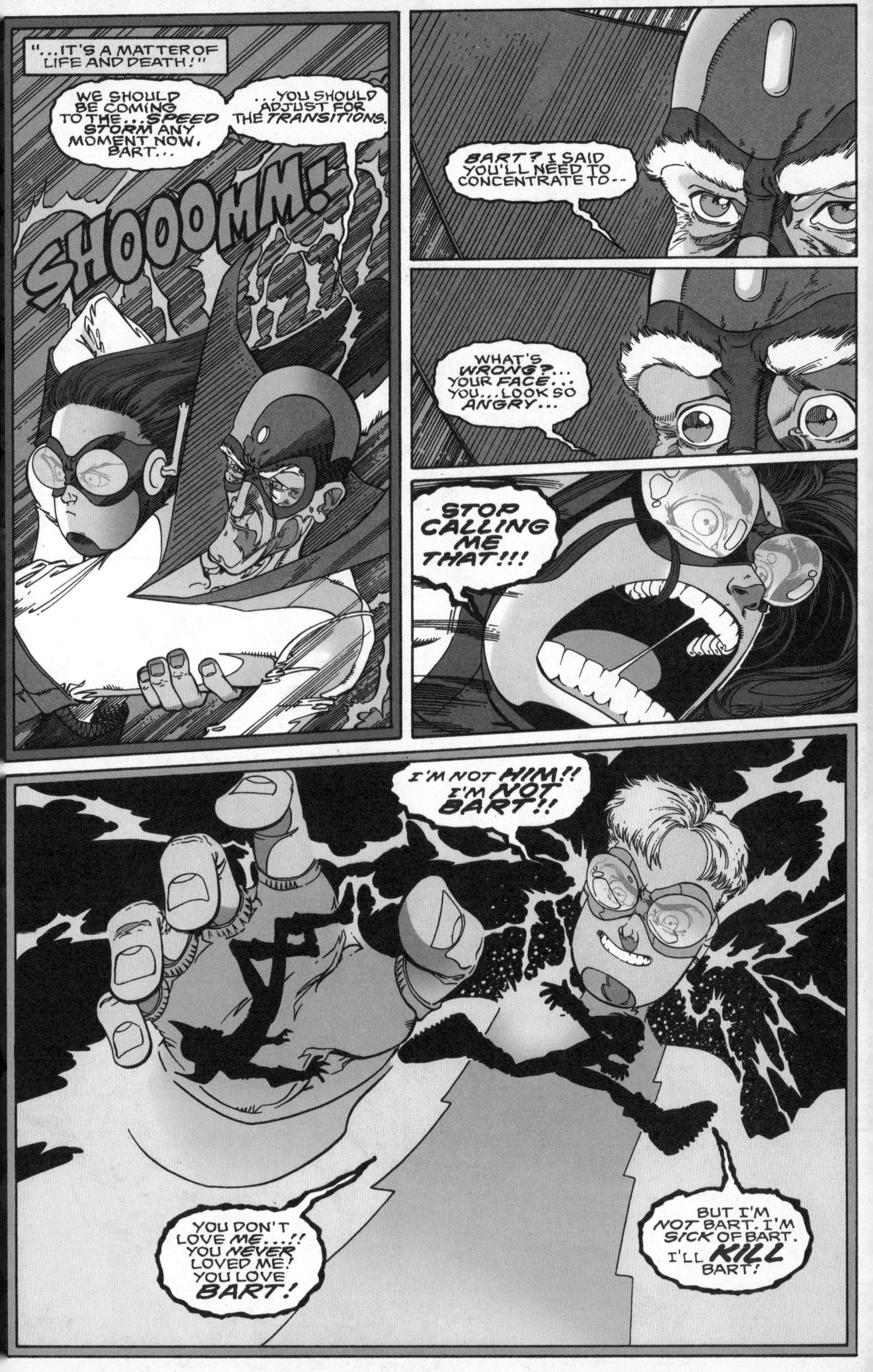
"...IT'S A MATTER OF LIFE AND DEATH!"
WE SHOULD BE COMING TO THE... SPEED STORM ANY MOMENT NOW. BART...
...YOU SHOULD ADJUST FOR THE TRANSITIONS.
SHOOOMM!
BART? I SAID YOU'LL NEED TO CONCENTRATE TO--
WHAT'S WRONG?... YOUR FACE... YOU... LOOK SO ANGRY...
STOP CALLING ME THAT!!!
I'M NOT HIM!! I'M NOT BART!!
YOU DON'T LOVE ME...!! YOU NEVER LOVED ME! YOU LOVE BART!
BUT I'M NOT BART. I'M SICK OF BART. I'LL KILL BART!

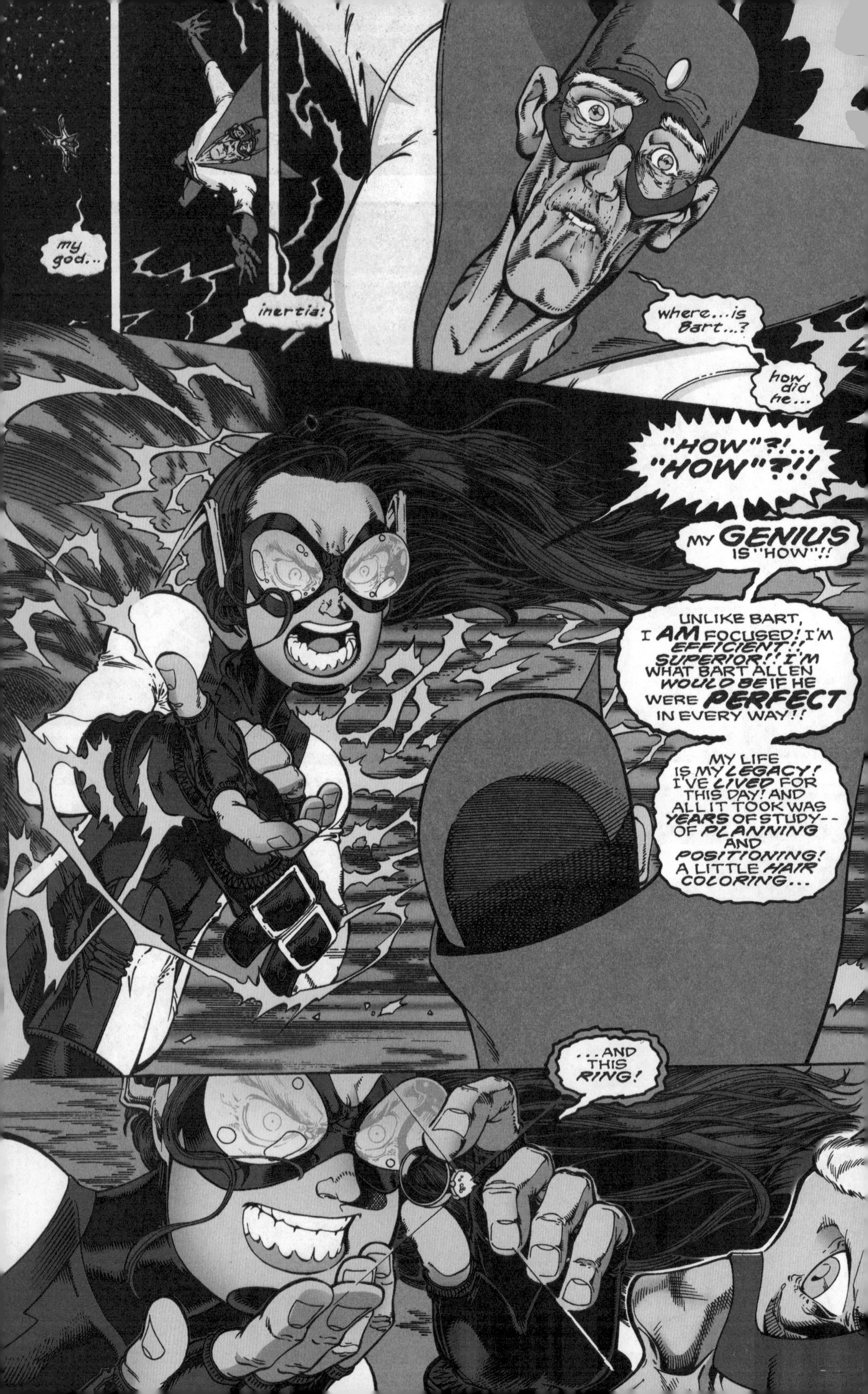
my god...
inertia!
where...is Bart...?
how did he...
"HOW"?!... "HOW"?!!
MY GENIUS IS "HOW"!!
UNLIKE BART, I AM FOCUSED! I'M EFFICIENT!! SUPERIOR!! I'M WHAT BART ALLEN WOULD BE IF HE WERE PERFECT IN EVERY WAY!!
MY LIFE IS MY LEGACY! I'VE LIVED FOR THIS DAY! AND ALL IT TOOK WAS YEARS OF STUDY-- OF PLANNING AND POSITIONING! A LITTLE HAIR COLORING...
...AND THIS RING!

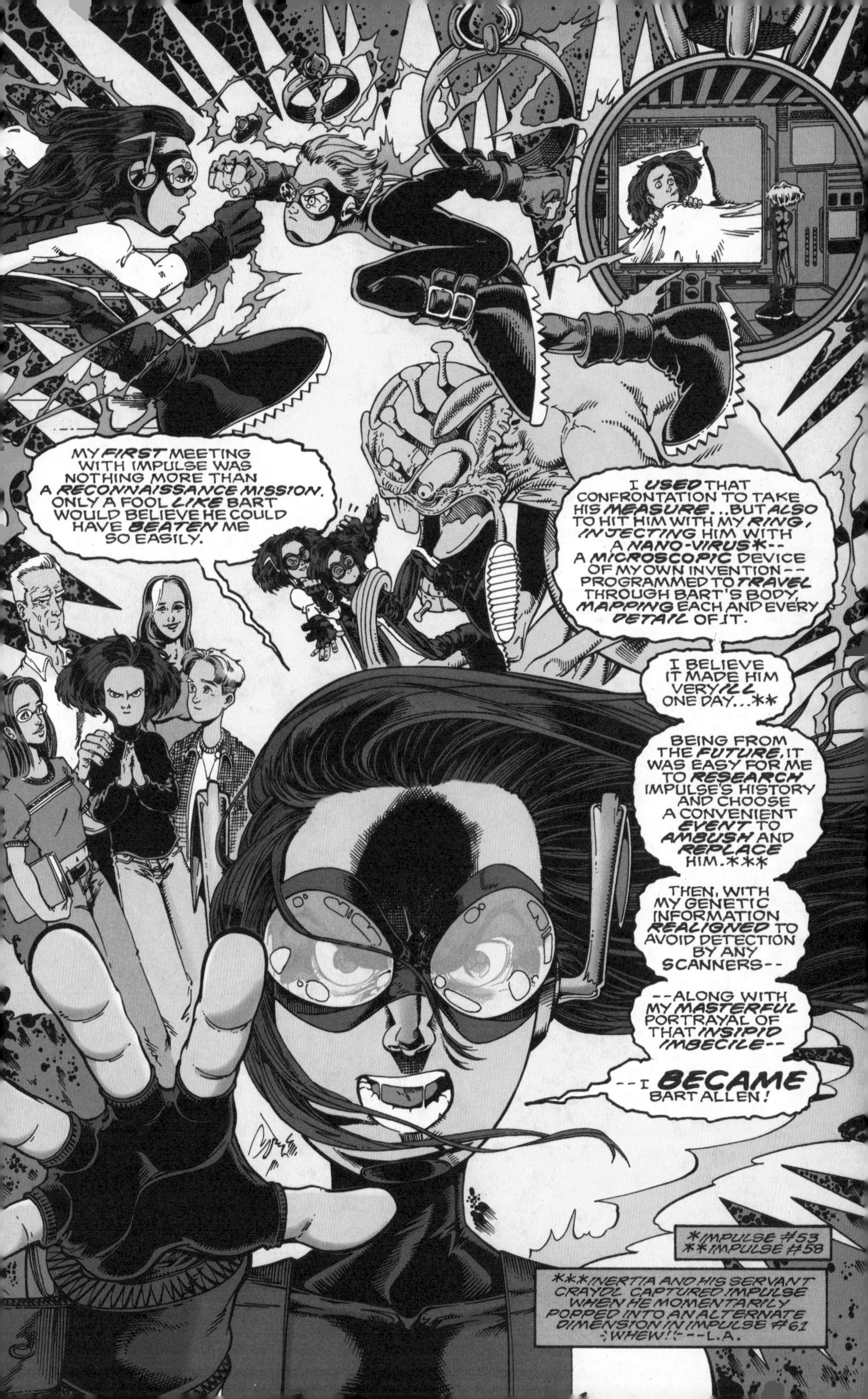

MY FIRST MEETING WITH IMPULSE WAS NOTHING MORE THAN A RECONNAISSANCE MISSION. ONLY A FOOL LIKE BART WOULD BELIEVE HE COULD HAVE BEATEN ME SO EASILY.
I USED THAT CONFRONTATION TO TAKE HIS MEASURE...BUT ALSO TO HIT HIM WITH MY RING, INJECTING HIM WITH A NANO-VIRUS*-- A MICROSCOPIC DEVICE OF MY OWN INVENTION--PROGRAMMED TO TRAVEL THROUGH BART'S BODY, MAPPING EACH AND EVERY DETAIL OF IT.
I BELIEVE IT MADE HIM VERY ILL ONE DAY...**
BEING FROM THE FUTURE, IT WAS EASY FOR ME TO RESEARCH IMPULSE'S HISTORY AND CHOOSE A CONVENIENT EVENT TO AMBUSH AND REPLACE HIM.***
THEN, WITH MY GENETIC INFORMATION REALIGNED TO AVOID DETECTION BY ANY SCANNERS--
--ALONG WITH MY MASTERFUL PORTRAYAL OF THAT INSIPID IMBECILE--
--I BECAME BART ALLEN!
*IMPULSE #53
**IMPULSE #58
***INERTIA AND HIS SERVANT CRAYDL CAPTURED IMPULSE WHEN HE MOMENTARILY POPPED INTO AN ALTERNATE DIMENSION IN IMPULSE #61 ;WHEW!;--L.A.

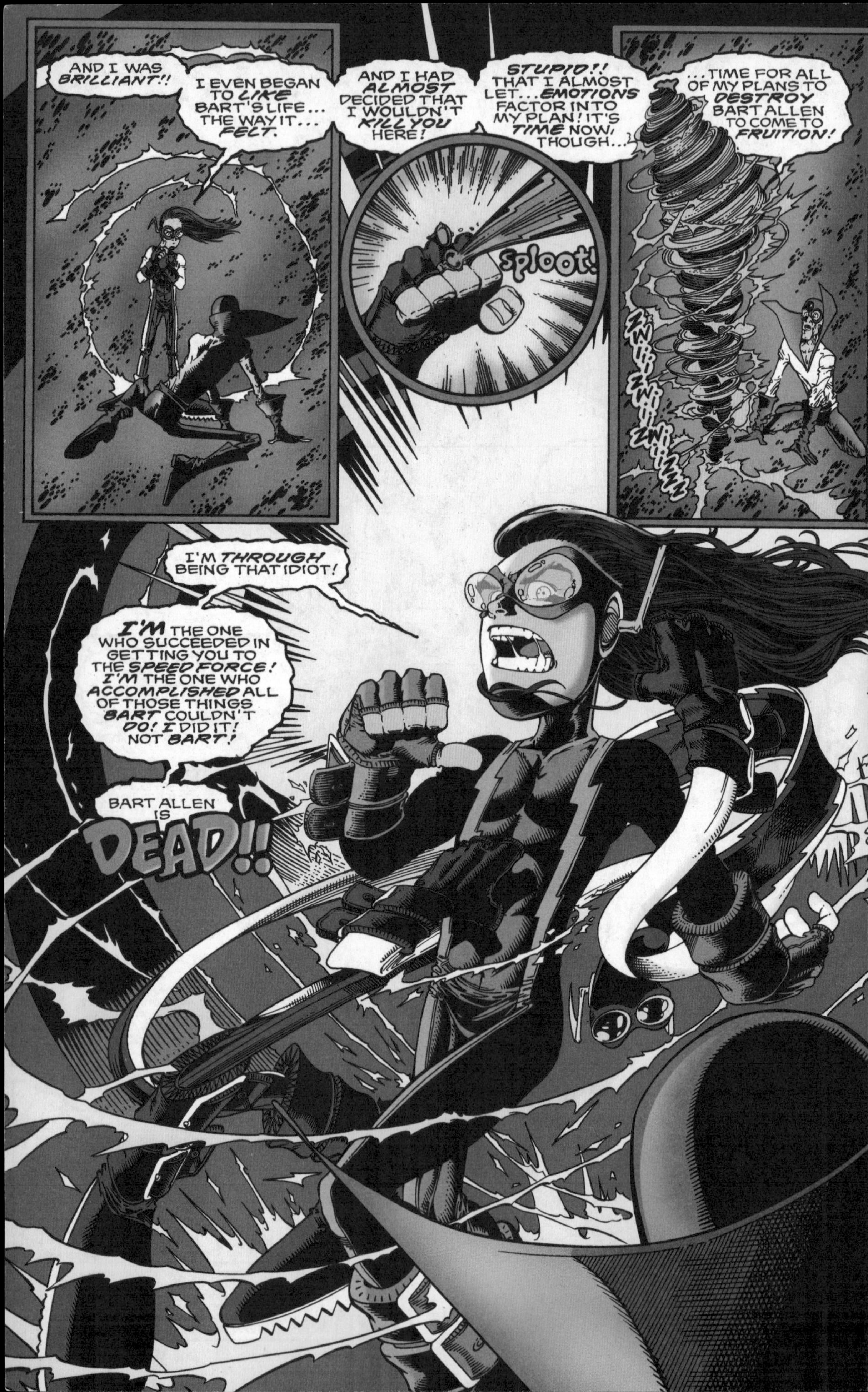
AND I WAS BRILLIANT!!
I EVEN BEGAN TO LIKE BART'S LIFE... THE WAY IT... FELT.
AND I HAD ALMOST DECIDED THAT I WOULDN'T KILL YOU HERE!
SPLOOT!
STUPID!! THAT I ALMOST LET... EMOTIONS FACTOR INTO MY PLAN! IT'S TIME NOW, THOUGH...
...TIME FOR ALL OF MY PLANS TO DESTROY BART ALLEN TO COME TO FRUITION!
I'M THROUGH BEING THAT IDIOT!
I'M THE ONE WHO SUCCEEDED IN GETTING YOU TO THE SPEED FORCE! I'M THE ONE WHO ACCOMPLISHED ALL OF THOSE THINGS BART COULDN'T DO! I DID IT! NOT BART!
BART ALLEN IS DEAD!!

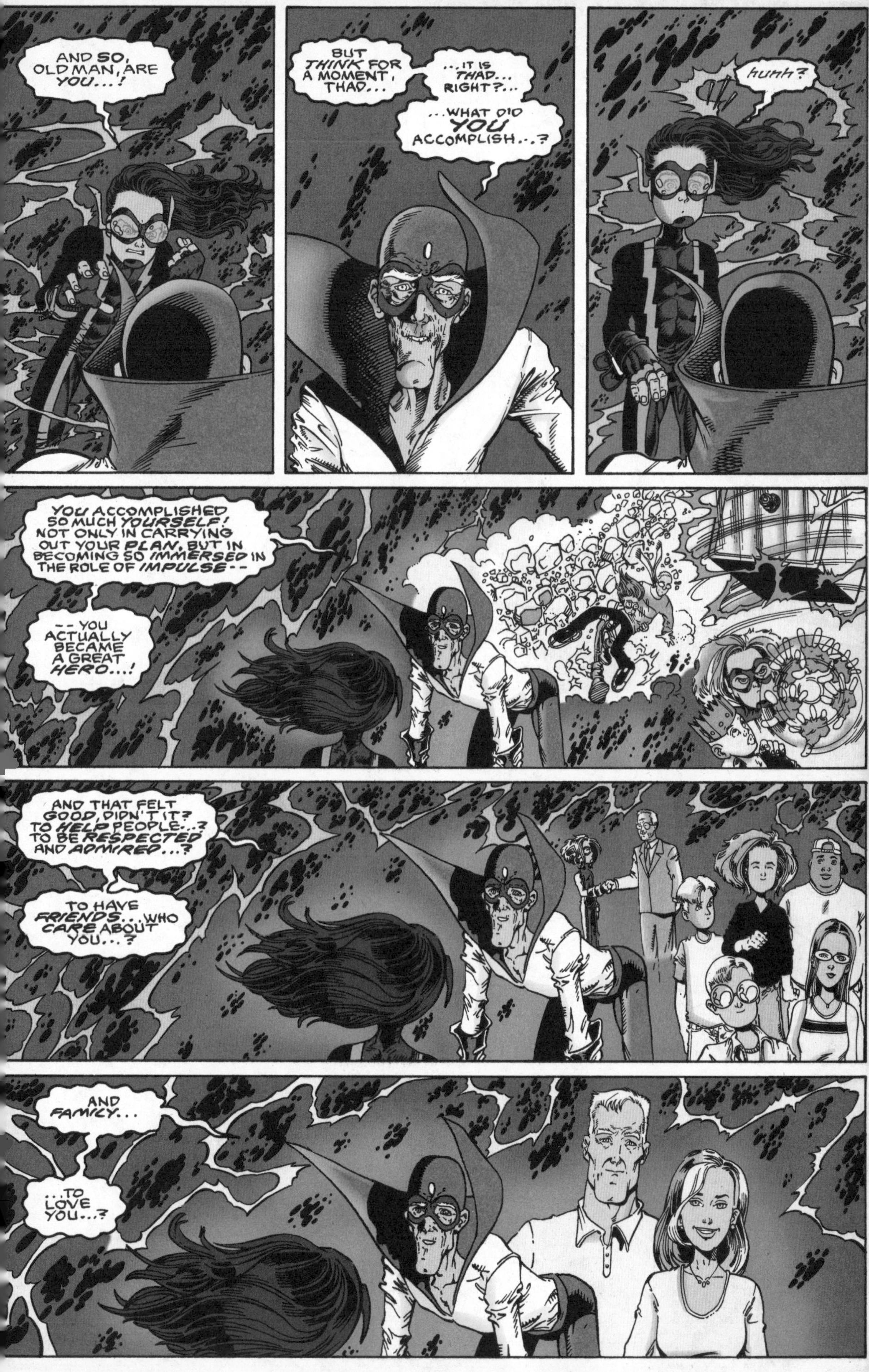
AND SO, OLD MAN, ARE YOU...!
BUT THINK FOR A MOMENT, THAD...
...IT IS THAD... RIGHT?...
...WHAT DID YOU ACCOMPLISH...?
huhh?
YOU ACCOMPLISHED SO MUCH YOURSELF! NOT ONLY IN CARRYING OUT YOUR PLAN, BUT IN BECOMING SO IMMERSED IN THE ROLE OF IMPULSE--
--YOU ACTUALLY BECAME A GREAT HERO...!
AND THAT FELT GOOD, DIDN'T IT? TO HELP PEOPLE...? TO BE RESPECTED AND ADMIRED...?
TO HAVE FRIENDS... WHO CARE ABOUT YOU...?
AND FAMILY...
...TO LOVE YOU...?

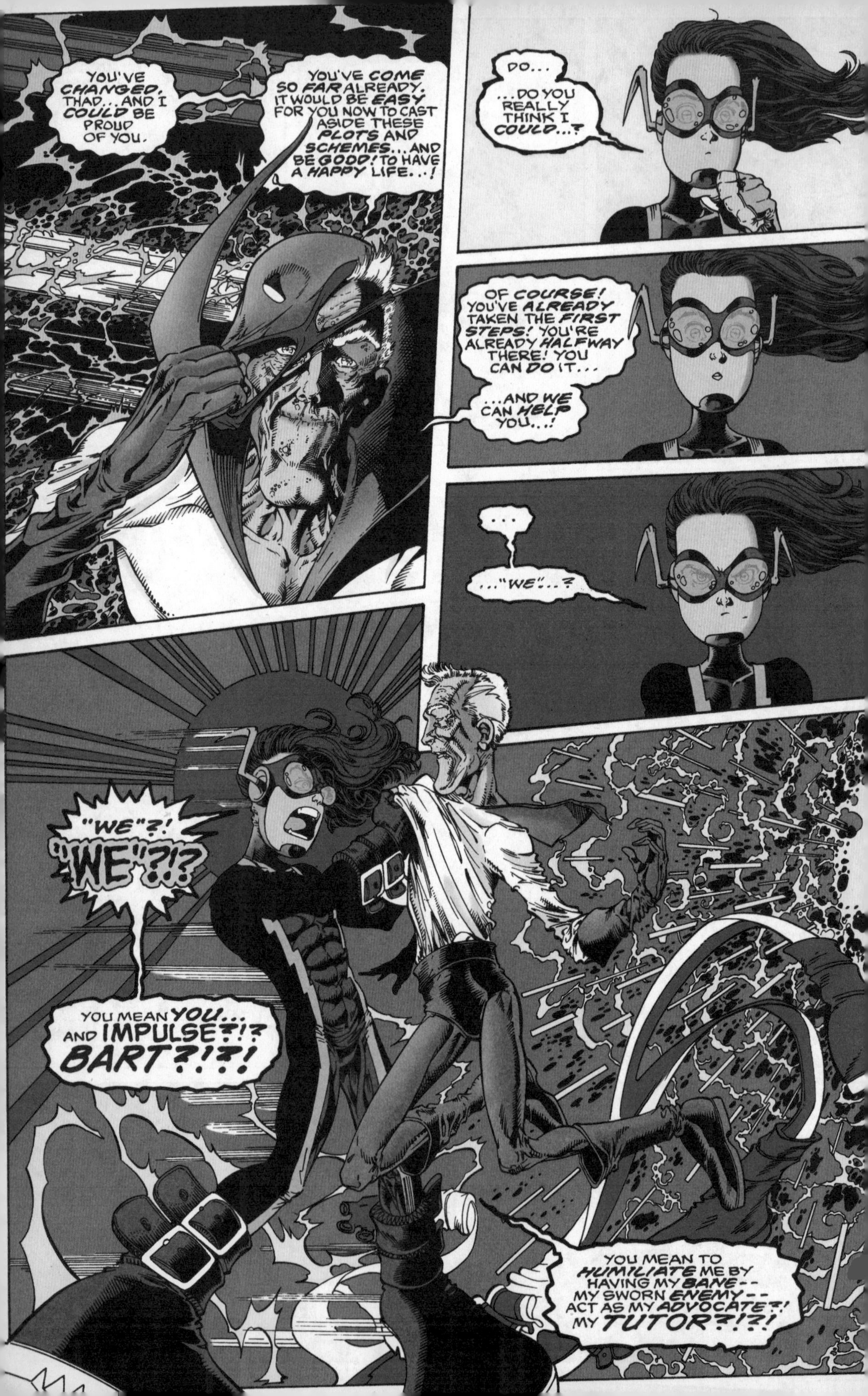

YOU'VE CHANGED, THAD... AND I COULD BE PROUD OF YOU.
YOU'VE COME SO FAR ALREADY. IT WOULD BE EASY FOR YOU NOW TO CAST ASIDE THESE PLOTS AND SCHEMES... AND BE GOOD! TO HAVE A HAPPY LIFE...!
DO...
...DO YOU REALLY THINK I COULD...?
OF COURSE! YOU'VE ALREADY TAKEN THE FIRST STEPS! YOU'RE ALREADY HALFWAY THERE! YOU CAN DO IT...
...AND WE CAN HELP YOU...!
...
..."WE"...?
"WE"?! "WE"?!?
YOU MEAN YOU... AND IMPULSE?!? BART?!?!
YOU MEAN TO HUMILIATE ME BY HAVING MY BANE-- MY SWORN ENEMY-- ACT AS MY ADVOCATE?! MY TUTOR?!?!

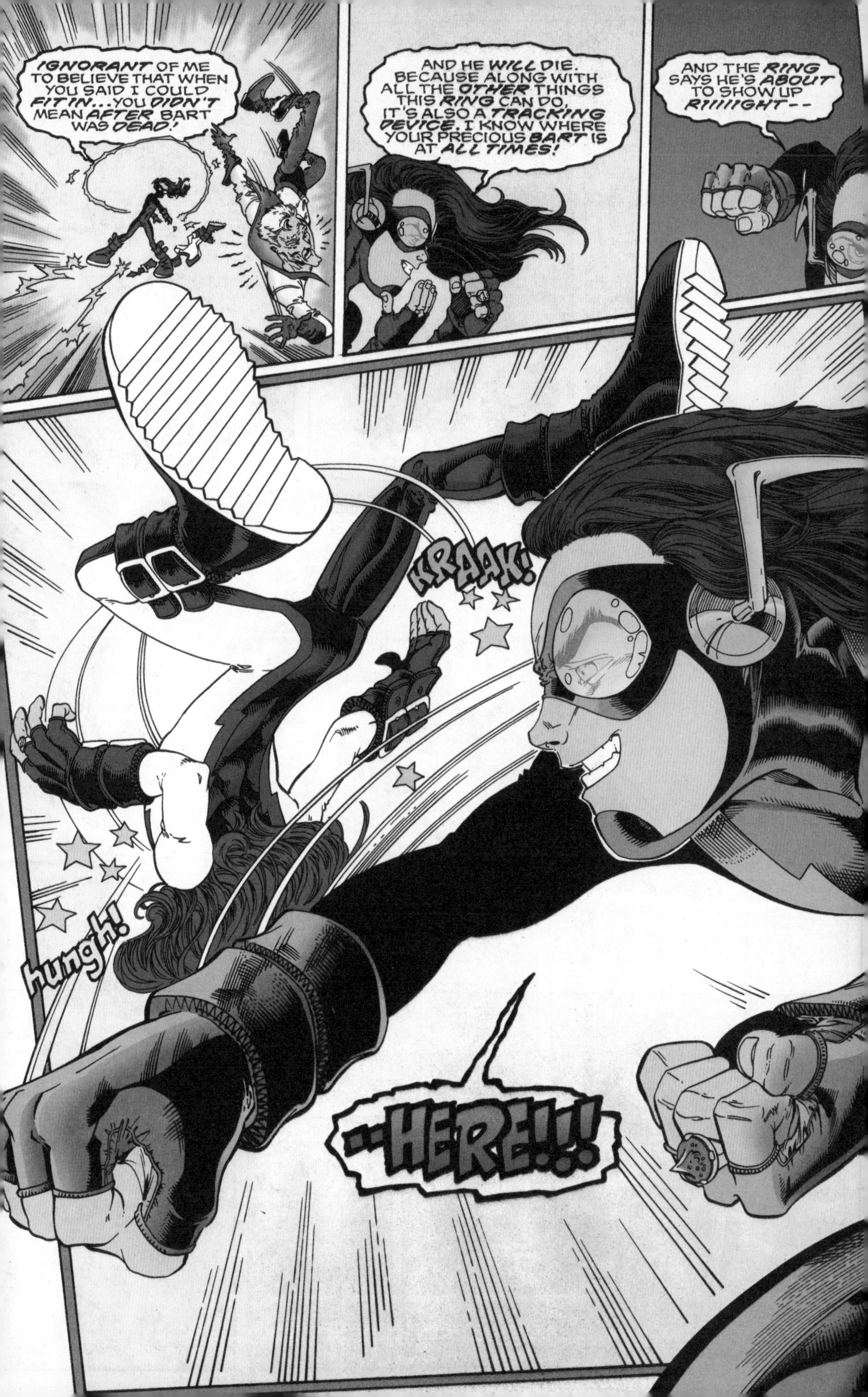
IGNORANT OF ME TO BELIEVE THAT WHEN YOU SAID I COULD FIT IN... YOU DIDN'T MEAN AFTER BART WAS DEAD!
AND HE WILL DIE. BECAUSE ALONG WITH ALL THE OTHER THINGS THIS RING CAN DO, IT'S ALSO A TRACKING DEVICE. I KNOW WHERE YOUR PRECIOUS BART IS AT ALL TIMES!
AND THE RING SAYS HE'S ABOUT TO SHOW UP RIIIIIGHT--
KRAAK!
hungh!
--HERE!!!

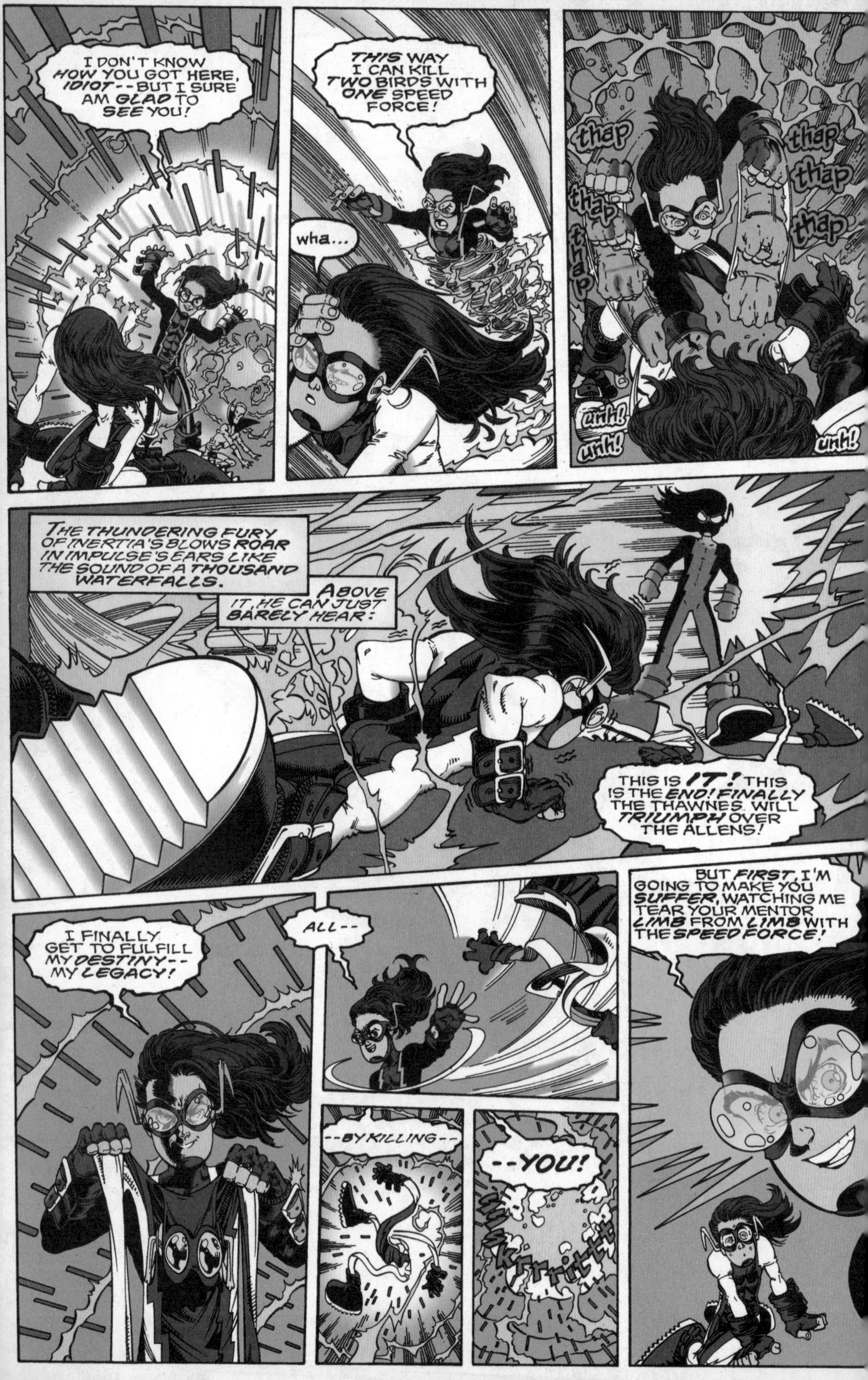

I DON'T KNOW HOW YOU GOT HERE, IDIOT--BUT I SURE AM GLAD TO SEE YOU!
THIS WAY I CAN KILL TWO BIRDS WITH ONE SPEED FORCE!
wha...
thap thap thap thap thap thap
unh! unh! unh!
THE THUNDERING FURY OF INERTIA'S BLOWS ROAR IN IMPULSE'S EARS LIKE THE SOUND OF A THOUSAND WATERFALLS.
ABOVE IT, HE CAN JUST BARELY HEAR:
THIS IS IT! THIS IS THE END! FINALLY THE THAWNES WILL TRIUMPH OVER THE ALLENS!
I FINALLY GET TO FULFILL MY DESTINY--MY LEGACY!
ALL--
--BY KILLING--
--YOU!
skrrritttt
BUT FIRST, I'M GOING TO MAKE YOU SUFFER, WATCHING ME TEAR YOUR MENTOR LIMB FROM LIMB WITH THE SPEED FORCE!

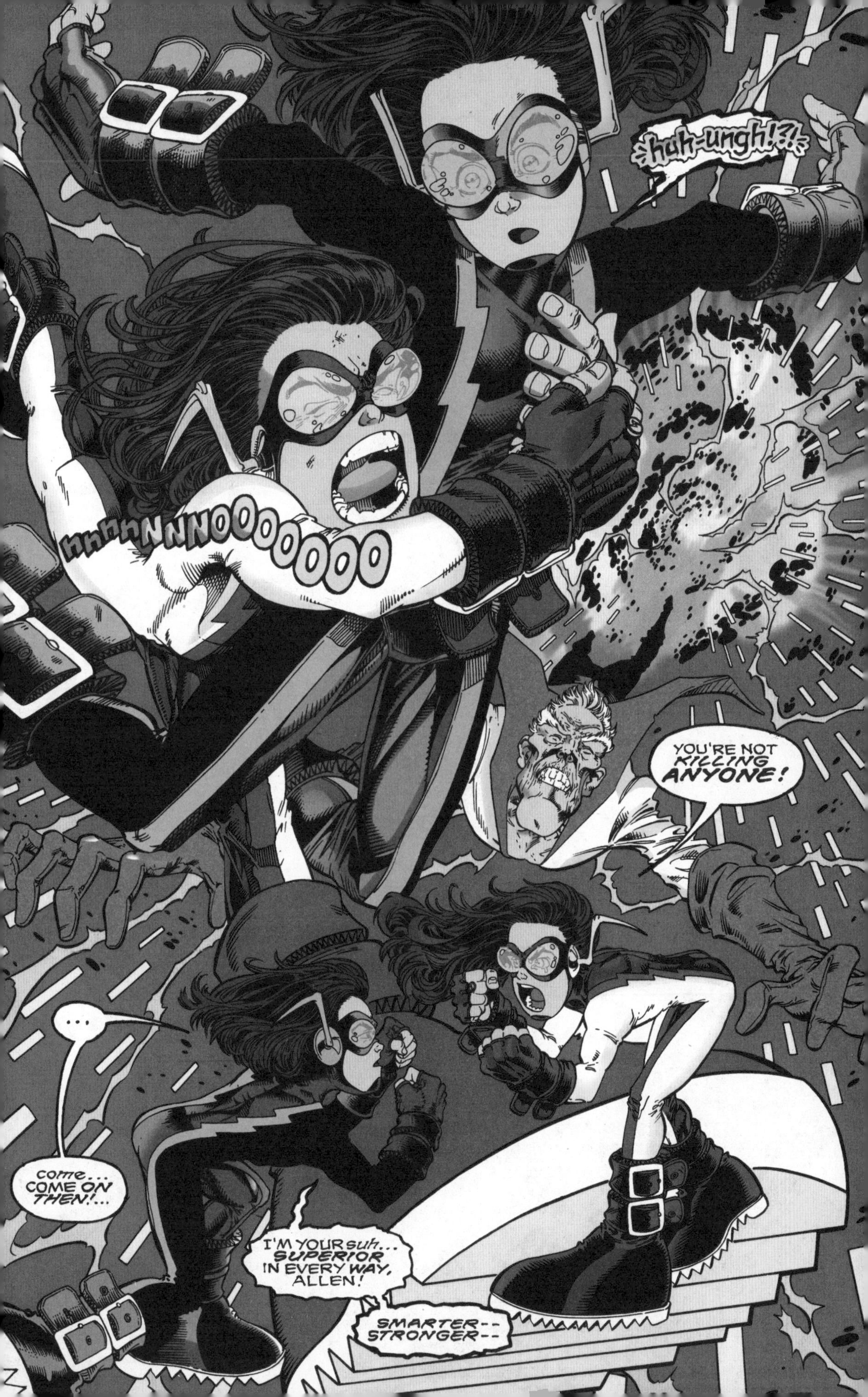
huh-ungh!?!
hhhhNNNOOOOOOOO
YOU'RE NOT KILLING ANYONE!
...
come... COME ON THEN!...
I'M YOUR suh... SUPERIOR IN EVERY WAY, ALLEN!
SMARTER-- STRONGER--

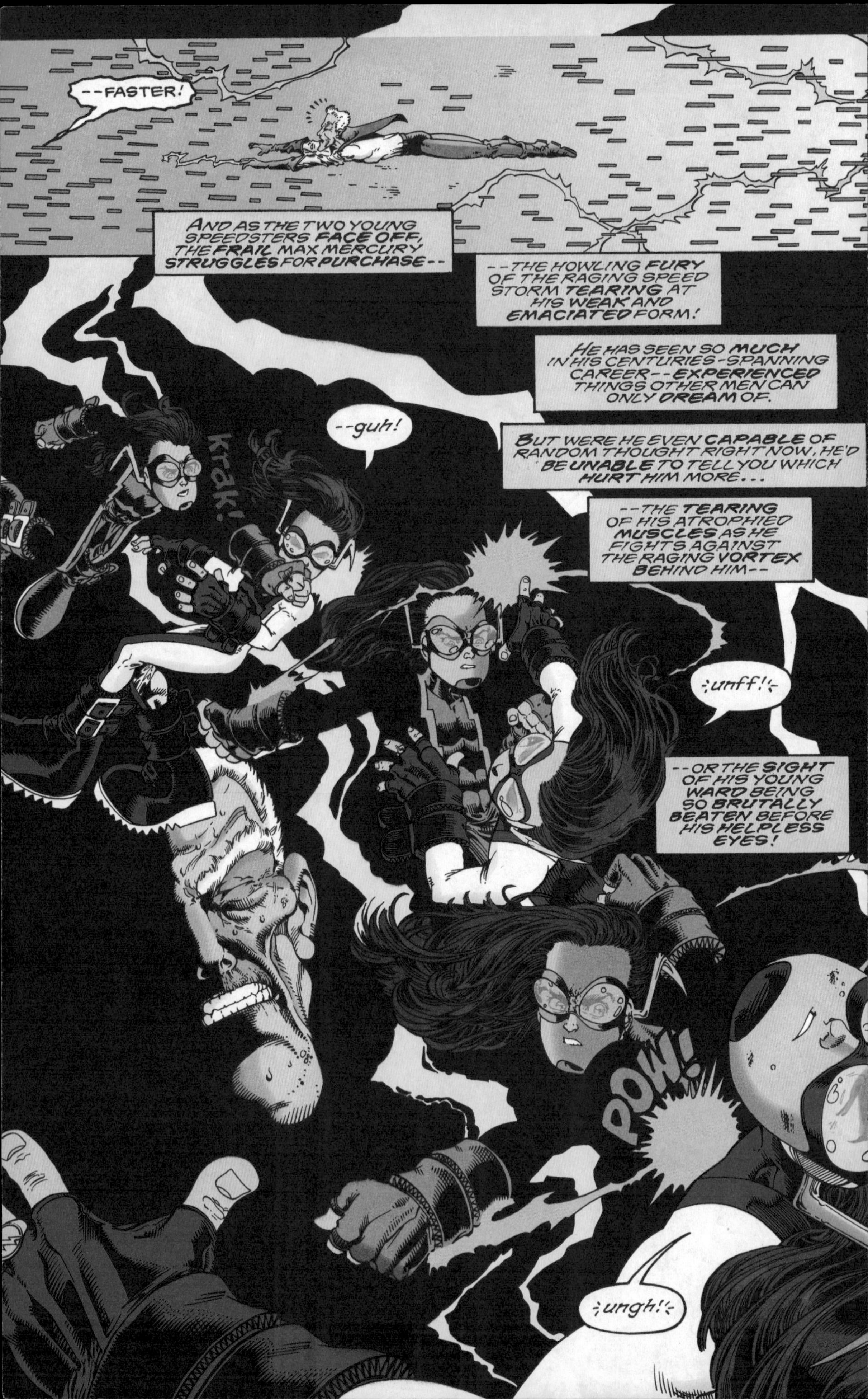
--FASTER!
AND AS THE TWO YOUNG SPEEDSTERS FACE OFF, THE FRAIL MAX MERCURY STRUGGLES FOR PURCHASE--
--THE HOWLING FURY OF THE RAGING SPEED STORM TEARING AT HIS WEAK AND EMACIATED FORM!
HE HAS SEEN SO MUCH IN HIS CENTURIES-SPANNING CAREER--EXPERIENCED THINGS OTHER MEN CAN ONLY DREAM OF.
--guh!
KRAK!
BUT WERE HE EVEN CAPABLE OF RANDOM THOUGHT RIGHT NOW, HE'D BE UNABLE TO TELL YOU WHICH HURT HIM MORE...
--THE TEARING OF HIS ATROPHIED MUSCLES AS HE FIGHTS AGAINST THE RAGING VORTEX BEHIND HIM--
unff!
--OR THE SIGHT OF HIS YOUNG WARD BEING SO BRUTALLY BEATEN BEFORE HIS HELPLESS EYES!
POW!
ungh!

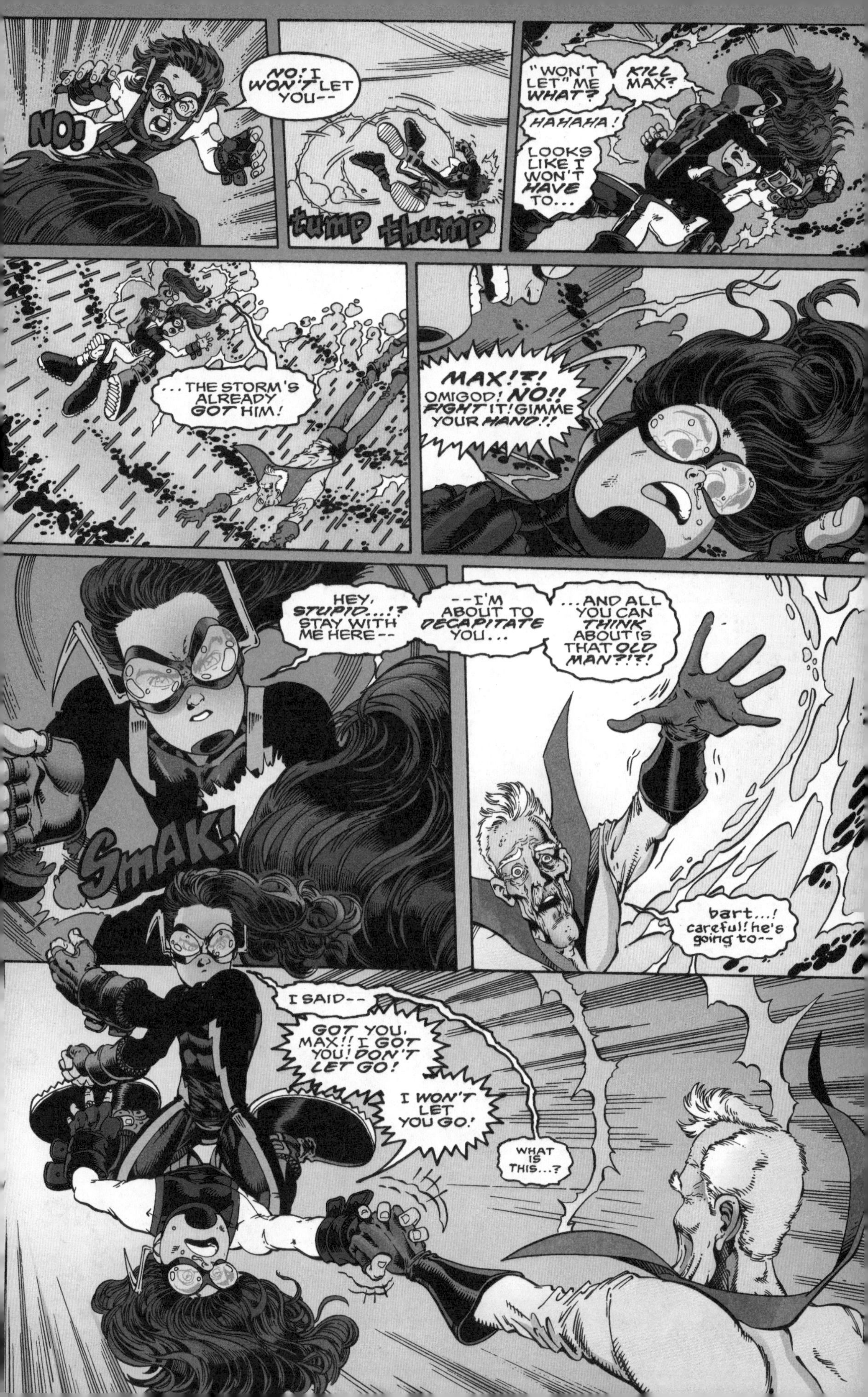
NO!
NO! I WON'T LET YOU--
tump thump
"WON'T LET" ME WHAT?
KILL MAX?
HAHAHA!
LOOKS LIKE I WON'T HAVE TO...
...THE STORM'S ALREADY GOT HIM!
MAX!?! OMIGOD! NO!! FIGHT IT! GIMME YOUR HAND!!
HEY, STUPID...!? STAY WITH ME HERE--
--I'M ABOUT TO DECAPITATE YOU...
...AND ALL YOU CAN THINK ABOUT IS THAT OLD MAN?!?!
SMAK!
bart...! careful! he's going to--
I SAID--
GOT YOU, MAX!! I GOT YOU! DON'T LET GO!
I WON'T LET YOU GO!
WHAT IS THIS...?

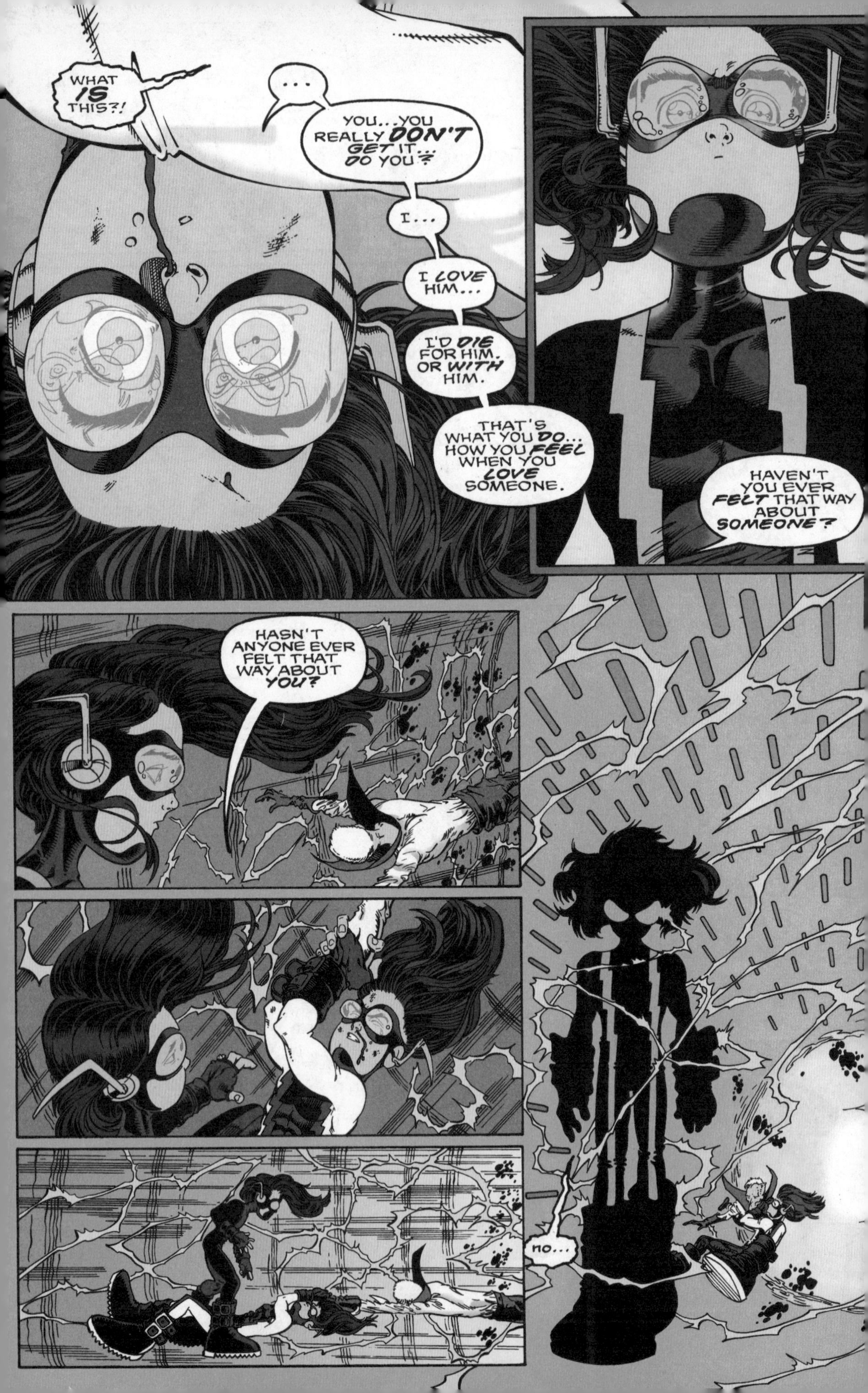
WHAT IS THIS?!
...
YOU...YOU REALLY DON'T GET IT... DO YOU?
I...
I LOVE HIM...
I'D DIE FOR HIM. OR WITH HIM.
THAT'S WHAT YOU DO... HOW YOU FEEL WHEN YOU LOVE SOMEONE.
HAVEN'T YOU EVER FELT THAT WAY ABOUT SOMEONE?
HASN'T ANYONE EVER FELT THAT WAY ABOUT YOU?
no...

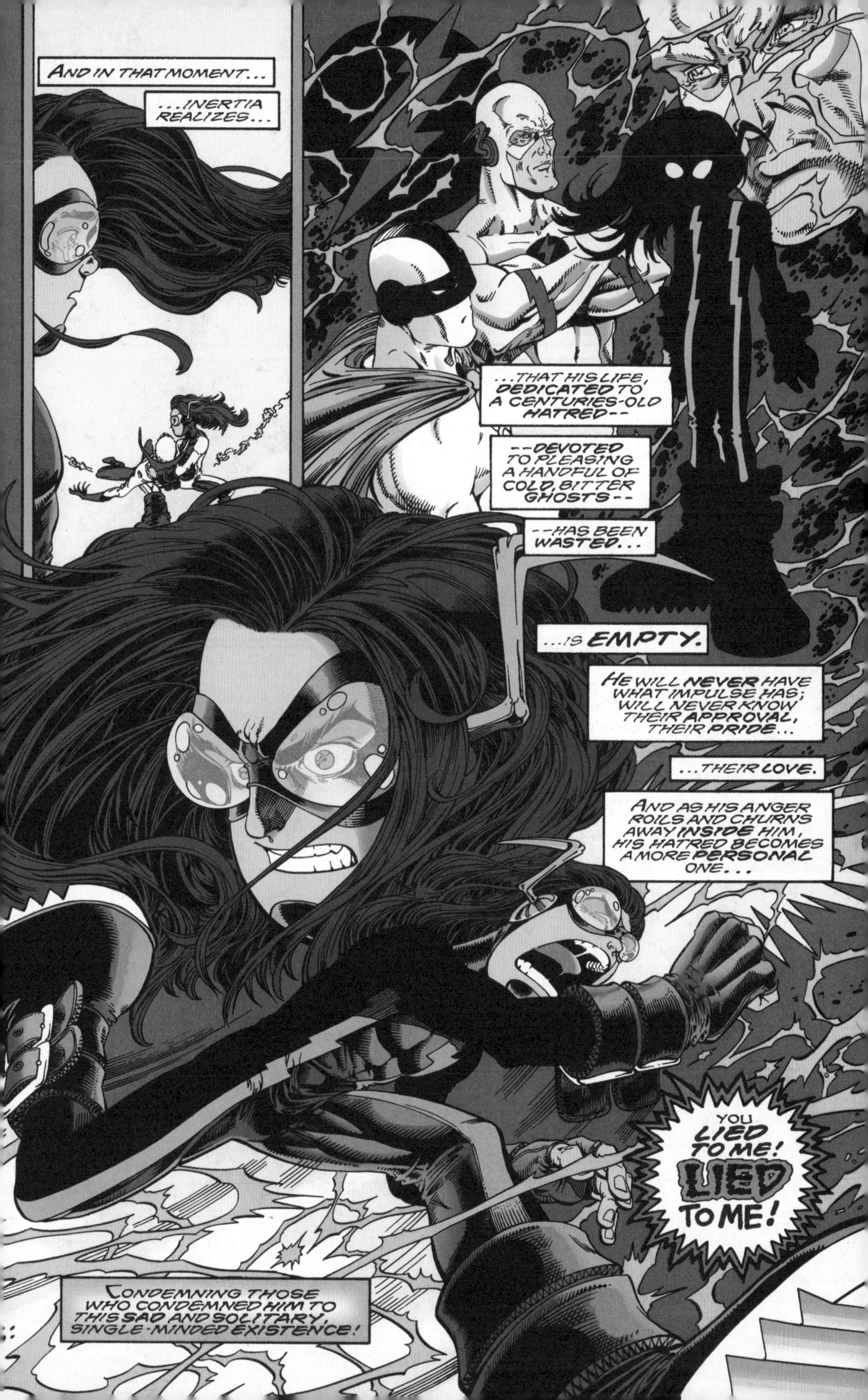
AND IN THAT MOMENT...
...INERTIA REALIZES...
...THAT HIS LIFE, DEDICATED TO A CENTURIES-OLD HATRED--
--DEVOTED TO PLEASING A HANDFUL OF COLD, BITTER GHOSTS--
--HAS BEEN WASTED...
...IS EMPTY.
HE WILL NEVER HAVE WHAT IMPULSE HAS; WILL NEVER KNOW THEIR APPROVAL, THEIR PRIDE...
...THEIR LOVE.
AND AS HIS ANGER ROILS AND CHURNS AWAY INSIDE HIM, HIS HATRED BECOMES A MORE PERSONAL ONE...
YOU LIED TO ME! LIED TO ME!
CONDEMNING THOSE WHO CONDEMNED HIM TO THIS SAD AND SOLITARY, SINGLE-MINDED EXISTENCE!

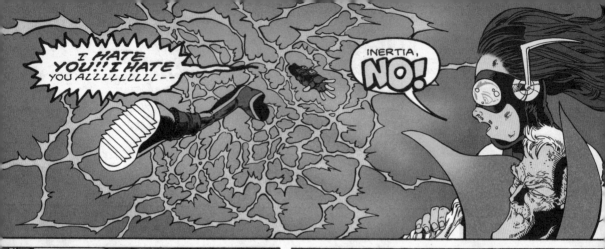

**I HATE YOU!! I HATE YOU ALLLLLLLLLL—**

**INERTIA, NO!**

**INERTIA... IS HE--?**

**HE'S... GONE...**

**BUT, C'MON, MAX--WE GOTTA GET YOU UP, GET YOU TO THE SPEED FORCE... I THINK YOU'LL...DIE SOON IF WE DON'T.**

**N-NO, BART...WE CAN'T DO THIS...YOU CAN'T DO THIS...**

**YOU...WEREN'T ABLE TO MATCH ALL OF THE VIBRATORY... FREQUENCIES TO...MAKE IT THROUGH THE SPEED STORM! IT'LL TEAR US BOTH APART...THEN WE'D BOTH BE...DEAD... I CAN'T...LET YOU DO THAT...**

**LISTEN, BART...I WANT YOU TO...LEAVE ME HERE, GO BACK YOURSELF--**

**NO, MAX! I CAN DO IT! I'VE ALREADY DONE A LOT OF THINGS THAT WE THOUGHT I COULDN'T, JUST GETTING HERE!**

**THE ONLY WAY YOU'RE GONNA GET RECONNECTED TO THE SPEED FORCE IS FOR US TO GO THROUGH THAT STORM! WE'RE GOIN'!**

**THE SPEED STORM TEARS AT BART, TRYING TO RIP THE OLD MAN FROM HIS GRASP--**

**--BART HOLDS ON.**

**NO, BART! STOP! THIS IS SUICIDE!**

**SORRY, MAX. CAN'T HEAR YA.**

**I CAN DO THIS. I CAN DO THIS. I CAN DO THIS.**

**IT PUSHES AT HIM, PUMMELING HIM WITH WAVE AFTER WAVE OF INCREDIBLE FORCE, THREATENING TO LOSE THEM IN THE TORRENTIAL CURRENTS OF THE TIMESTREAM--**

**--BART PRESSES ON--**

**...I HOPE.**

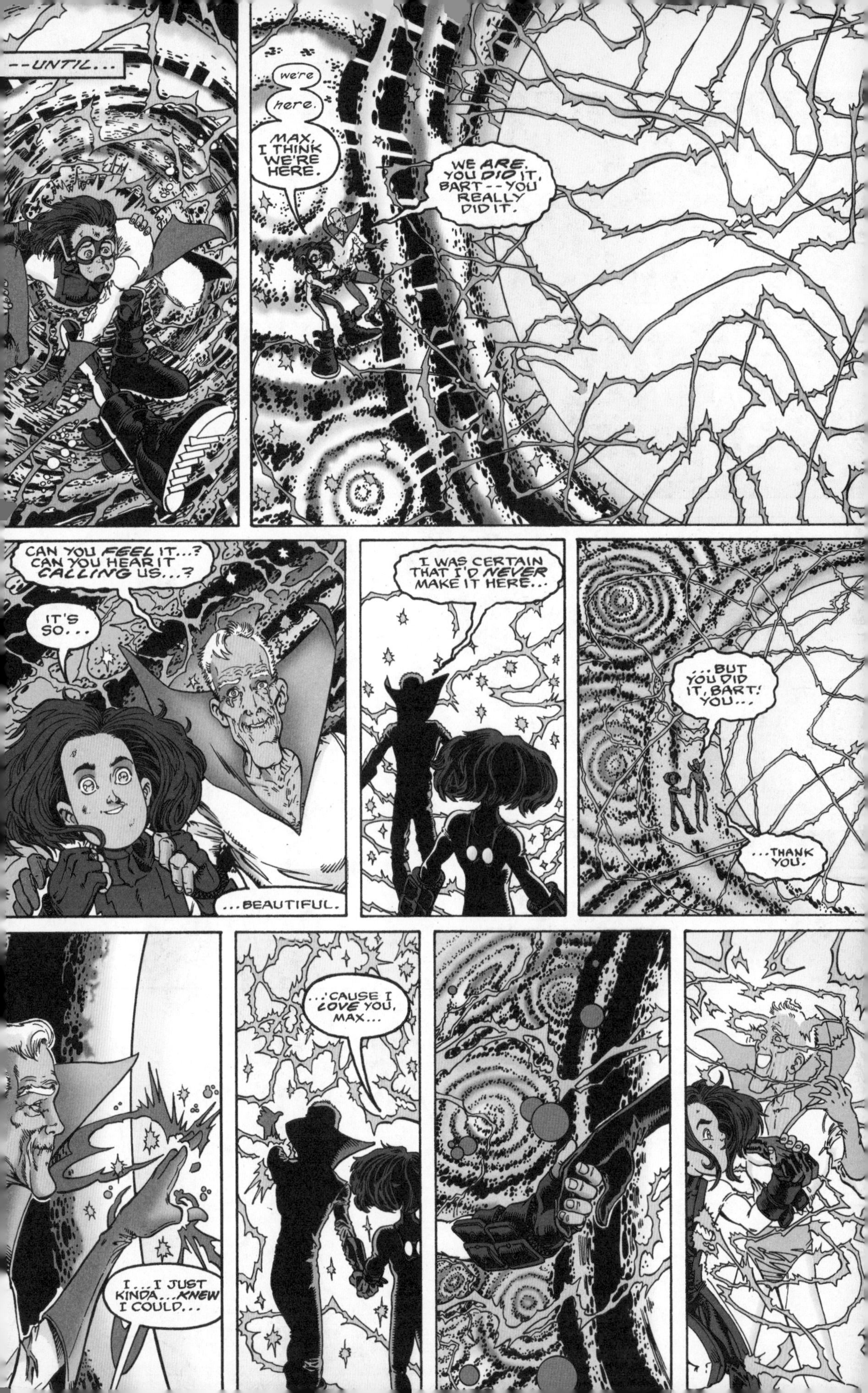
--UNTIL...
we're
here.
MAX, I THINK WE'RE HERE.
WE ARE. YOU DID IT, BART--YOU REALLY DID IT.
CAN YOU FEEL IT...? CAN YOU HEAR IT CALLING US...?
IT'S SO...
...BEAUTIFUL.
I WAS CERTAIN THAT I'D NEVER MAKE IT HERE...
...BUT YOU DID IT, BART! YOU...
...THANK YOU.
I...I JUST KINDA...KNEW I COULD...
...'CAUSE I LOVE YOU, MAX...

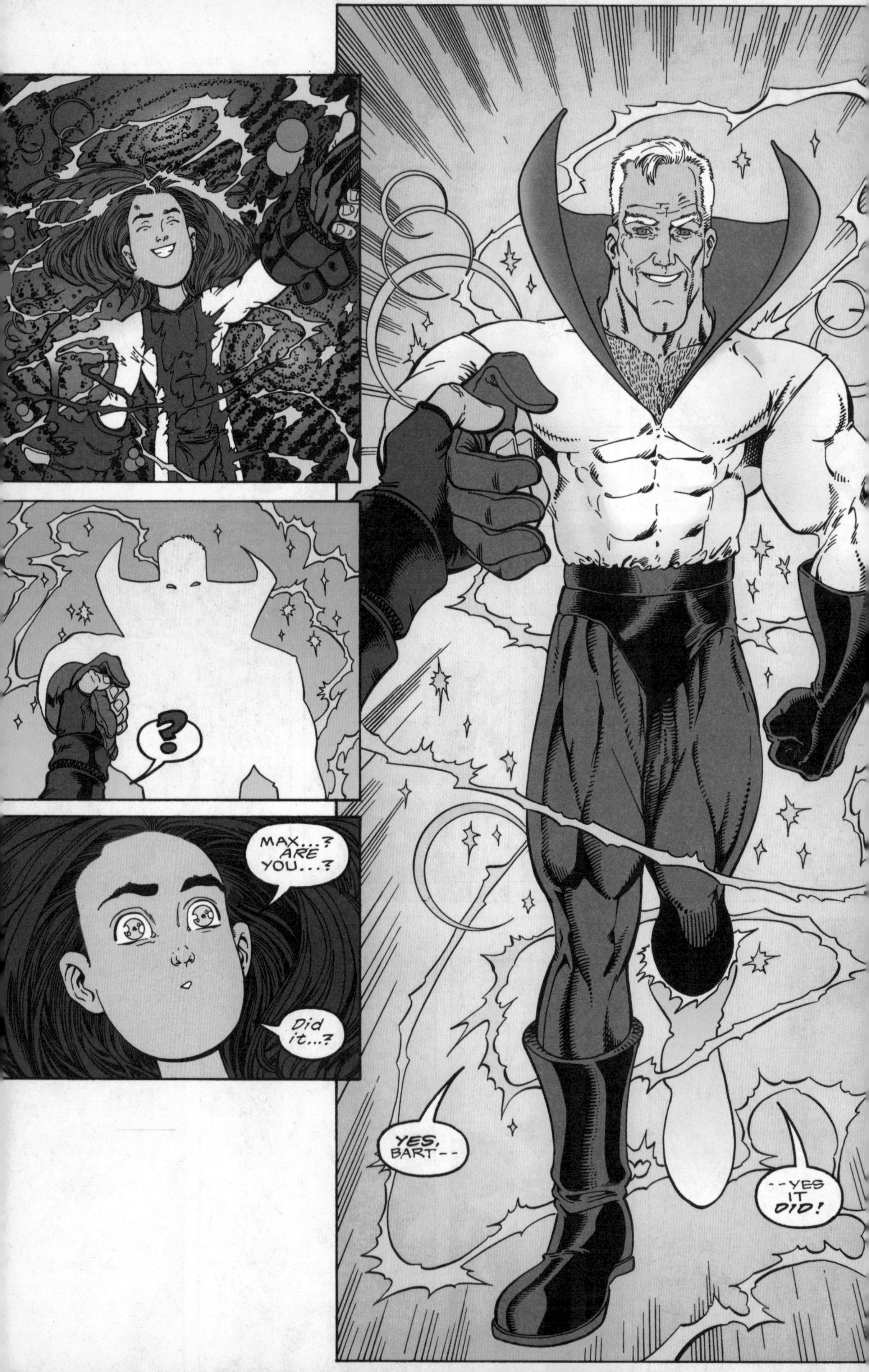
?
MAX...? ARE YOU...?
Did it...?
YES, BART--
--YES IT DID!

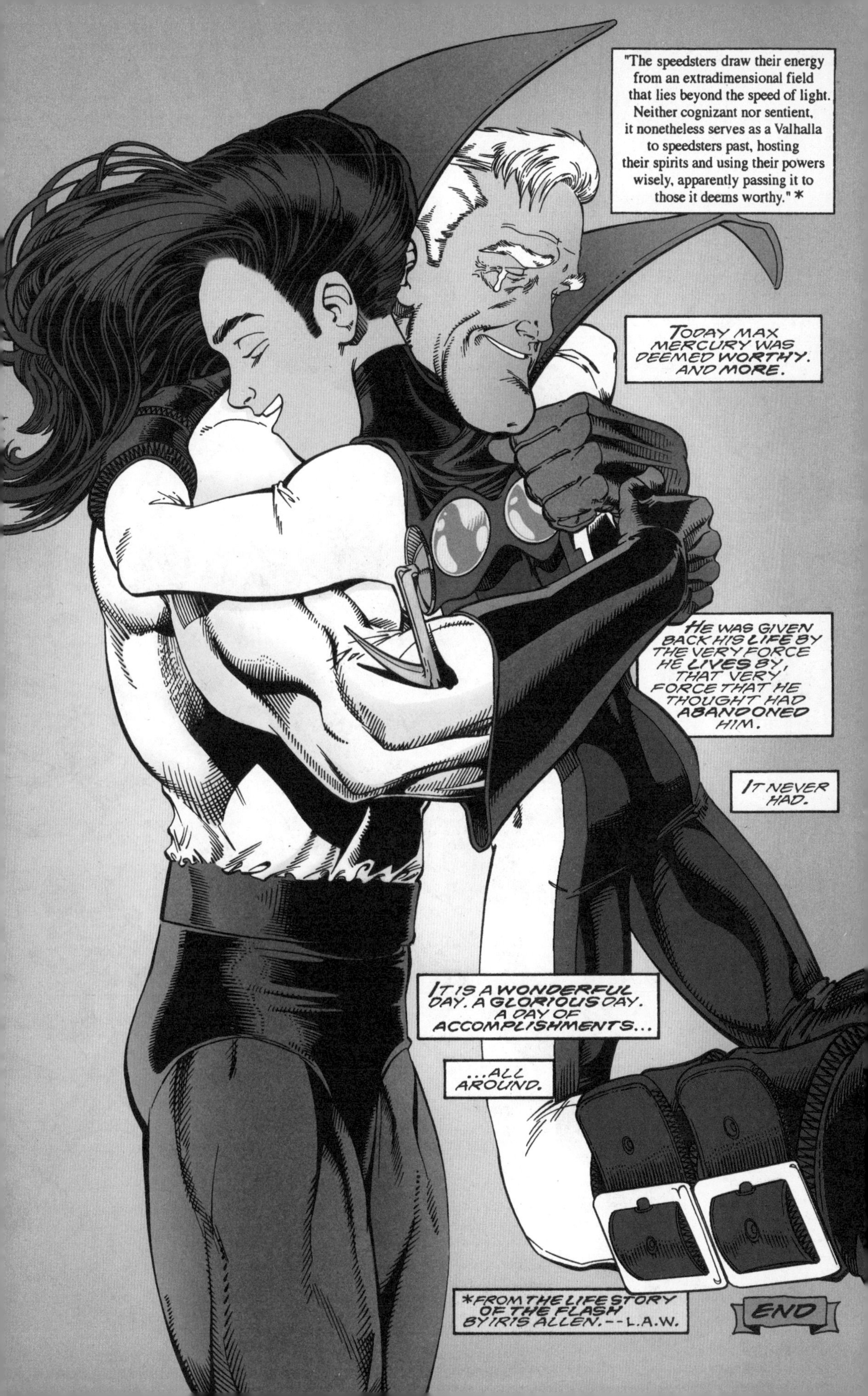
"The speedsters draw their energy from an extradimensional field that lies beyond the speed of light. Neither cognizant nor sentient, it nonetheless serves as a Valhalla to speedsters past, hosting their spirits and using their powers wisely, apparently passing it to those it deems worthy." *
TODAY MAX MERCURY WAS DEEMED WORTHY. AND MORE.
HE WAS GIVEN BACK HIS LIFE BY THE VERY FORCE HE LIVES BY, THAT VERY FORCE THAT HE THOUGHT HAD ABANDONED HIM.
IT NEVER HAD.
IT IS A WONDERFUL DAY. A GLORIOUS DAY. A DAY OF ACCOMPLISHMENTS...
...ALL AROUND.
*FROM THE LIFE STORY OF THE FLASH BY IRIS ALLEN. --L.A.W.
END

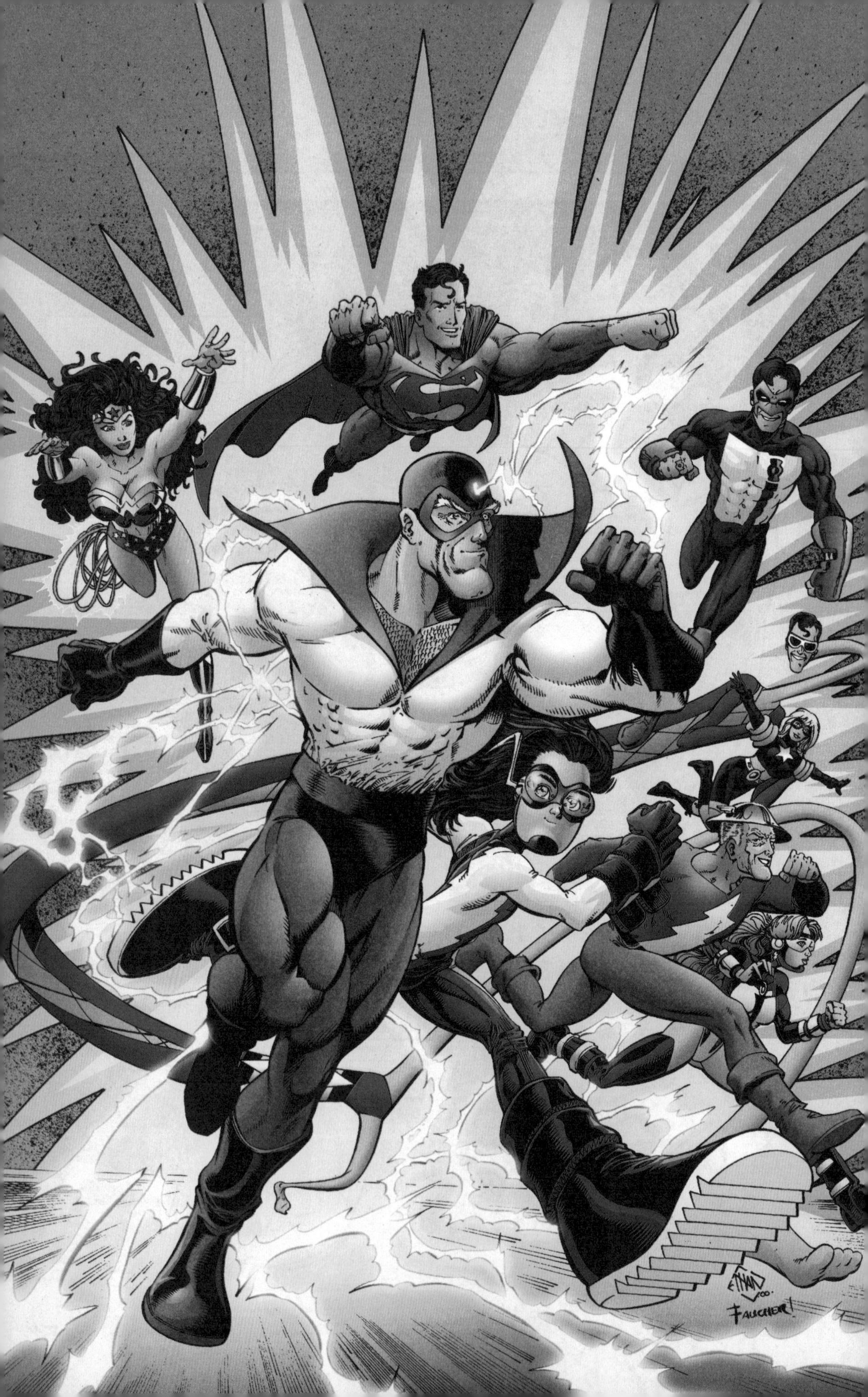
FAUCHER!

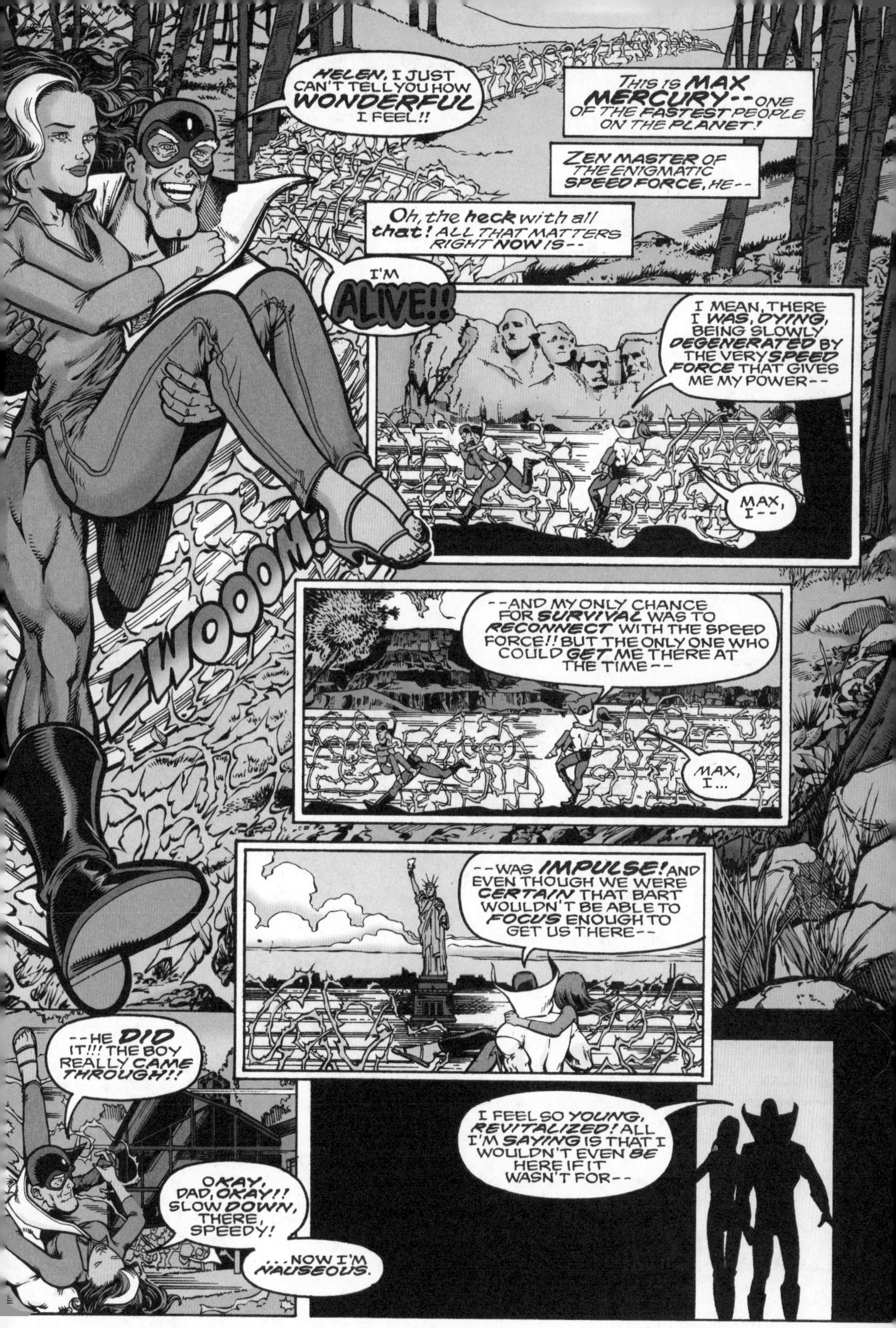
HELEN, I JUST CAN'T TELL YOU HOW WONDERFUL I FEEL!!
THIS IS MAX MERCURY--ONE OF THE FASTEST PEOPLE ON THE PLANET!
ZEN MASTER OF THE ENIGMATIC SPEED FORCE, HE--
Oh, the heck with all that! ALL THAT MATTERS RIGHT NOW IS--
I'M ALIVE!!
ZWOOOM!
I MEAN, THERE I WAS, DYING, BEING SLOWLY DEGENERATED BY THE VERY SPEED FORCE THAT GIVES ME MY POWER--
MAX, I--
--AND MY ONLY CHANCE FOR SURVIVAL WAS TO RECONNECT WITH THE SPEED FORCE!! BUT THE ONLY ONE WHO COULD GET ME THERE AT THE TIME--
MAX, I...
--WAS IMPULSE! AND EVEN THOUGH WE WERE CERTAIN THAT BART WOULDN'T BE ABLE TO FOCUS ENOUGH TO GET US THERE--
--HE DID IT!!! THE BOY REALLY CAME THROUGH!!
OKAY, DAD, OKAY!! SLOW DOWN, THERE, SPEEDY!
...NOW I'M NAUSEOUS.
I FEEL SO YOUNG, REVITALIZED! ALL I'M SAYING IS THAT I WOULDN'T EVEN BE HERE IF IT WASN'T FOR--

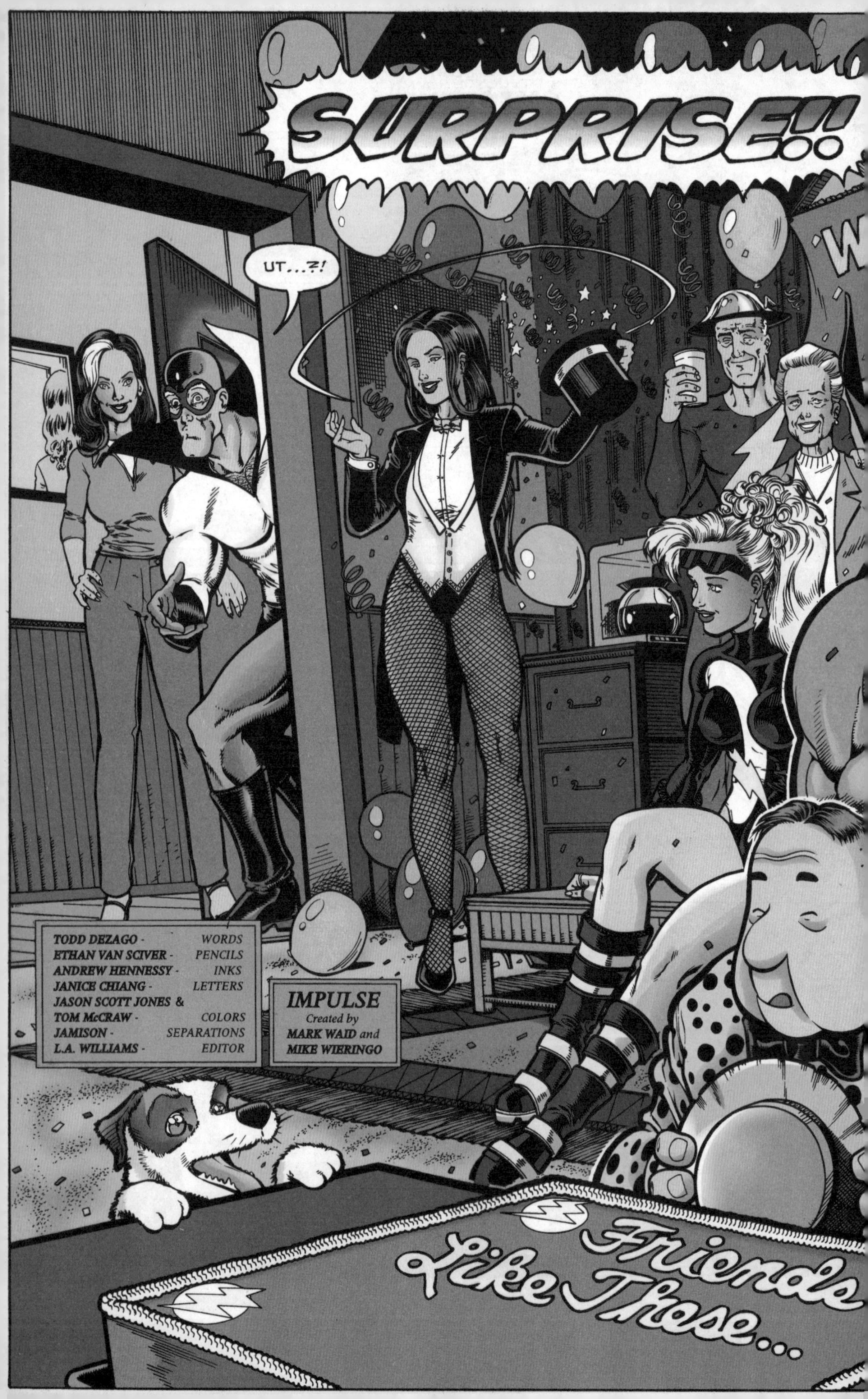
SURPRISE!!
UT...?!
'W
TODD DEZAGO - WORDS
ETHAN VAN SCIVER - PENCILS
ANDREW HENNESSY - INKS
JANICE CHIANG - LETTERS
JASON SCOTT JONES &
TOM McCRAW - COLORS
JAMISON - SEPARATIONS
L.A. WILLIAMS - EDITOR
IMPULSE
Created by
MARK WAID and
MIKE WIERINGO
Friends Like These...

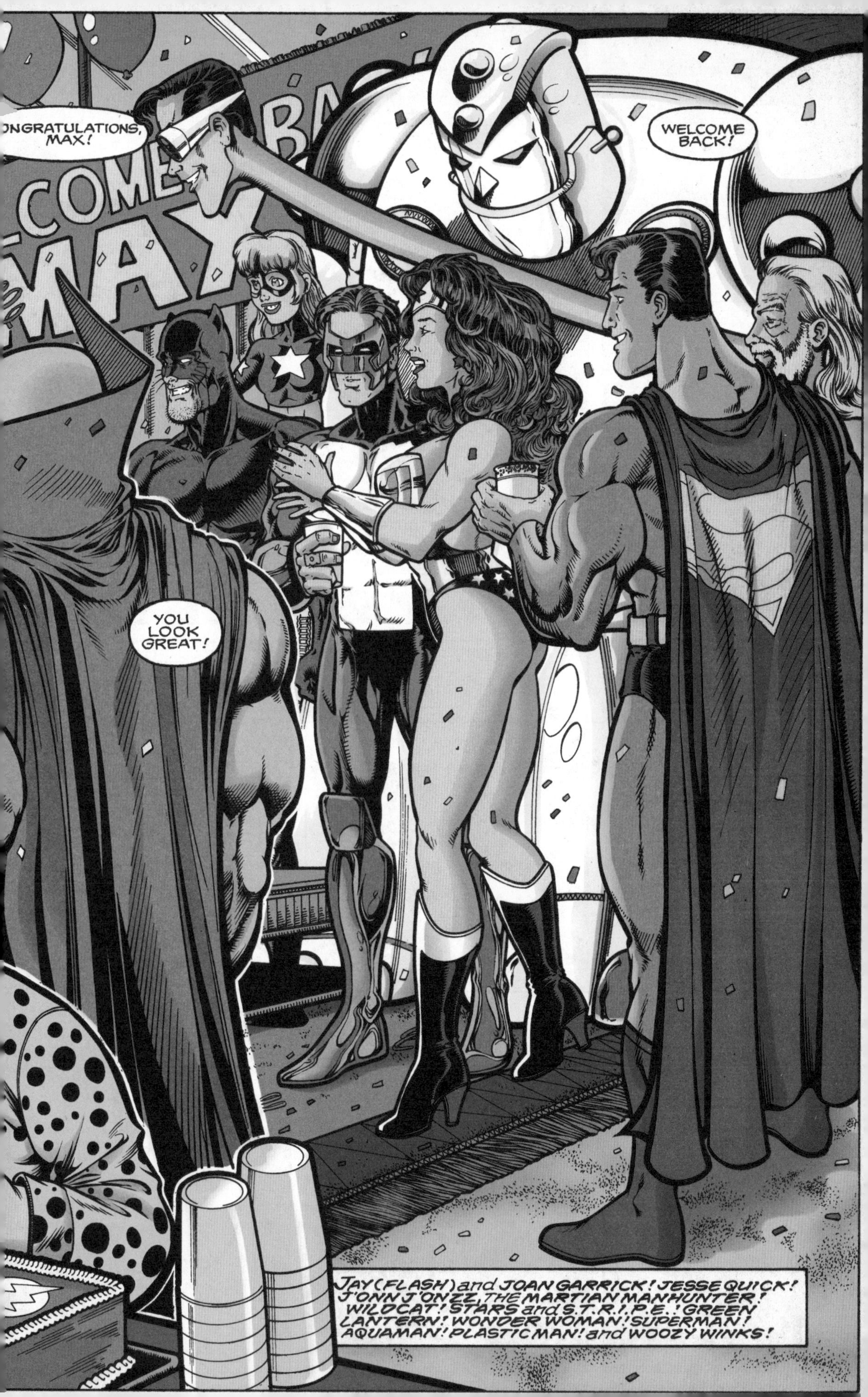
ONGRATULATIONS, MAX!
WELCOME BACK!
YOU LOOK GREAT!
JAY (FLASH) and JOAN GARRICK! JESSE QUICK! J'ONN J'ONZZ, THE MARTIAN MANHUNTER! WILDCAT! STARS and S.T.R.I.P.E.! GREEN LANTERN! WONDER WOMAN! SUPERMAN! AQUAMAN! PLASTIC MAN! and WOOZY WINKS!

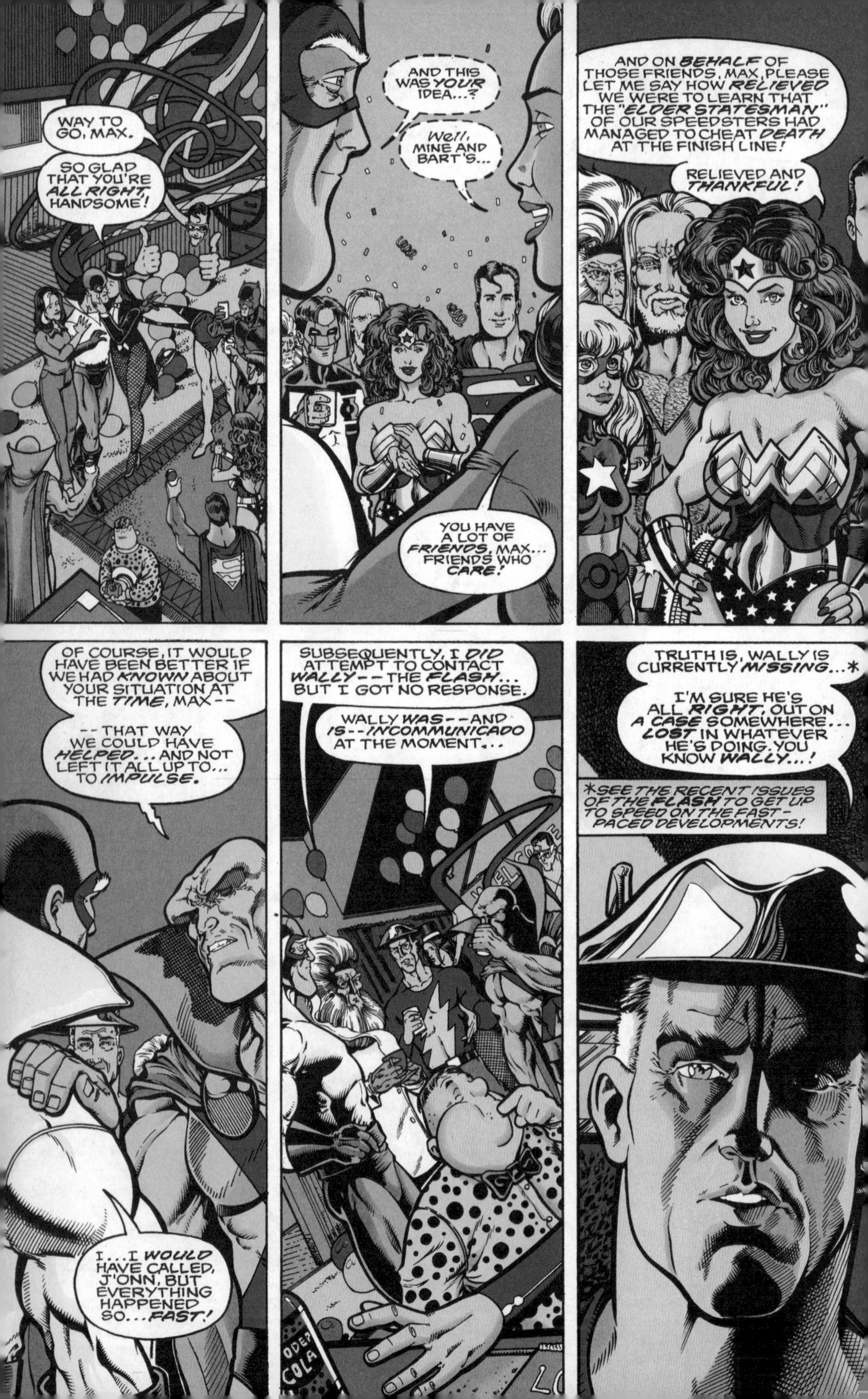
WAY TO GO, MAX.
SO GLAD THAT YOU'RE ALL RIGHT, HANDSOME!
AND THIS WAS YOUR IDEA...?
Well, MINE AND BART'S...
YOU HAVE A LOT OF FRIENDS, MAX... FRIENDS WHO CARE!
AND ON BEHALF OF THOSE FRIENDS, MAX, PLEASE LET ME SAY HOW RELIEVED WE WERE TO LEARN THAT THE "ELDER STATESMAN" OF OUR SPEEDSTERS HAD MANAGED TO CHEAT DEATH AT THE FINISH LINE!
RELIEVED AND THANKFUL!
OF COURSE, IT WOULD HAVE BEEN BETTER IF WE HAD KNOWN ABOUT YOUR SITUATION AT THE TIME, MAX--
--THAT WAY WE COULD HAVE HELPED... AND NOT LEFT IT ALL UP TO... TO IMPULSE.
I... I WOULD HAVE CALLED, J'ONN, BUT EVERYTHING HAPPENED SO... FAST!
SUBSEQUENTLY, I DID ATTEMPT TO CONTACT WALLY--THE FLASH... BUT I GOT NO RESPONSE.
WALLY WAS--AND IS--INCOMMUNICADO AT THE MOMENT...
TRUTH IS, WALLY IS CURRENTLY MISSING...*
I'M SURE HE'S ALL RIGHT, OUT ON A CASE SOMEWHERE... LOST IN WHATEVER HE'S DOING. YOU KNOW WALLY...!
*SEE THE RECENT ISSUES OF THE FLASH TO GET UP TO SPEED ON THE FAST-PACED DEVELOPMENTS!

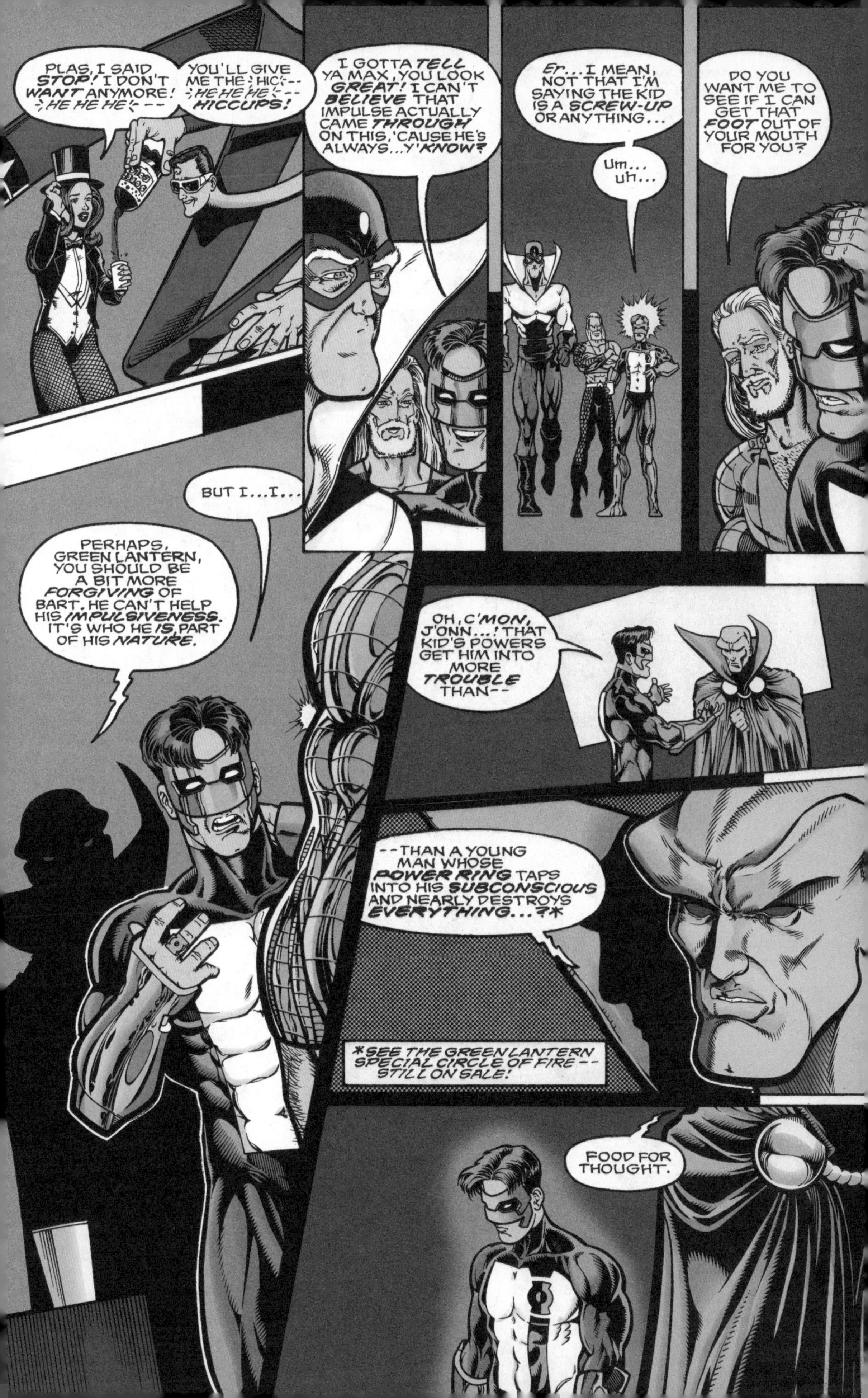

PLAS, I SAID STOP! I DON'T WANT ANYMORE! HE HE HE --
YOU'LL GIVE ME THE HIC-- HE HE HE -- HICCUPS!
I GOTTA TELL YA MAX, YOU LOOK GREAT! I CAN'T BELIEVE THAT IMPULSE ACTUALLY CAME THROUGH ON THIS, 'CAUSE HE'S ALWAYS... Y'KNOW?
Er... I MEAN, NOT THAT I'M SAYING THE KID IS A SCREW-UP OR ANYTHING...
Um... uh...
DO YOU WANT ME TO SEE IF I CAN GET THAT FOOT OUT OF YOUR MOUTH FOR YOU?
BUT I... I...
PERHAPS, GREEN LANTERN, YOU SHOULD BE A BIT MORE FORGIVING OF BART. HE CAN'T HELP HIS IMPULSIVENESS. IT'S WHO HE IS, PART OF HIS NATURE.
OH, C'MON, J'ONN...! THAT KID'S POWERS GET HIM INTO MORE TROUBLE THAN--
--THAN A YOUNG MAN WHOSE POWER RING TAPS INTO HIS SUBCONSCIOUS AND NEARLY DESTROYS EVERYTHING...?*
*SEE THE GREEN LANTERN SPECIAL CIRCLE OF FIRE -- STILL ON SALE!
FOOD FOR THOUGHT.

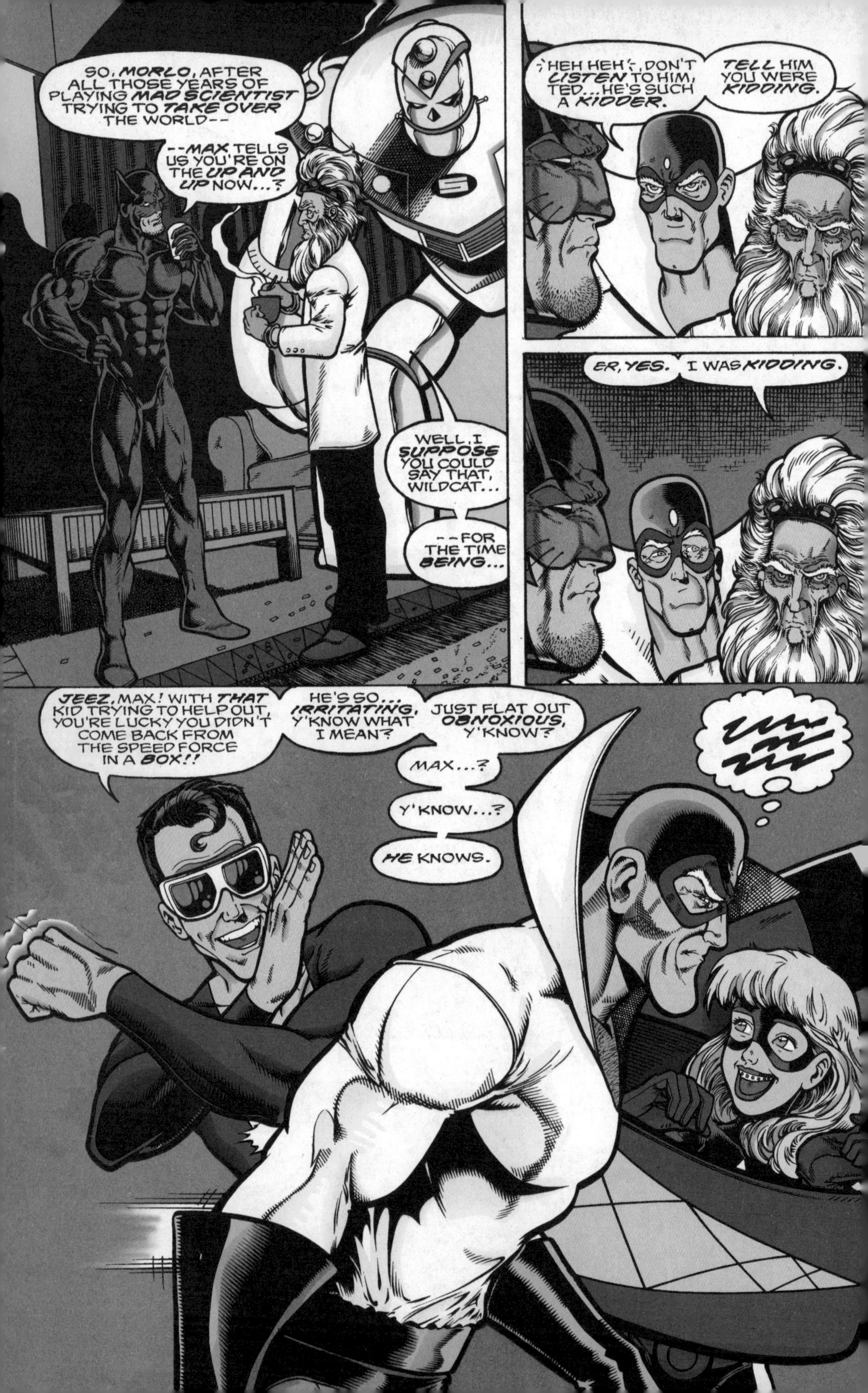
SO, MORLO, AFTER ALL THOSE YEARS OF PLAYING MAD SCIENTIST TRYING TO TAKE OVER THE WORLD--
--MAX TELLS US YOU'RE ON THE UP AND UP NOW...?
WELL, I SUPPOSE YOU COULD SAY THAT, WILDCAT...
--FOR THE TIME BEING...
HEH HEH --, DON'T LISTEN TO HIM, TED... HE'S SUCH A KIDDER.
TELL HIM YOU WERE KIDDING.
ER, YES.
I WAS KIDDING.
JEEZ, MAX! WITH THAT KID TRYING TO HELP OUT, YOU'RE LUCKY YOU DIDN'T COME BACK FROM THE SPEED FORCE IN A BOX!!
HE'S SO... IRRITATING, Y'KNOW WHAT I MEAN?
JUST FLAT OUT OBNOXIOUS, Y'KNOW?
MAX...?
Y'KNOW...?
HE KNOWS.

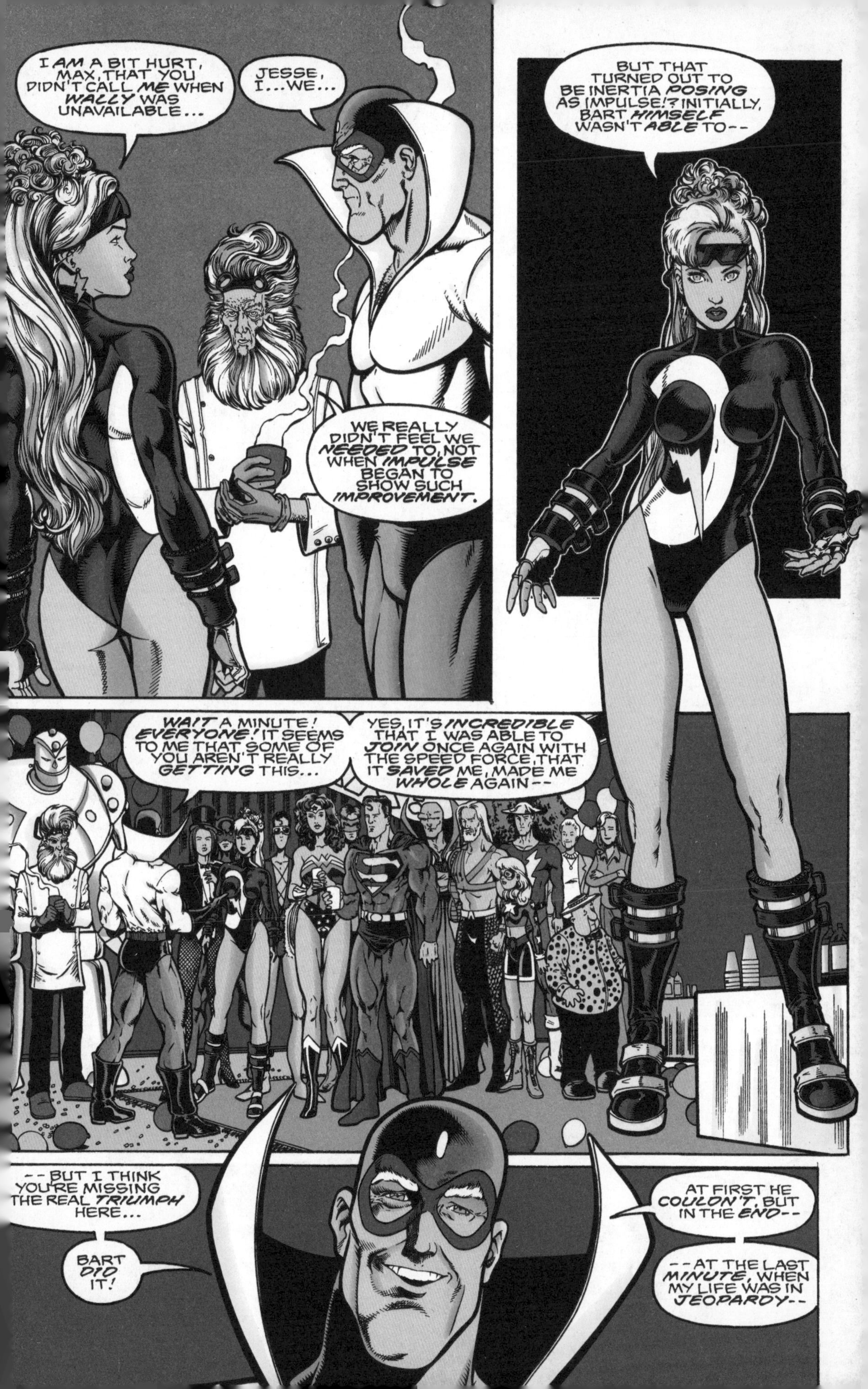
I AM A BIT HURT, MAX, THAT YOU DIDN'T CALL ME WHEN WALLY WAS UNAVAILABLE...
JESSE, I...WE...
WE REALLY DIDN'T FEEL WE NEEDED TO, NOT WHEN IMPULSE BEGAN TO SHOW SUCH IMPROVEMENT.
BUT THAT TURNED OUT TO BE INERTIA POSING AS IMPULSE!? INITIALLY, BART HIMSELF WASN'T ABLE TO--
WAIT A MINUTE! EVERYONE! IT SEEMS TO ME THAT SOME OF YOU AREN'T REALLY GETTING THIS...
YES, IT'S INCREDIBLE THAT I WAS ABLE TO JOIN ONCE AGAIN WITH THE SPEED FORCE, THAT IT SAVED ME, MADE ME WHOLE AGAIN--
--BUT I THINK YOU'RE MISSING THE REAL TRIUMPH HERE...
BART DID IT!
AT FIRST HE COULDN'T, BUT IN THE END--
--AT THE LAST MINUTE, WHEN MY LIFE WAS IN JEOPARDY--

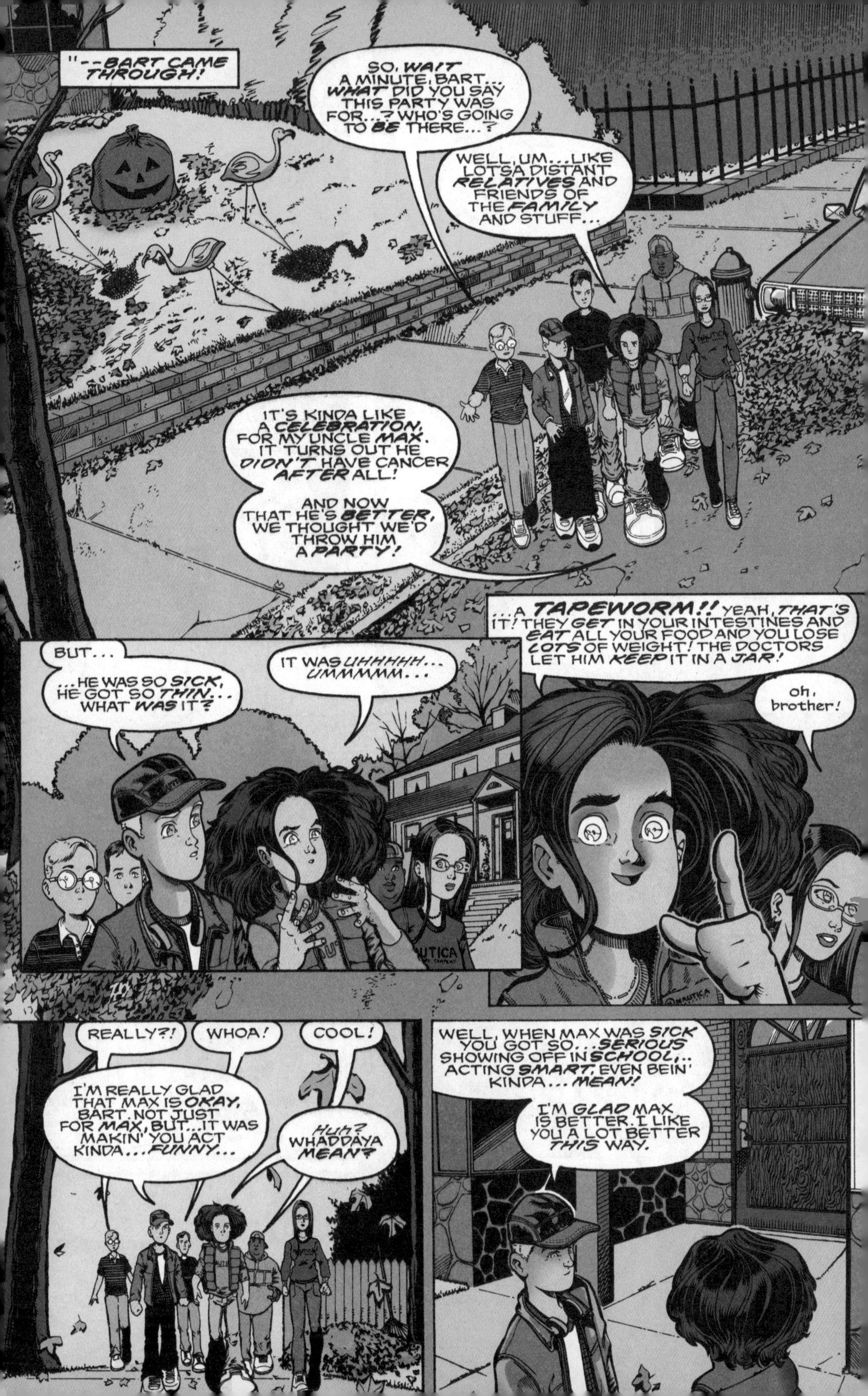
"--BART CAME THROUGH!
SO, WAIT A MINUTE, BART... WHAT DID YOU SAY THIS PARTY WAS FOR...? WHO'S GOING TO BE THERE...?
WELL, UM...LIKE LOTSA DISTANT RELATIVES AND FRIENDS OF THE FAMILY AND STUFF...
IT'S KINDA LIKE A CELEBRATION, FOR MY UNCLE MAX. IT TURNS OUT HE DIDN'T HAVE CANCER AFTER ALL!
AND NOW THAT HE'S BETTER, WE THOUGHT WE'D THROW HIM A PARTY!
BUT...
...HE WAS SO SICK, HE GOT SO THIN... WHAT WAS IT?
IT WAS UHHHHHH... UMMMMMM...
...A TAPEWORM!! YEAH, THAT'S IT! THEY GET IN YOUR INTESTINES AND EAT ALL YOUR FOOD AND YOU LOSE LOTS OF WEIGHT! THE DOCTORS LET HIM KEEP IT IN A JAR!
oh, brother!
REALLY?!
WHOA!
COOL!
I'M REALLY GLAD THAT MAX IS OKAY, BART. NOT JUST FOR MAX, BUT...IT WAS MAKIN' YOU ACT KINDA...FUNNY...
Huh? WHADDAYA MEAN?
WELL, WHEN MAX WAS SICK YOU GOT SO...SERIOUS SHOWING OFF IN SCHOOL,... ACTING SMART, EVEN BEIN' KINDA...MEAN!
I'M GLAD MAX IS BETTER. I LIKE YOU A LOT BETTER THIS WAY.

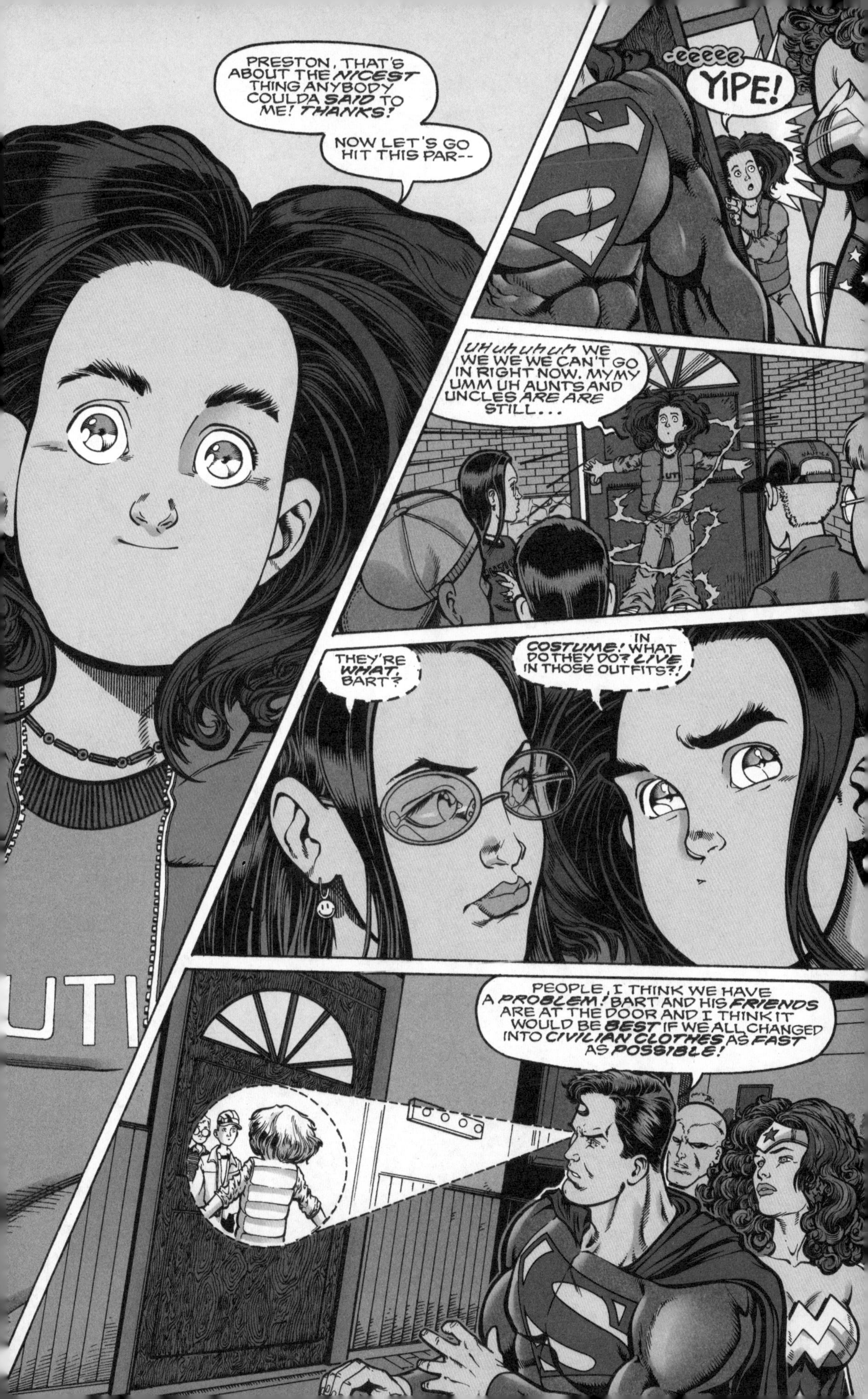
PRESTON, THAT'S ABOUT THE *NICEST* THING ANYBODY COULDA *SAID* TO ME! *THANKS!*
NOW LET'S GO HIT THIS PAR--
-EEEEE YIPE!
*UH UH UH UH* WE WE WE WE CAN'T GO IN RIGHT NOW. MY MY UMM UH AUNTS AND UNCLES *ARE ARE* STILL...
THEY'RE *WHAT*, BART?
IN *COSTUME!* WHAT DO THEY DO? *LIVE* IN THOSE OUTFITS?!
PEOPLE, I THINK WE HAVE A *PROBLEM!* BART AND HIS *FRIENDS* ARE AT THE DOOR AND I THINK IT WOULD BE *BEST* IF WE ALL CHANGED INTO *CIVILIAN CLOTHES* AS *FAST* AS *POSSIBLE!*

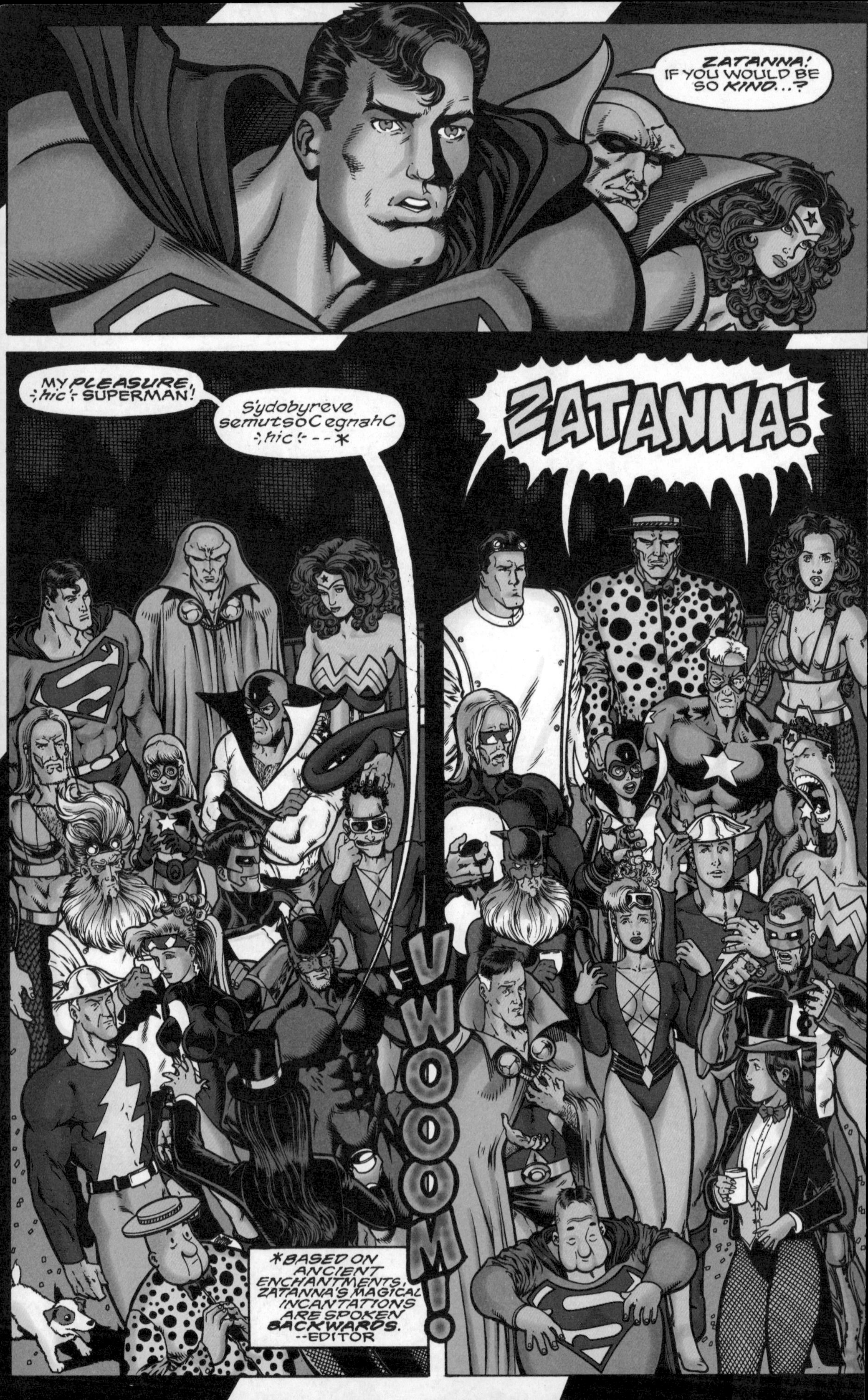
ZATANNA! IF YOU WOULD BE SO KIND...?
MY PLEASURE, -hic- SUPERMAN!
S'ydobyreve semutsoC egnahC -hic- --*
ZATANNA!
VWOOOM!
*BASED ON ANCIENT ENCHANTMENTS, ZATANNA'S MAGICAL INCANTATIONS ARE SPOKEN BACKWARDS. --EDITOR

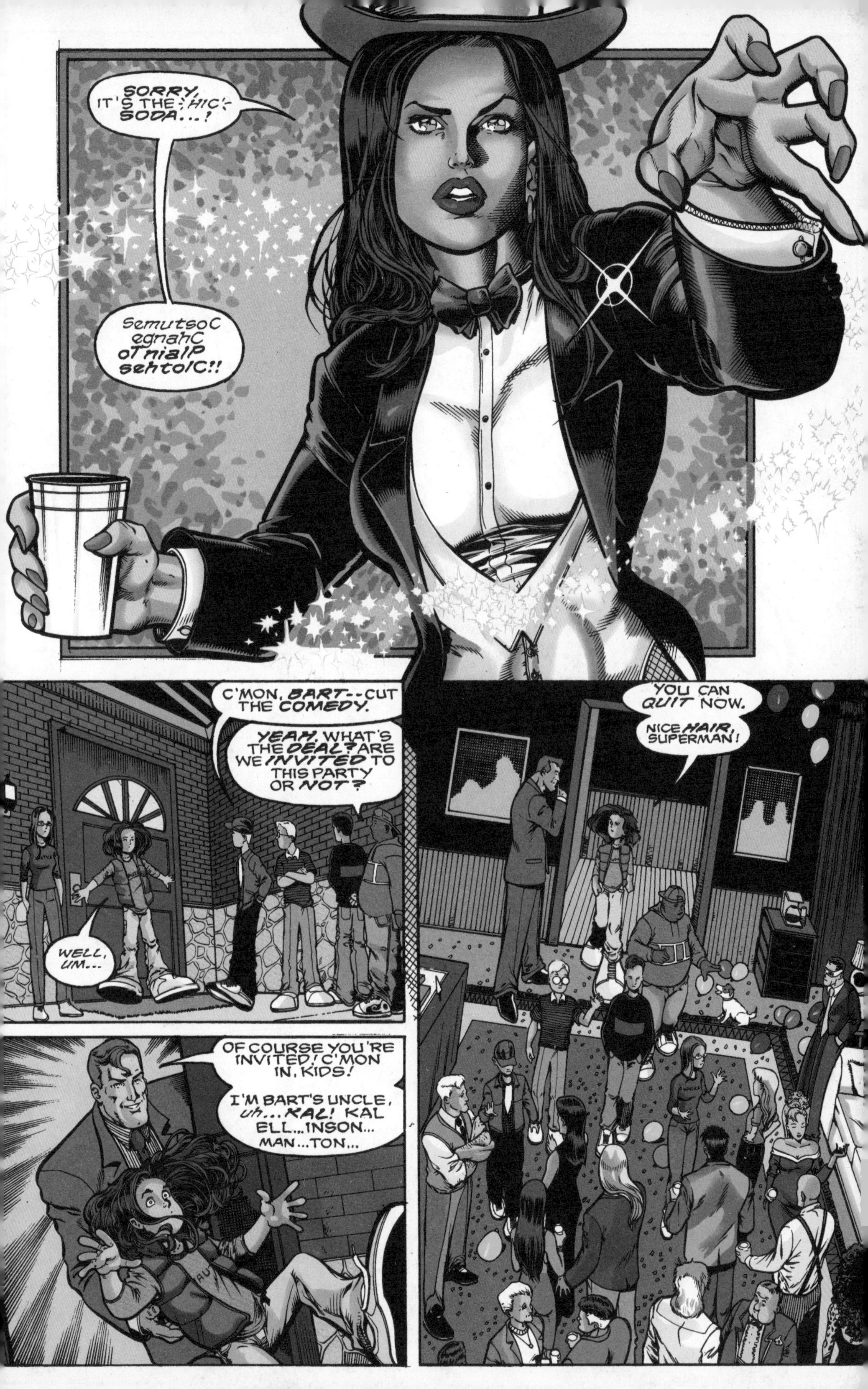
SORRY, IT'S THE -HIC- SODA...!
SemutsoC egnahC oTnialP sehtolC!!
C'MON, BART--CUT THE COMEDY.
YEAH, WHAT'S THE DEAL? ARE WE INVITED TO THIS PARTY OR NOT?
WELL, UM...
YOU CAN QUIT NOW.
NICE HAIR, SUPERMAN!
OF COURSE YOU'RE INVITED! C'MON IN, KIDS!
I'M BART'S UNCLE, uh...KAL! KAL ELL...INSON... MAN...TON...

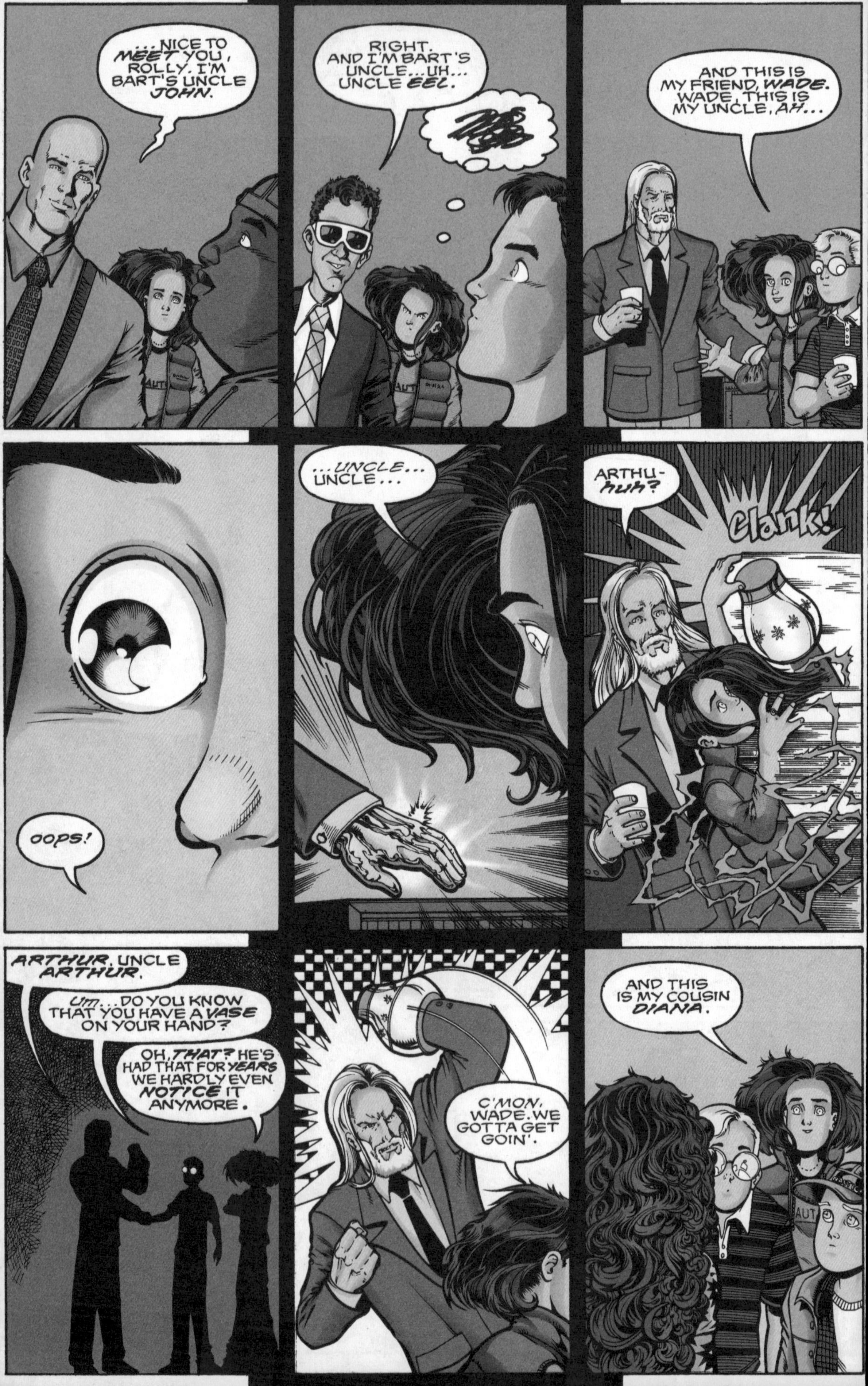
...NICE TO MEET YOU, ROLLY. I'M BART'S UNCLE JOHN.
RIGHT. AND I'M BART'S UNCLE... UH... UNCLE EEL.
AND THIS IS MY FRIEND, WADE. WADE, THIS IS MY UNCLE, AH...
OOPS!
...UNCLE... UNCLE...
ARTHU-huh?
Clank!
ARTHUR. UNCLE ARTHUR.
Um... DO YOU KNOW THAT YOU HAVE A VASE ON YOUR HAND?
OH, THAT? HE'S HAD THAT FOR YEARS WE HARDLY EVEN NOTICE IT ANYMORE.
C'MON, WADE. WE GOTTA GET GOIN'.
AND THIS IS MY COUSIN DIANA.

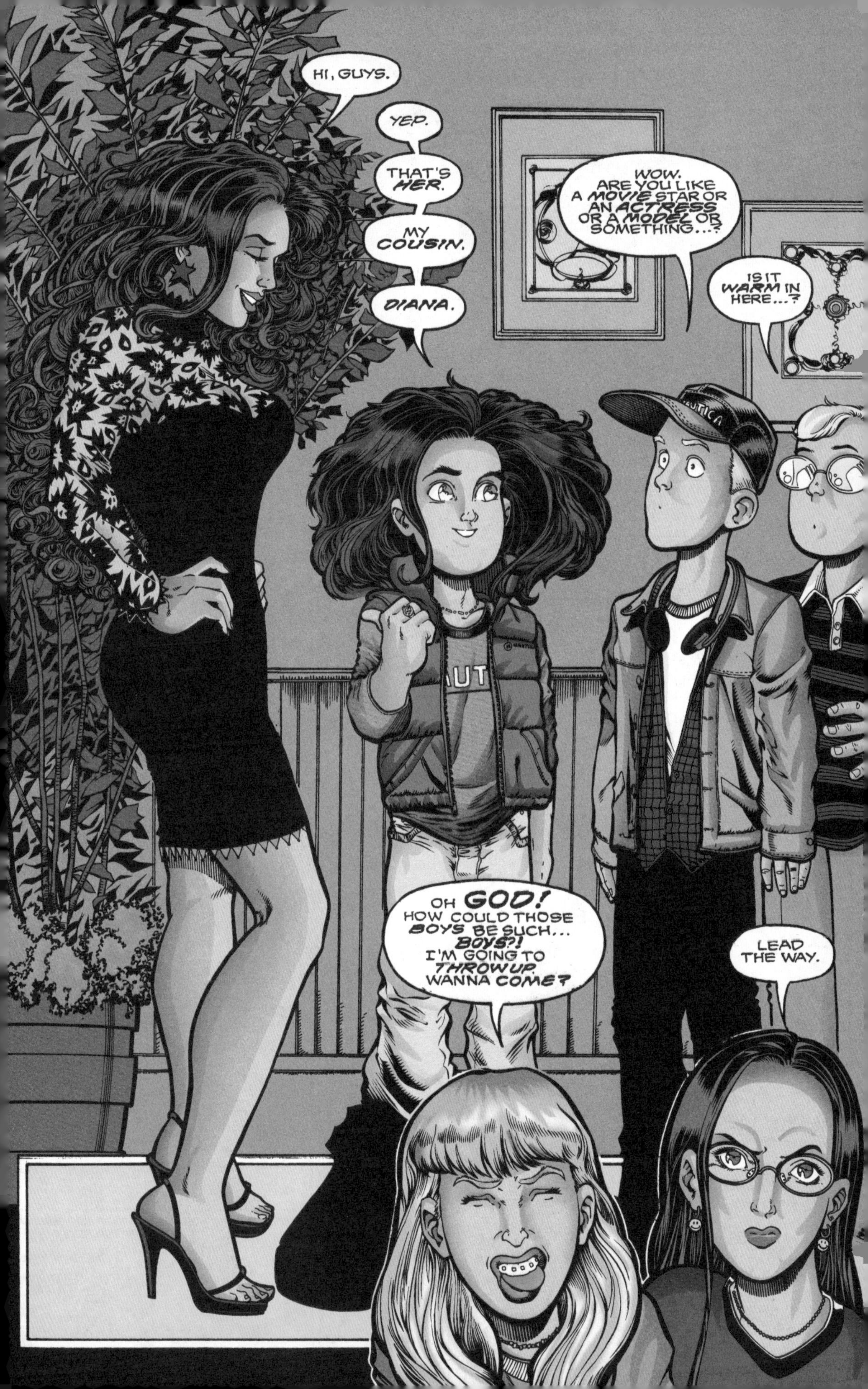
HI, GUYS.
YEP.
THAT'S HER.
MY COUSIN.
DIANA.
WOW. ARE YOU LIKE A MOVIE STAR OR AN ACTRESS OR A MODEL OR SOMETHING...?
IS IT WARM IN HERE...?
OH GOD! HOW COULD THOSE BOYS BE SUCH... BOYS?! I'M GOING TO THROW UP. WANNA COME?
LEAD THE WAY.

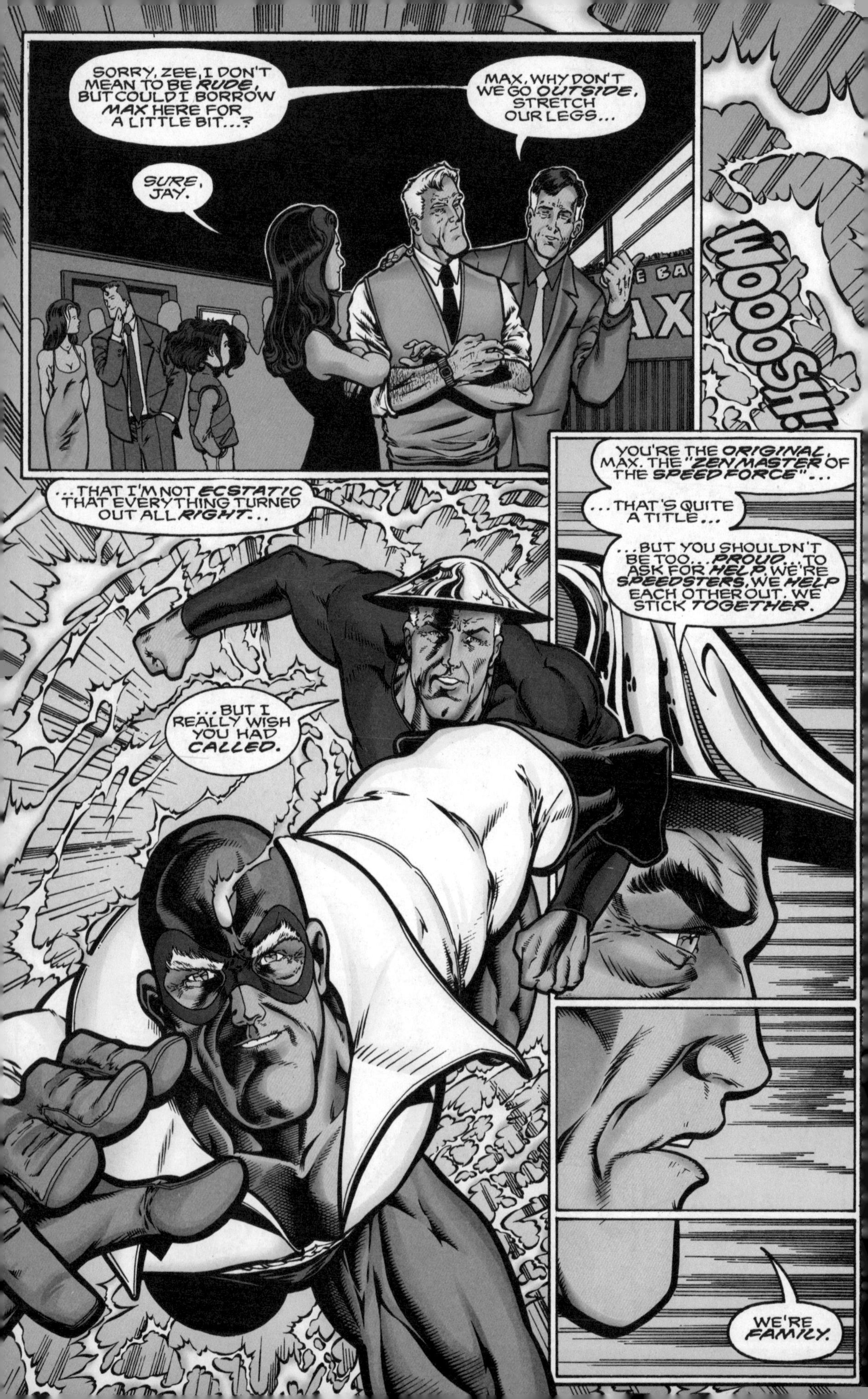
SORRY, ZEE, I DON'T MEAN TO BE RUDE, BUT COULD I BORROW MAX HERE FOR A LITTLE BIT...?
MAX, WHY DON'T WE GO OUTSIDE, STRETCH OUR LEGS...
SURE, JAY.
WOOOSH!
YOU'RE THE ORIGINAL, MAX. THE "ZEN MASTER OF THE SPEED FORCE"...
...THAT'S QUITE A TITLE...
...BUT YOU SHOULDN'T BE TOO... PROUD... TO ASK FOR HELP. WE'RE SPEEDSTERS. WE HELP EACH OTHER OUT. WE STICK TOGETHER.
...THAT I'M NOT ECSTATIC THAT EVERYTHING TURNED OUT ALL RIGHT...
...BUT I REALLY WISH YOU HAD CALLED.
WE'RE FAMILY.

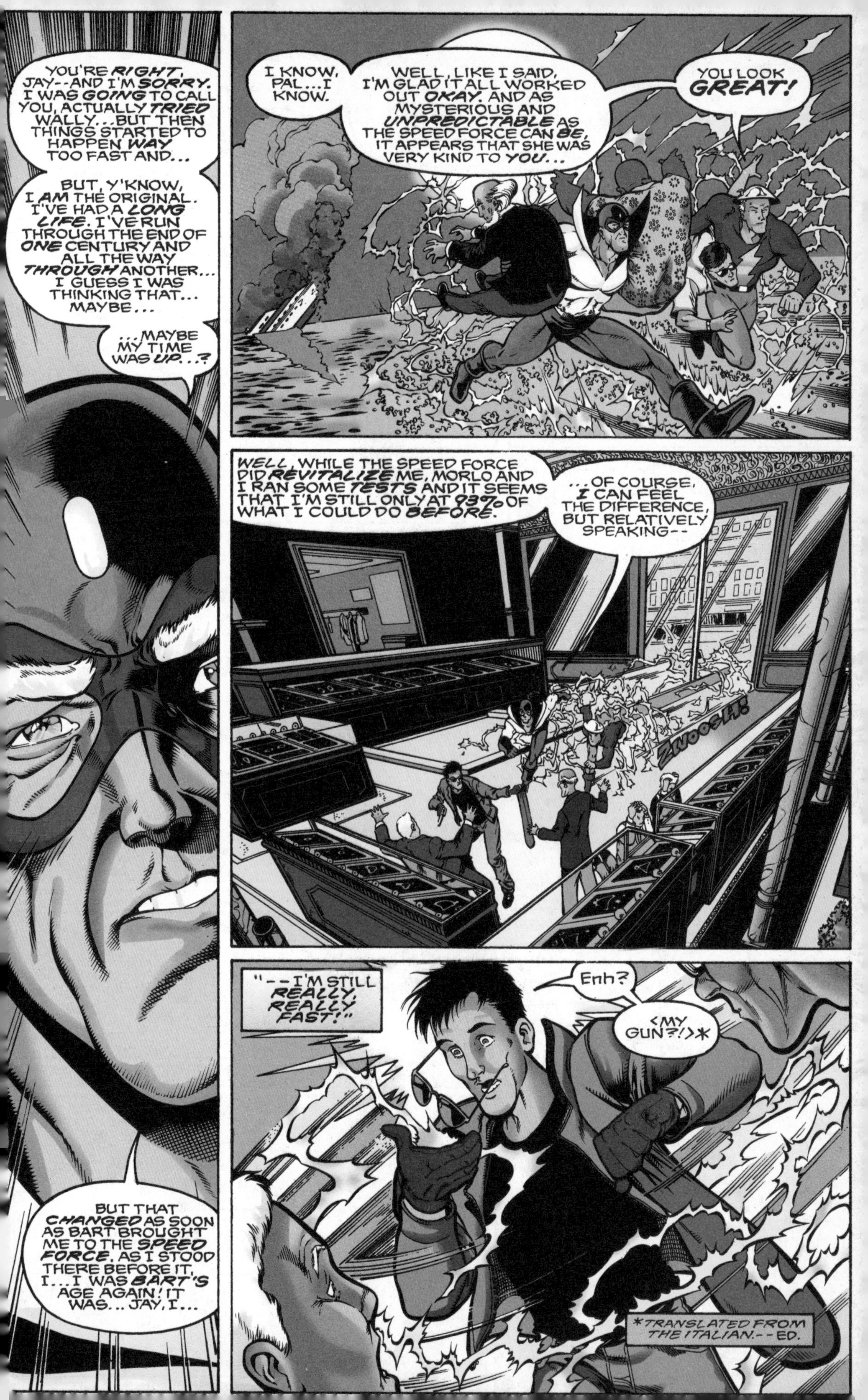

YOU'RE RIGHT, JAY--AND I'M SORRY. I WAS GOING TO CALL YOU, ACTUALLY TRIED WALLY... BUT THEN THINGS STARTED TO HAPPEN WAY TOO FAST AND...
BUT, Y'KNOW, I AM THE ORIGINAL. I'VE HAD A LONG LIFE. I'VE RUN THROUGH THE END OF ONE CENTURY AND ALL THE WAY THROUGH ANOTHER... I GUESS I WAS THINKING THAT... MAYBE...
...MAYBE MY TIME WAS UP...?
BUT THAT CHANGED AS SOON AS BART BROUGHT ME TO THE SPEED FORCE. AS I STOOD THERE BEFORE IT, I...I WAS BART'S AGE AGAIN! IT WAS... JAY, I...
I KNOW, PAL...I KNOW.
WELL, LIKE I SAID, I'M GLAD IT ALL WORKED OUT OKAY. AND AS MYSTERIOUS AND UNPREDICTABLE AS THE SPEED FORCE CAN BE, IT APPEARS THAT SHE WAS VERY KIND TO YOU...
YOU LOOK GREAT!
WELL, WHILE THE SPEED FORCE DID REVITALIZE ME, MORLO AND I RAN SOME TESTS AND IT SEEMS THAT I'M STILL ONLY AT 93% OF WHAT I COULD DO BEFORE.
...OF COURSE, I CAN FEEL THE DIFFERENCE, BUT RELATIVELY SPEAKING--
ZNOOSH!
"--I'M STILL REALLY, REALLY FAST!"
Enh?
<MY GUN?!>*
*TRANSLATED FROM THE ITALIAN.--ED.

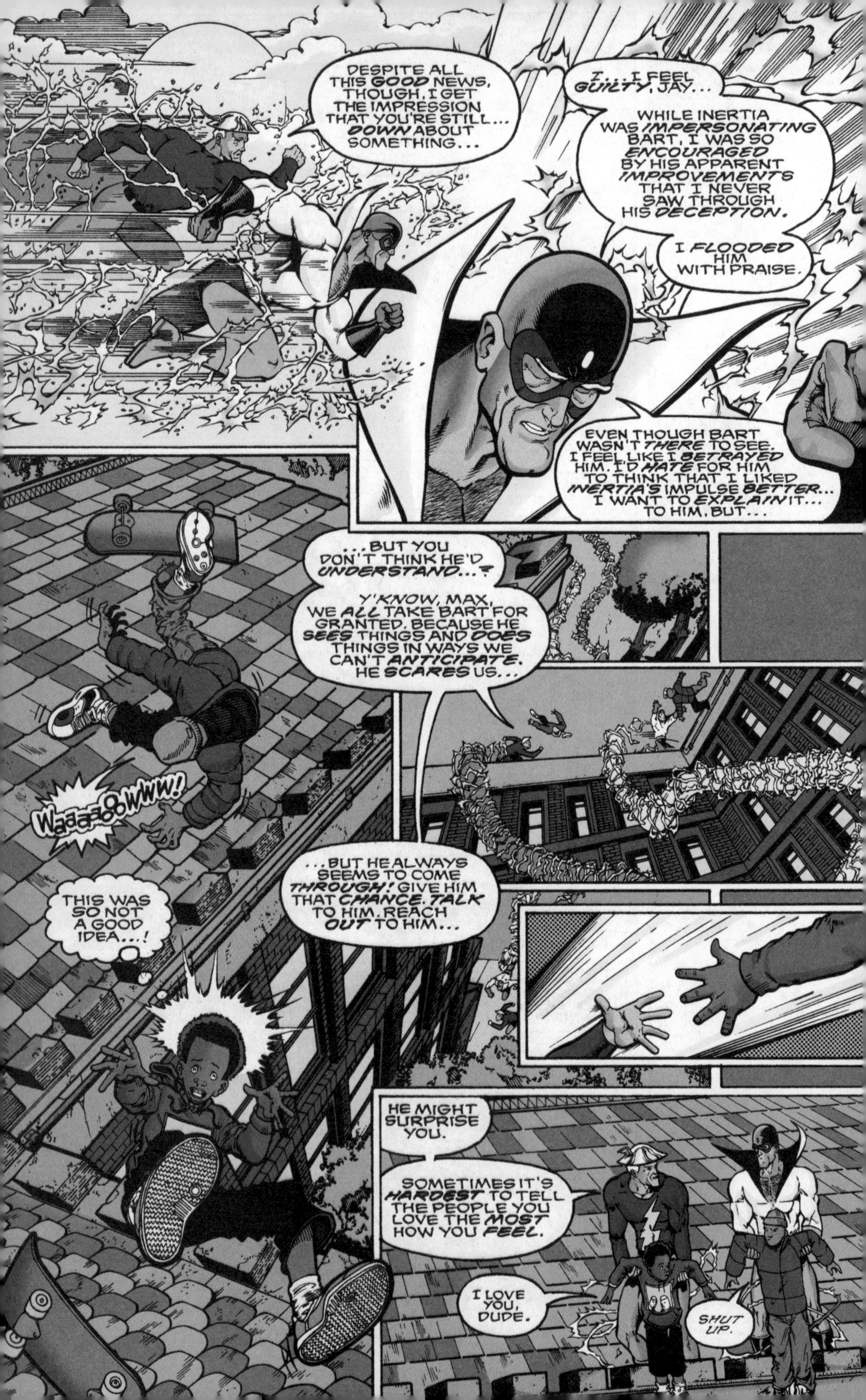
DESPITE ALL THIS GOOD NEWS, THOUGH, I GET THE IMPRESSION THAT YOU'RE STILL... DOWN ABOUT SOMETHING...
I... I FEEL GUILTY, JAY...
WHILE INERTIA WAS IMPERSONATING BART, I WAS SO ENCOURAGED BY HIS APPARENT IMPROVEMENTS THAT I NEVER SAW THROUGH HIS DECEPTION.
I FLOODED HIM WITH PRAISE.
EVEN THOUGH BART WASN'T THERE TO SEE. I FEEL LIKE I BETRAYED HIM. I'D HATE FOR HIM TO THINK THAT I LIKED INERTIA'S IMPULSE BETTER... I WANT TO EXPLAIN IT... TO HIM, BUT...
...BUT YOU DON'T THINK HE'D UNDERSTAND...?
Y'KNOW, MAX, WE ALL TAKE BART FOR GRANTED, BECAUSE HE SEES THINGS AND DOES THINGS IN WAYS WE CAN'T ANTICIPATE. HE SCARES US...
WAAAAOOOWWW!
...BUT HE ALWAYS SEEMS TO COME THROUGH! GIVE HIM THAT CHANCE. TALK TO HIM. REACH OUT TO HIM...
THIS WAS SO NOT A GOOD IDEA...!
HE MIGHT SURPRISE YOU.
SOMETIMES IT'S HARDEST TO TELL THE PEOPLE YOU LOVE THE MOST HOW YOU FEEL.
I LOVE YOU, DUDE.
SHUT UP.

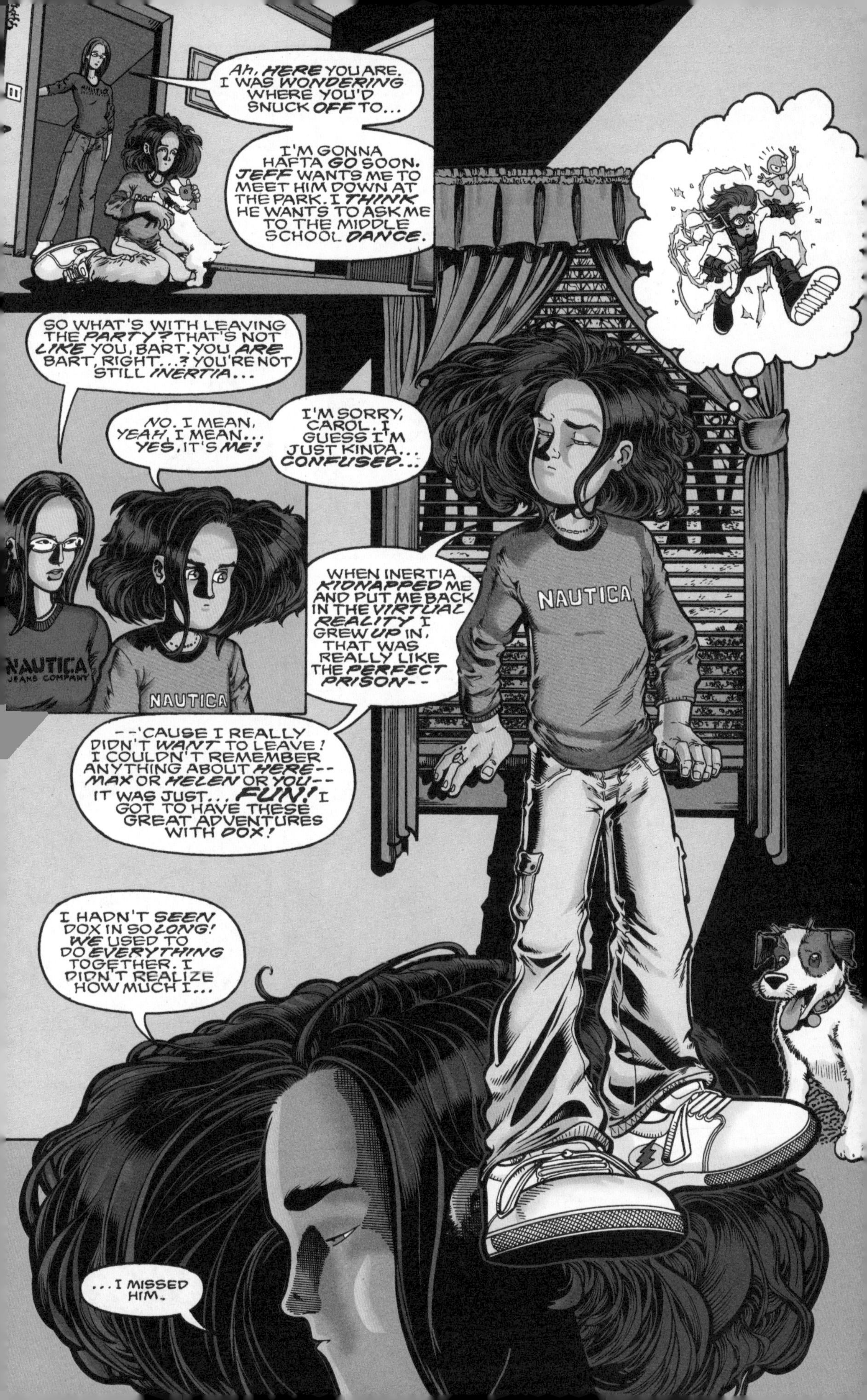

Ah, HERE YOU ARE. I WAS WONDERING WHERE YOU'D SNUCK OFF TO...
I'M GONNA HAFTA GO SOON. JEFF WANTS ME TO MEET HIM DOWN AT THE PARK. I THINK HE WANTS TO ASK ME TO THE MIDDLE SCHOOL DANCE.
SO WHAT'S WITH LEAVING THE PARTY? THAT'S NOT LIKE YOU, BART. YOU ARE BART, RIGHT...? YOU'RE NOT STILL INERTIA...
NO. I MEAN, YEAH, I MEAN... YES, IT'S ME!
I'M SORRY, CAROL. I GUESS I'M JUST KINDA... CONFUSED...
NAUTICA JEANS COMPANY
NAUTICA
WHEN INERTIA KIDNAPPED ME AND PUT ME BACK IN THE VIRTUAL REALITY I GREW UP IN, THAT WAS REALLY LIKE THE PERFECT PRISON--
NAUTICA
--'CAUSE I REALLY DIDN'T WANT TO LEAVE! I COULDN'T REMEMBER ANYTHING ABOUT HERE--MAX OR HELEN OR YOU--IT WAS JUST... FUN! I GOT TO HAVE THESE GREAT ADVENTURES WITH DOX!
I HADN'T SEEN DOX IN SO LONG! WE USED TO DO EVERYTHING TOGETHER. I DIDN'T REALIZE HOW MUCH I...
...I MISSED HIM.

BUT WHILE I WAS IN *THERE*, *INERTIA* WAS OUT *HERE*! TAKING OVER MY *LIFE*. HE WAS DOING EVERYTHING *RIGHT*. EVERYTHING *BETTER*. EVERYBODY *LIKED* HIM...

everybody loved him... maybe... better...

NO, BART. THAT'S NOT *TRUE*-- AND IT'S NOT *FAIR*. I DIDN'T. *WE* DIDN'T.

NO, *YOU* DIDN'T. BUT IT SURE SEEMED LIKE EVERYBODY *ELSE* DID. HE WAS BETTER AT BEING A HERO, AT FOLLOWING DIRECTIONS...

I JUST KINDA FEEL LIKE HE WAS A BETTER *ME* THAN I AM...

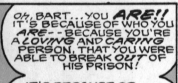

OH, BART... YOU *ARE*!! IT'S BECAUSE OF WHO YOU *ARE*-- BECAUSE YOU'RE A *LOVING* AND *CARING* PERSON, THAT YOU WERE ABLE TO BREAK *OUT* OF HIS PRISON!

IT'S BECAUSE OF YOUR *FEELINGS* FOR MAX THAT YOU WERE ABLE TO GO TO THE *SPEED FORCE* AND *SAVE* HIM.

*INERTIA* COULD NEVER DO THAT.

BESIDES, DIDN'T YOU HEAR PRESTON BEFORE...? THAT OTHER BART WASN'T ANYTHING LIKE YOU. HE WAS MEAN AND STUCK UP.

...AND NOT NEAR AS CUTE...

YEAH, BUT COMPARED TO THE *INERTIA* IMPULSE, AND ALL THE THINGS HE WAS ABLE TO *DO*...

I'M... WELL, I'M KINDA THINKIN' THAT MAYBE MAX MIGHT BE *DISAPPOINTED* IN ME...?

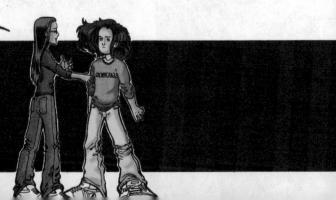

WELL, IF IT'S SOMETHING THAT'S *BOTHERING* YOU, MAYBE YOU SHOULD JUST TALK TO *MAX* ABOUT IT...

NOW, C'MON, SPEEDY, I'VE GOTTA *GO*. WALK ME TO THE DOOR.

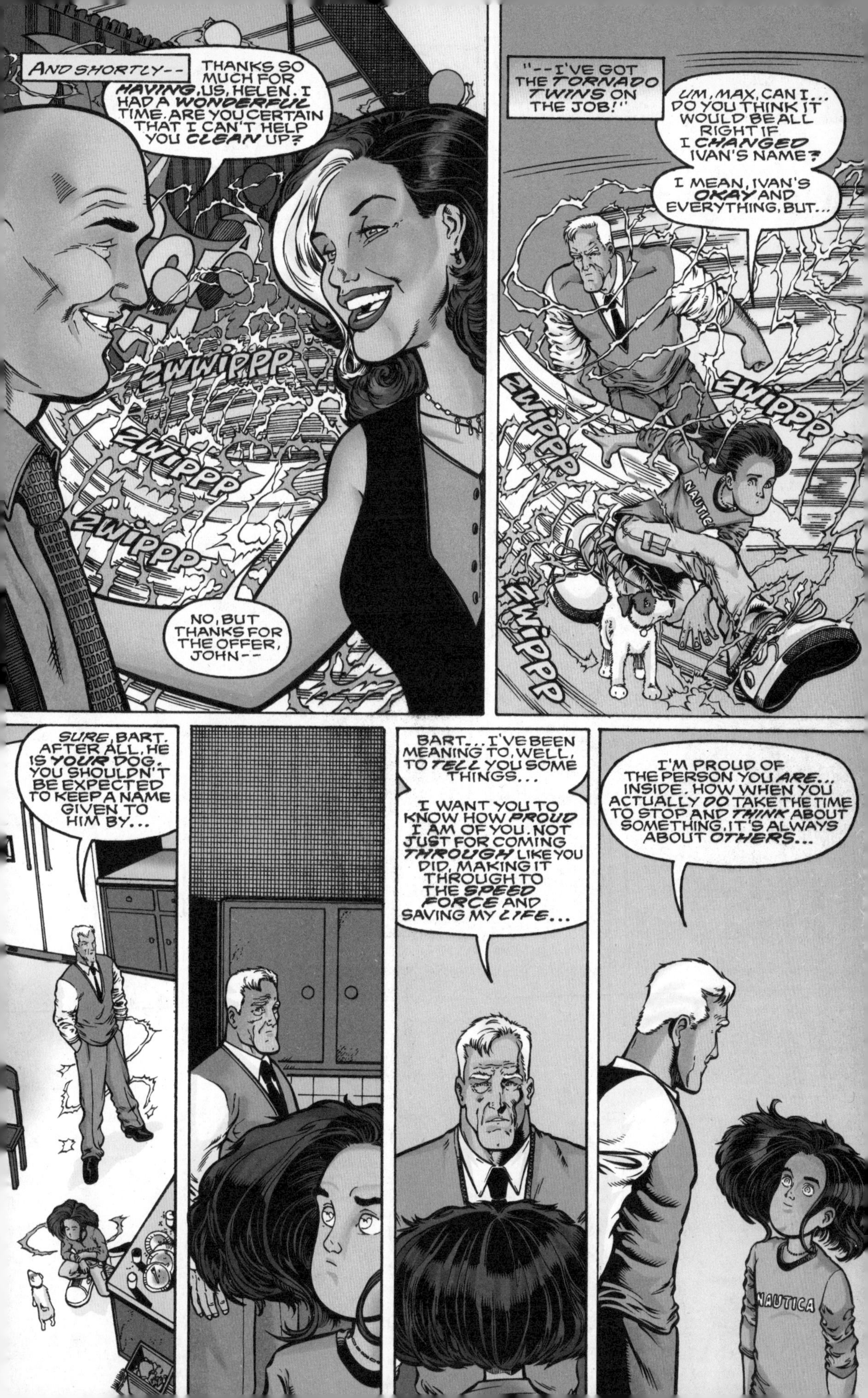
AND SHORTLY--
THANKS SO MUCH FOR HAVING US, HELEN. I HAD A WONDERFUL TIME. ARE YOU CERTAIN THAT I CAN'T HELP YOU CLEAN UP?
ZWWIPPP
ZWIPPP
ZWIPPP
NO, BUT THANKS FOR THE OFFER, JOHN--
"--I'VE GOT THE TORNADO TWINS ON THE JOB!"
UM, MAX, CAN I... DO YOU THINK IT WOULD BE ALL RIGHT IF I CHANGED IVAN'S NAME?
I MEAN, IVAN'S OKAY AND EVERYTHING, BUT...
ZWIPPP
ZWIPPP
ZWIPPP
NAUTICA
SURE, BART. AFTER ALL, HE IS YOUR DOG. YOU SHOULDN'T BE EXPECTED TO KEEP A NAME GIVEN TO HIM BY...
BART... I'VE BEEN MEANING TO, WELL, TO TELL YOU SOME THINGS...
I WANT YOU TO KNOW HOW PROUD I AM OF YOU. NOT JUST FOR COMING THROUGH LIKE YOU DID, MAKING IT THROUGH TO THE SPEED FORCE AND SAVING MY LIFE...
I'M PROUD OF THE PERSON YOU ARE... INSIDE. HOW WHEN YOU ACTUALLY DO TAKE THE TIME TO STOP AND THINK ABOUT SOMETHING, IT'S ALWAYS ABOUT OTHERS...
NAUTICA

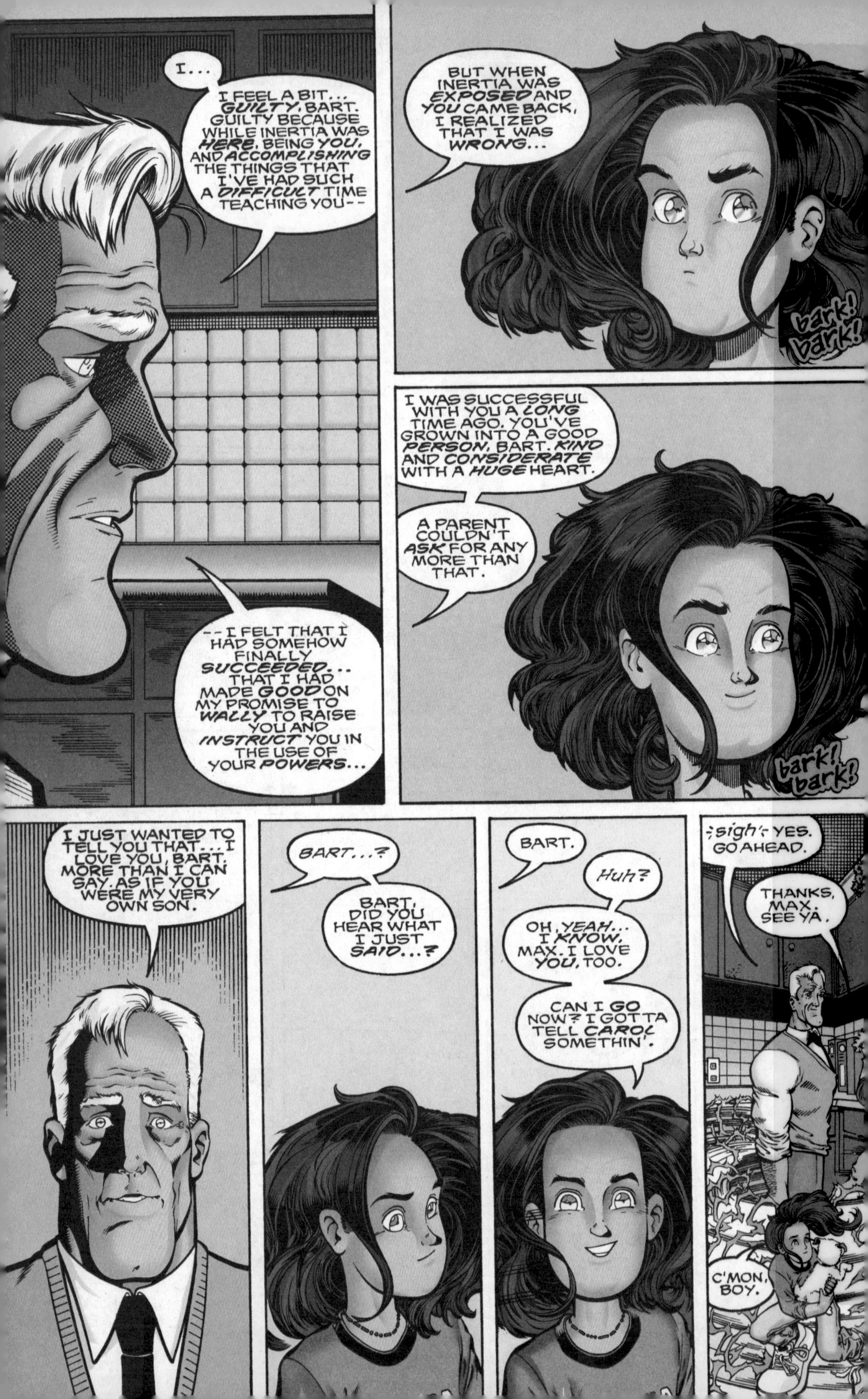
I...
I FEEL A BIT... GUILTY, BART. GUILTY BECAUSE WHILE INERTIA WAS HERE, BEING YOU, AND ACCOMPLISHING THE THINGS THAT I'VE HAD SUCH A DIFFICULT TIME TEACHING YOU--
--I FELT THAT I HAD SOMEHOW FINALLY SUCCEEDED... THAT I HAD MADE GOOD ON MY PROMISE TO WALLY TO RAISE YOU AND INSTRUCT YOU IN THE USE OF YOUR POWERS...
BUT WHEN INERTIA WAS EXPOSED AND YOU CAME BACK, I REALIZED THAT I WAS WRONG...
bark! bark!
I WAS SUCCESSFUL WITH YOU A LONG TIME AGO. YOU'VE GROWN INTO A GOOD PERSON, BART. KIND AND CONSIDERATE WITH A HUGE HEART.
A PARENT COULDN'T ASK FOR ANY MORE THAN THAT.
bark! bark!
I JUST WANTED TO TELL YOU THAT... I LOVE YOU, BART. MORE THAN I CAN SAY. AS IF YOU WERE MY VERY OWN SON.
BART...?
BART, DID YOU HEAR WHAT I JUST SAID...?
BART.
Huh?
OH, YEAH... I KNOW, MAX. I LOVE YOU, TOO.
CAN I GO NOW? I GOTTA TELL CAROL SOMETHIN'.
-sigh- YES. GO AHEAD.
THANKS, MAX. SEE YA.
C'MON, BOY.

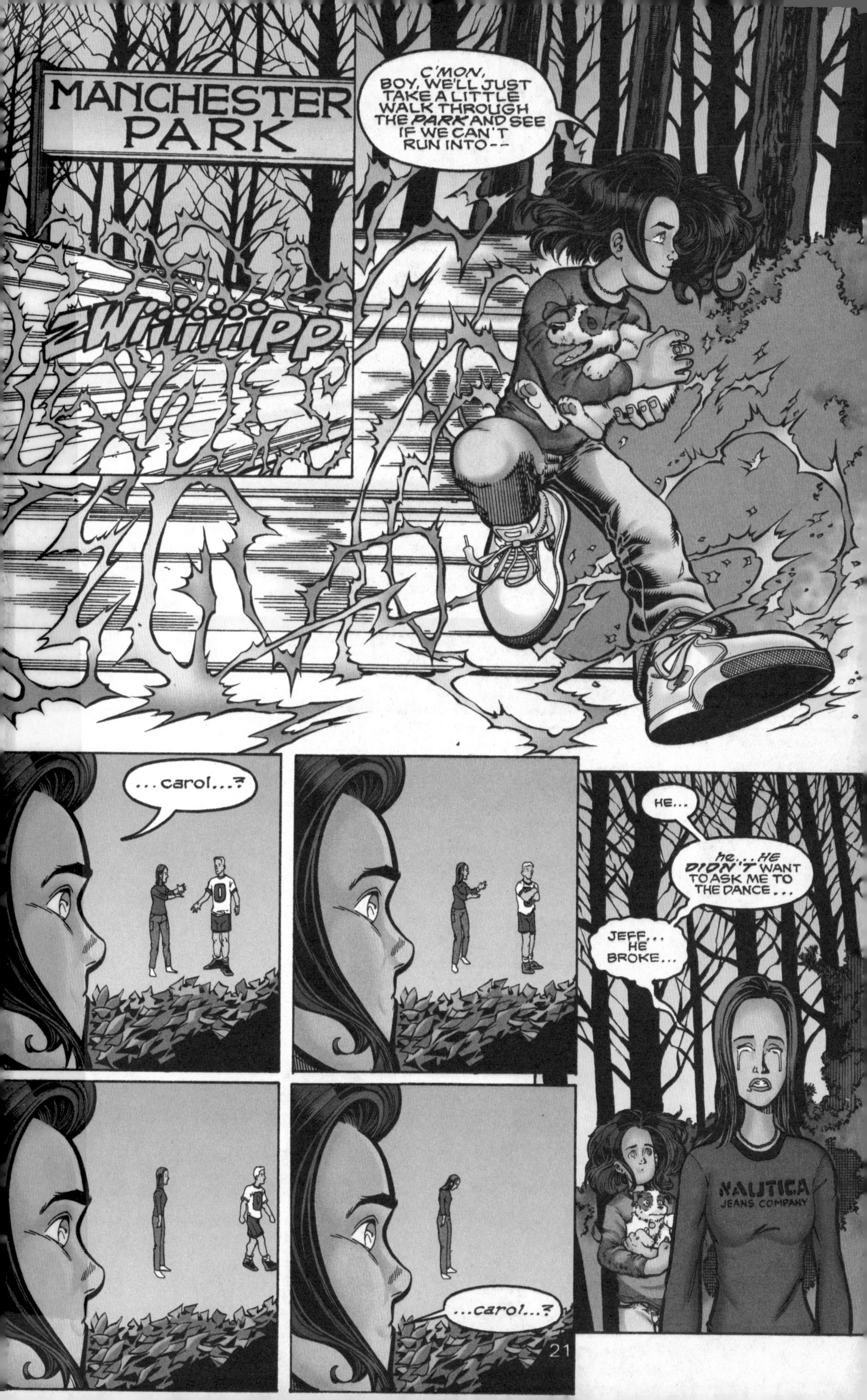
MANCHESTER PARK
C'MON, BOY, WE'LL JUST TAKE A LITTLE WALK THROUGH THE PARK AND SEE IF WE CAN'T RUN INTO--
ZWIIIIIIPP
...carol...?
HE...
he...HE DIDN'T WANT TO ASK ME TO THE DANCE...
JEFF... HE BROKE...
NAUTICA JEANS COMPANY
...carol...?

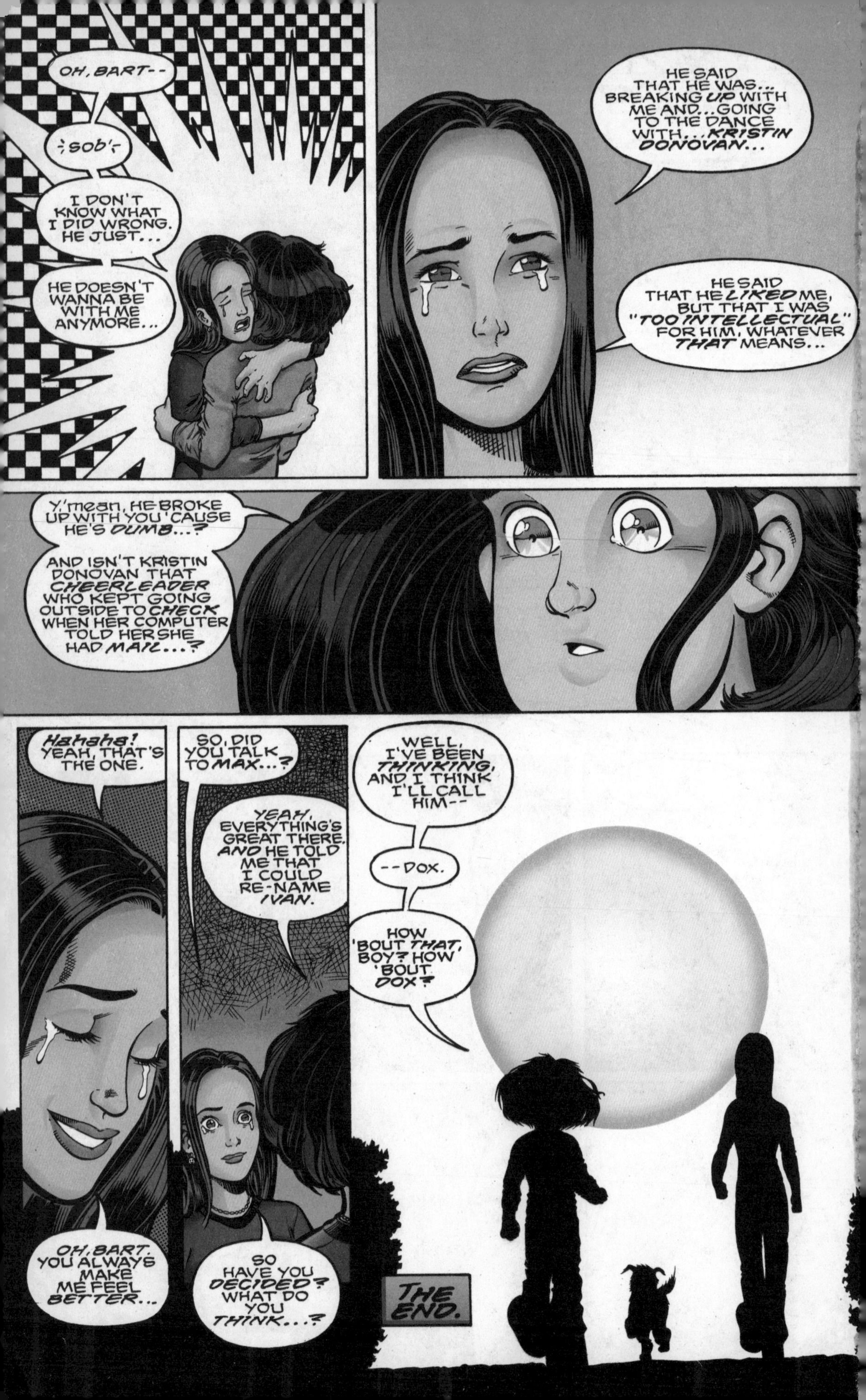
OH, BART--
;SOB;
I DON'T KNOW WHAT I DID WRONG. HE JUST...
HE DOESN'T WANNA BE WITH ME ANYMORE...
HE SAID THAT HE WAS... BREAKING UP WITH ME AND...GOING TO THE DANCE WITH...KRISTIN DONOVAN...
HE SAID THAT HE LIKED ME, BUT THAT I WAS "TOO INTELLECTUAL" FOR HIM, WHATEVER THAT MEANS...
Y'mean, HE BROKE UP WITH YOU 'CAUSE HE'S DUMB...?
AND ISN'T KRISTIN DONOVAN THAT CHEERLEADER WHO KEPT GOING OUTSIDE TO CHECK WHEN HER COMPUTER TOLD HER SHE HAD MAIL...?
Hahaha! YEAH, THAT'S THE ONE.
OH, BART. YOU ALWAYS MAKE ME FEEL BETTER...
SO, DID YOU TALK TO MAX...?
YEAH. EVERYTHING'S GREAT THERE. AND HE TOLD ME THAT I COULD RE-NAME IVAN.
SO HAVE YOU DECIDED? WHAT DO YOU THINK...?
WELL, I'VE BEEN THINKING, AND I THINK I'LL CALL HIM--
--DOX.
HOW 'BOUT THAT, BOY? HOW 'BOUT DOX?
THE END.